SPANISH/EN
BUSINESS GLO

DATE DUE

JUN - 2 2004	
JUN 1 4 2004	

BRODART   Cat. No. 23-221

In the same series

French Business Correspondence
Stuart Williams and Nathalie McAndrew-Cazorla

German Business Correspondence
Paul Hartley and Gertrud Robins

Italian Business Correspondence
Vincent Edwards and Gianfranca Gessa Shepheard

Spanish Business Correspondence
Michael Gorman and María-Luisa Henson

*French Business Situations**
Stuart Williams and Nathalie McAndrew-Cazorla

*German Business Situations**
Paul Hartley and Gertrud Robins

*Italian Business Situations**
Vincent Edwards and Gianfranca Gessa Shepheard

*Spanish Business Situations**
Michael Gorman and María-Luisa Henson

Manual of Business French
Stuart Williams and Nathalie McAndrew-Cazorla

Manual of Business German
Paul Hartley and Gertrud Robins

Manual of Business Italian
Vincent Edwards and Gianfranca Gessa Shepheard

Manual of Business Spanish
Michael Gorman and María-Luisa Henson

German/English Business Glossary
Paul Hartley and Gertrud Robins

French/English Business Glossary
Stuart Williams and Nathalie McAndrew-Cazorla

Italian/English Business Glossary
Vincent Edwards and Gianfranca Gessa Shepheard

* Accompanying cassettes available

SPANISH/ENGLISH BUSINESS GLOSSARY

Michael Gorman
and
María-Luisa Henson

London and New York

Michael Gorman and **María-Luisa Henson** are Senior Lecturers in Spanish at the School of Languages and European Studies, University of Wolverhampton.

First published 1997
by Routledge
11 New Fetter Lane, London EC4P 4EE

Simultaneously published in the USA and Canada
by Routledge
29 West 35th Street, New York, NY 10001

©1997 Michael Gorman and María-Luisa Henson

Typeset in Rockwell and Univers by Routledge
Printed and bound in Great Britain by TJ International Ltd, Padstow, Cornwall

British Library Cataloguing in Publication Data
A catalogue record for this book is available from the British Library

Library of Congress Cataloguing in Publication Data
A catalogue record for this book is available from the Library of Congress

ISBN 0–415–16043–X

Business Glossary

Key to glossary

Grammatical abbreviations

abbr	abbreviation
adj	adjective
adv	adverb
conj	conjunction
det	determiner
n	noun
nf	feminine noun
nfpl	plural feminine noun
nm	masculine noun
nmpl	plural masculine noun
pp	past participle
pref	prefix
prep	preposition
vb	verb

Symbols

* denotes slang term
(US) term particular to USA
(GB) term particular to Great Britain
(LAm) term particular to Latin American country/countries

NB: Contexts are given in parentheses after term and part of speech or before multiple translations

Parts of speech are provided for all headwords and for translations where appropriate. Subterms are only supplied with parts of speech where it is considered necessary to indicate gender or to avoid ambiguity

Latin American variants are given after main Spanish term. Multiple Latin American variants are separated from each other by semicolons. The part of speech is always provided for Latin American variants of Spanish terms where the part of speech differs from that of Spanish term. Where there is no part of speech indicated for a Latin American variant, the part of speech is the same as that of Spanish term

Spanish–English

abandonar *vb* abandon *vb*, quit *vb*
abandono *nm* neglect *n*, withdrawal *n*, desertion *n*
abastecedor, -ora *nm,f* supplier *n*
abastecer *vb* supply *vb* **abastecer algo a crédito** supply sth on trust
abogado, -ada *nm,f* solicitor *n*, lawyer (US) *n* **abogado que actúa únicamente en el juicio oral** barrister *n*, lawyer (US) *n*
abogar *vb* defend *vb*, champion *vb* **abogar por** advocate
abolición *nf* abolition *n*
abolir *vb* abolish *vb*
abonar *vb* pay *vb* **abonar algo en una cuenta** credit sth to an account, pay sth into an account
abreviación *nf* abbreviation *n*
abreviado *adj* abbreviated *adj*
abreviar *vb* abbreviate *vb*
abreviatura *nf* abbreviation *n*
abrir *vb* (market) open *vb*, open up *vb* **abrir una cuenta** open an account
absentismo *nm* absenteeism *n*
absoluto *adj* absolute *adj*, total *adj*
absorber *vb* absorb *vb* **absorber existencias sobrantes** absorb surplus stock
absorción *nf* takeover *n*
abundancia *nf* abundance *n*, wealth *n*
abusar *vb* abuse *vb* **abusar de** abuse *vb*
abuso *nm* abuse *n* **abuso de confianza** abuse of confidence **abuso de poder** abuse of power
acabar *vb* complete *vb* (end) turn out *vb* **acabar con un proyecto** kill a project
acápite *nm* (LAm) heading *n*, paragraph *n*, section *n*
acatar *vb* comply *vb*, obey *vb* **acatar las normas** observe the rules
accesibilidad *nf* accessibility *n*
acceso *nm* access *n*
accidente *nm* accident *n* **accidente laboral** industrial accident
acción *nf* action *n*, share *n* **acción cotizada** listed share, listed stock (US) **acciones** *nfpl* stocks and shares **acciones cotiza-**

bles en bolsa listed securities **acciones que se cotizan en Bolsa** quoted shares, quoted stocks (US) **acciones emitidas sin aumento de capital** watered capital **acción industrial, paro** (LAm) industrial action **acción nominativa** registered share **acción ordinaria** ordinary share, ordinary stock (US) **acción al portador** bearer share **acción de Tesoro** government bond
accionista *nmf* shareholder *n*, stockholder *n* **accionista apoderado, -ada** nominee shareholder
aceleración *nf* acceleration *n*
acelerar *vb* accelerate *vb*, expedite *vb*
aceptación *nf* acceptance *n* **aceptación de mercado** market acceptance **aceptación por parte del consumidor** consumer acceptance **aceptación con reservas** qualified acceptance
aceptar *vb* accept *vb* **aceptar la entrega de** accept delivery of
aclarar *vb* (sort out) resolve *vb*, clarify *vb*
aconsejar *vb* recommend *vb*, warn *vb* **aconsejarle a alguien sobre algo** advise sb about sth
acordado *adj* agreed *adj*
acotación *nf* limit *n*
acreedor, -ora *nm,f* creditor *n* **acreedor, -ora hipotecario, -ria** mortgagee
acta *nm* record *n* **el acta de la reunión** the minutes of the meeting **actas de conferencia** conference proceedings
activo *nm* asset *n* **activo circulante** floating assets **activo congelado** frozen assets **activo disponible** liquid assets, quick assets **activo fijo** capital assets, fixed assets **activo intangible** intangible asset **activo material** tangible asset **activo neto** net(t) assets **activo nominal** nominal assets **activos ficticios** fictitious assets **activos financieros** financial assets **activos ocultos** hidden assets **activo tangible** tangible asset

actuación *nf* (behaviour) performance *n*, action *n*

actual, moderno (LAm) *adj* up-to-date *adj*

actualizar *vb* (records) update *vb*

actuar *vb* act *vb*

actuario, -ria *nm,f* actuary *n*, Clerk of Court *n* **actuario de seguros** (insurance) actuary

acudir *vb* attend *vb*, come *vb* **acudir a una cita** keep an appointment

acuerdo *nm* agreement *n*, treaty *n*, understanding *n* **de acuerdo con** in accordance with **acuerdo entre caballeros** gentleman's agreement **acuerdo comercial** commercial treaty, trade agreement **acuerdo de cuotas** quota agreement **acuerdo de pago de suma única** lump sum settlement **acuerdo no escrito** verbal agreement **acuerdo fiduciario** trust agreement **acuerdo global** package deal **acuerdo laboral** working agreement **Acuerdo Monetario Europeo (AME)** European Monetary Agreement (EMA) **acuerdo mutuo** compromise **acuerdo oficial** formal agreement **acuerdo salarial** wage(s) agreement, wage(s) settlement **por acuerdo tácito** by tacit agreement **acuerdo de trueque** barter agreement **acuerdo verbal** verbal agreement **de común acuerdo** by mutual agreement

acumulación *nf* accrual *n* **acumulación de trabajo atrasado** backlog

acumulado *adj* accumulated *adj*

acumular *vb* accumulate *vb*, hoard *vb*

acuñar *vb* mint *vb*

acusar *vb* accuse *vb* **acusar recibo de algo** acknowledge receipt of sth, confirm receipt of sth

adaptación *nf* adaptation *n*, adjustment *n*

adaptar *vb* adjust *vb*, (adapt) tailor *vb*

adecuado *adj* (price) keen *adj*, appropriate *adj*

adelantar *vb* (salary) advance *vb*, bring forward *vb*

adelanto *nm* (on salary) advance *n*, cash advance *n*, progress *n*

adeudar *vb* (account) debit *vb*, owe *vb*

adición *nf* (LAm) bill *n*

adjuntar *vb* enclose *vb*

adjunto *adj* attached *adj*, enclosed *adj*, deputy *adj*

administración *nf* administration *n*, government *n* **administración de aduanas e impuestos sobre el consumo** the Board of Customs and Excise **administración de empresas, gestión** (LAm) management **administración pública** civil service

administrador, -ora *nm,f* administrator *n*, bailiff *n*, bursar *n*

administrar *vb* administer *vb*, manage *vb*

administrativo, -iva *nm, f* clerical worker *n*, white-collar worker *n*

adquirido *adj* vested *adj*, acquired *adj*

adquirir *vb* acquire *vb*, purchase *vb*, (company) take over *vb*

adquisición *nf* acquisition *n*, buy-out *n*, purchase *n*, takeover *n* **adquisición apalancada de empresas** LBO (leveraged buy-out) *abbr* **adquisición de una empresa por sus propios directivos** management buy-out

aduana *nf* customs *npl*

aduanero, -era *nm,f* customs inspector *n*, customs officer *n*

advertencia *nf* reminder *n*, warning *n*

advertir *vb* warn *vb*

aeropuerto *nm* airport *n*

afán *nm* keenness *n*, effort *n* **con afán de lucro** for pecuniary gain

afectado *adj* affected *adj* **muy afectado** hard-hit

afilado *adj* (competition) keen *adj*

afiliación *nf* affiliation *n*, membership *n* **afiliación sindical** union membership

afirmación *nf* statement *n*

aflojar *vb* (market) weaken *vb*

afueras, colonias (LAm) *nfpl* suburbs *npl*

agencia *nf* agency *n* **agencia de colocaciones** employment agency, Jobcentre (GB), Job centre, job shop **agencia de empleo** employment agency **agencia exprés** express agency **Agencia Federal** Federal Bureau (US) **agencia de informes comerciales** credit agency **agencia inmobiliaria** estate agency, real estate agency (US) **agencia de prensa** news agency **agencia de publicidad** advertising agency **agencias generales** general agencies (US) **agencia de trabajo** employment agency **agencia de transporte, agencia de fletes** (LAm) forwarding agency **agencia de venta de localidades** ticket agency **agencia de viajes** travel agency

agenda *nf* agenda *n*, timetable *n*, diary *n*

agente *nmf* agent *n*, representative *n* **agente de bolsa** commission broker, jobber, stockbroker **agente de cambio** foreign exchange dealer **agente comercial** broker, sales representative **agente**

de despacho, agente de flete de mercancías (LAm) forwarding agent **agente expedidor** shipping broker **agente fiscal** fiscal agent **agente general** general agent **agente de importación** import agent **agente inmobiliario, -ria** estate agent, real estate agent, realtor (US) **agente al por mayor** (buyer of debts) factor **agente mediador, -ora** dealer **agente oficial** authorized dealer **agente que recibe una comisión elevada porque garantiza el pago** del credere agent **agentes de bolsa** brokerage firm **agente de seguros** insurance agent, insurance broker, insurance representative **agente de transportes, agente fletero** (LAm) forwarder, forwarding agent, freight forwarder, transport agent

agotamiento nm depletion n, exhaustion n

agotar vb (reserves) exhaust vb

agrario adj agrarian adj

agricultura nf agriculture n, farming n

agrimensor, -ora nm,f surveyor n **agrimensor colegiado** chartered surveyor

agroindustria nf agribusiness n

agrónomo, -oma nm,f agronomist n

agrupación nf syndicate n **agrupación temporal de empresas** collaborative venture, joint venture

ahorrar vb save (time, money) vb **que ahorra tiempo** time-saving

ahorro nm saving n **ahorro neto** net(t) saving **ahorros** savings

aire nm air n, look n **con aire acondicionado** air-conditioned

ajustar vb adjust vb **ajustar las cifras** adjust the figures **ajustar el presupuesto** balance the budget

ajuste nm adjustment n **ajuste definitivo** final settlement **ajuste por suma fija** lump sum settlement

albañil nmf bricklayer n, builder n

alcance nm range n, reach n **de gran alcance** wide-ranging **de largo alcance** long-range

alcista 1. adj upward adj 2. nmf (stock exchange) bull n

alguacil nmf bailiff n

aliciente nm incentive n

aliviar vb moderate vb, relieve vb

almacén, bodega (LAm) nm, nf warehouse n **en almacén** ex factory/works, ex store/warehouse, in stock **almacén de depósito** bonded warehouse **grandes almacenes, tienda de departamentos** (LAm) department store

almacenaje nm warehousing n **almacenaje de datos** information storage

almacenamiento nm storage n

alojamiento nm accommodation n **alojamiento hotelero** hotel accommodation

alquilar, arrendar; rentar (LAm) vb hire vb (property) let vb (house, office) rent vb **se alquila, se arrienda; se renta** (LAm) for hire

alquiler, arriendo (LAm) nm hire n, hire charges npl, rent n, rental n **alquiler de maquinaria** plant hire, tool hire

alza nf (in bank rate) rise n **alza de la demanda** boom in demand

amarrar vb moor vb, fasten vb

ambiente nm atmosphere n **ambiente laboral** working environment

ámbito nm terms of reference npl, ambit n **de ámbito nacional** nationwide prep

amigable adj user-friendly adj

amo, ama nm,f boss n, owner n

amortización nf amortization n, depreciation n, redemption n

amortizar vb amortize vb, depreciate vb, redeem vb, write down vb

ampliación nf expansion n

ampliar vb enlarge vb, expand vb **ampliar la capacidad** expand capacity **ampliar la gama** extend the range

amplio adj comprehensive adj, wide--ranging adj

análisis nm analysis n **análisis de cifras** (of figures) breakdown **análisis coste--beneficio** cost-benefit analysis **análisis de costes, análisis de costos** (LAm) cost breakdown **análisis económico** economic analysis **análisis funcional** functional analysis **análisis horizontal** horizontal analysis **análisis de mercado** market analysis **análisis de mercados** market research **análisis de necesidades** needs assessment **análisis numérico** numerical analysis **análisis de riesgos** risk analysis **análisis de sistemas** systems analysis **análisis de tendencias** trend analysis

analista nm analyst n **analista de sistemas** systems analyst

analizar vb analyze vb **sin analizar** (unprocessed) raw

anexo nm enclosure n, appendix n

anfitrión, -ona nm,f host n

año nm year n **al año** per annum **por año** per annum **año fiscal** financial year, fiscal year, tax year

anotar vb note vb, record vb

antecedentes *nmpl* record *n*, track record *n*
antedatar *vb* backdate *vb*
antedicho *adj* above-mentioned *adj*
antelación *nf* notice *n*, priority *n*
anticipar *vb* anticipate *vb*, advance *vb*
anticuado *adj* obsolete *adj*, out-of-date *adj*
antigüedad *nf* seniority *n*
anual *adj* yearly *adj*
anualidad *nf* annuity *n*
anulación *nf* annulment *n*, cancellation *n*, write-off *n*
anular *vb* rescind *vb* (debts) write off *vb*
anular un contrato cancel a contract
anular un pedido cancel an order
anunciar, hacerle réclame a (LAm) *vb* advertise *vb*, announce *vb*
anuncio, aviso; réclame (LAm) *nm* advertisement *n*, bulletin *n* **anuncio por palabras, aviso clasificado** (LAm) classified advertisement **anuncio publicitario, aviso** (LAm) newspaper advertisement **anuncios clasificados, avisos clasificados** (LAm) small ads
aparato *nm* machine *n*, appliance *n* **aparato estatal** machinery of government
aparecer *vb* appear *vb*, come out *vb*
apartado *nm* box *n*, section *n* **apartado de correos, apartado postal; casilla postal** (LAm) box number, PO box
apelación *nf* appeal *n*
apelar *vb* appeal *vb*
aplazado *adj* (tax) deferred *adj*, postponed *adj*
aplazar *vb* adjourn *vb*, postpone *vb*, defer *vb* (to next period) hold over *vb*
aplicación *nf* enforcement *n*
aplicar *vb* (policy) enforce *vb* **aplicar por** (LAm) apply for
apoderado, -ada *nm,f* (power) proxy *n*, agent *n*
aportación *nf* contribution *n* **sin aportaciones por parte del empleado** non-contributory
aportar, hacer aportes (LAm) *vb* contribute *vb*
apostador, -ora *nm,f* stakeholder *n*
apoyar *vb* support *vb*
apoyo *nm* backing *n*
apreciación *nf* appreciation *n*
apremiante *adj* urgent *adj*
aprendiz, -iza *nm,f* apprentice *n*, trainee *n*
aprendizaje *nm* apprenticeship *n*, training *n* **aprendizaje asistido por ordenador** (CAL), **aprendizaje asistido por**

computadora (LAm) computer-aided learning (CAL)
apretón *nm* handshake *n*, hug *n* **apretón de manos** handshake
aprobación *nf* approval *n*, endorsement *n*, seal *n*
aprobar *vb* approve *vb*, vote *vb*
apropiación *nf* appropriation *n*
apropiado *adj* relevant *adj*, suitable *adj*
aprovechar *vb* exploit *vb*, make use *vb* **aprovechar un mercado** tap a market
aprovecharse *vb* benefit *vb*, take advantage of *vb* **aprovecharse de la ocasión** seize an opportunity
aproximadamente *adv* approximately *adv*
aproximado *adj* approximate *adj*
aptitud *nf* ability *n*
apuntar *vb* write down *vb* **apuntar algo** make a note of sth
arancel *nm* tariff *n*
arbitraje *nm* arbitrage *n*, arbitration *n* **arbitraje laboral** industrial arbitration
arbitrar *vb* arbitrate *vb*
arbitrario *adj* arbitrary *adj*
árbitro, -tra *nm*, *f* arbitrator *n*, referee *n*
archivador, archivero (LAm) *nm* filing cabinet *n*
archivar *vb* file *vb*
archivo *nm* computer file *n*, file *n*, record *n*, register *n*
área *nf* **área de la bodega** hold area **área de trabajo** working area
argumento *nm* **argumentos** arguments, reasoning **argumentos de venta** sales talks
aritmética *nf* arithmetic *n*
arreglar *vb* repair *vb*, resolve *vb*, arrange *vb*
arreglo *nm* (agreement) arrangement *n*
arrendador, -ora, hacendado, -ada (LAm) *nm,f* landlord *n*, lessor *n*
arrendamiento *nm* leasehold *n*, rent *n*, rental *n* **arrendamiento de medios de producción** equipment leasing
arrendar, rentar (LAm) *vb* hire *vb*, lease *vb* (house, office) rent *vb* **se arrienda, se renta** (LAm) for hire
arrendatario, -ria *nm,f* leaseholder *n*, lessee *n*, tenant *n*
arriendo *nm* hire *n*, hire charge *n*, income *n* (LAm)
artículo *nm* item *n* **artículo de gancho** loss leader **artículo líder** market leader **artículo de mayor venta** market leader **artículos consignados, mercaderías en consignación** (LAm) goods on

consignment **artículos defectuosos** faulty goods **artículos de importación, mercaderías de importación** (LAm) import goods **artículos de lujo** luxury goods **artículos de mercería** dry goods **artículos perecederos, mercaderías perecederas** (LAm) perishable goods **artículos de primera necesidad** staple commodities **artículos de producción en serie, mercaderías a granel** (LAm) bulk goods **artículos de venta rápida, mercaderías de venta rápida** (LAm) fast-selling goods

artificial *adj* man-made *adj*

asalariado, -ada *nm,f* wage earner *n*, paid employee *n*

ascender *vb* (person) promote *vb*, upgrade *vb* **ascender a** amount to

ascenso *nm* (of person) promotion *n*

aseguradora *nf* insurance company *n*

asegurar *vb* indemnify *vb*, insure *vb*, warrant *vb* (risk) underwrite *vb* **asegurar la marcha de la empresa** keep the business running

asesor, -ora *nm,f* adviser/advisor *n*, consultant *n* **asesor comercial** marketing consultant **asesor económico** economic adviser **asesor de empresas** business consultant, management consultant **asesor financiero** financial consultant **asesor de inversiones** investment adviser **asesor de seguros** insurance representative

asesoramiento *nm* advice *n*

asesorar *vb* consult *vb* **asesorarle a alguien sobre algo** advise sb on sth

asesoría *nf* consultancy *n*, consultancy work *n*, consulting (US) *n* **asesoría financiera** financial consultancy

asiento *nm* seat *n*, entry *n* **asiento contable** ledger entry **asiento final** final entry

asignación *nf* appropriation *n*, allowance *n* **asignación de fondos** funding

asignar *vb* allocate *vb*, assign *vb*, budget for *vb*, commit *vb*

asistencia *nf* aid *n*, attendance *n* **asistencia económica al exterior** foreign aid **asistencia social** welfare

asistir *vb* attend *vb*, help *vb* **asistir a una entrevista** attend for interview

asociación *nf* partnership *n* **asociación comercial** trading partnership **asociación de estudiantes, gremio** (LAm) students' union **Asociación Europea de Libre Comercio** EFTA (European Free Trade Association) **asociación general** general partnership **asociación limitada** limited partnership

asociado, -ada *nm, f* associate *n*, partner *n*, joint vendor *n*

aspirante *nmf* (for job) candidate *n* **aspirante a un puesto directivo** trainee manager

astillero *nm* dockyard *n*, shipyard *n*

asumir *vb* assume *vb* **asumir responsabilidad de algo** take responsibility for sth

asunto *nm* matter *n*, subject *n* **Asunto** re **asunto urgente** a matter of urgency

ataque *nm* offence *n*, offense (US) *n*

atasco *nm* bottleneck *n*, obstruction *n*

atender *vb* attend to *vb* **atender una reclamación** meet a claim

atenerse a *vb* abide by *vb*

atestiguar *vb* witness *vb* **atestiguar una firma** witness a signature

atrasado *adj* in arrears *adj*, overdue *adj*

atrasarse *vb* be late *vb*, fall behind *vb* **atrasarse en los pagos** fall/get into arrears

atraso *nm* **atrasos** arrears *npl* **atrasos de sueldo** back pay

atribución *nf* **atribuciones** allocations, attributions **atribuciones y responsabilidades** terms of reference

auditor, -ora *nm,f* auditor *n*

auditoría *nf* audit *n* **auditoría externa** external audit **auditoría interna** internal audit

auge *nm* increase *n* **en auge** booming

aumentar *vb* boom *vb*, enlarge *vb*, escalate *vb*, expand *vb* (prices) bump up *vb*, improve *vb*, mark up *vb*, rise *vb* **aumentar la producción** increase output **aumentar de valor** gain in value

aumento *nm* boost *n*, mark up *n* (in earnings, inflation) rise *n* **aumento de capital** expansion of capital **aumento del coste de vida, aumento del costo de vida** (LAm) increase in the cost of living **aumento rápido de la demanda** boom in demand **aumentos de productividad** productivity gains **aumento de sueldo** pay increase/rise **aumento de ventas** sales growth

ausente *adj* absent *adj*, absentee *adj*

autoedición *nf* desk-top publishing *n*

autoevaluación *nf* self-assessment *n*

autofinanciación *nf* self-financing *n*

autogestión *nf* self-management *n*

automático *adj* automatic *adj*

automatización *nf* automation *n*

autónomo *adj* autonomous *adj*, self-employed *adj*

autoridad *nf* (official) authority *n*

autorización nf approval n, attestation n, licence n, warrant n

autorizar vb accredit vb, approve vb, authorize vb, license vb

autoservicio nm cash and carry n, supermarket n

autosuficiente adj self-sufficient adj

auxiliar adj auxiliary adj, junior adj

avalúo nm (LAm) appraisal n

avance nm (on salary) advance n, progress n **avance importante** breakthrough

avanzar vb (research, project) progress vb

avería nf fault n **avería importante** serious fault

averiado, descompuesto (LAm) adj out-of-action adj

avión nm aeroplane n **avión de carga** freighter

avisar vb notify vb, warn vb **avisar de algo** give notice of sth

aviso nm (suggestion) tip n warning n, advertisement (LAm) n **aviso por adelantado** advance notice **aviso de envío** advice note **aviso de expedición** advice note, remittance advice **aviso previo** advance notice **hasta nuevo aviso** until further notice

ayuda nf backing n **ayuda financiera** financial aid

ayudante nmf assistant n **ayudante de dirección** assistant manager

ayudar vb help vb **ayudar a salir de un apuro** tide over

ayuntamiento nm town council n, town hall n

azar nm chance n, random n **al azar** at random

baja nf (economic) decline n redundancy n, termination of employment n **a la baja** downward **baja por enfermedad, licencia por enfermedad** (LAm) sick leave

bajar vb decrease vb, (price, interest rate) lower vb

bajista nmf (stock exchange) bear n

bajón nm (economic) downturn n

balance nm stocktaking n, balance n **balance final** final balance **balance financiero** financial balance **balance fiscal** fiscal balance **balance general** balance sheet, financial statement **balance de situación** balance sheet

balanza nf balance n, scale n **balanza comercial** balance of trade, trade balance **balanza comercial favorable** favourable balance of trade **balanza comercial ne-**

gativa adverse balance of trade **balanza de pagos** balance of payments **balanza de pagos favorable** favourable balance of payments

banca nf banking n, banking system n **banca de depósito** commercial bank **banca electrónica** electronic banking

bancario, -ria nm,f (LAm) bank clerk n

bancarrota nf bankruptcy n **en bancarrota** bankrupt

banco nm bank n **banco central/de emisión** central bank **banco comercial** clearing bank, commercial bank **banco comercial de negocios** acceptance house **banco de compensación** clearing bank **banco de datos** data bank **banco de depósito** commercial bank **banco de direcciones** mailing list **banco emisor** bank of issue, issuing bank **Banco Europeo de Inversiones (BEI)** European Investment Bank (EIB) **banco extranjero** foreign bank **banco fundado antiguamente por cédula real** chartered bank **banco mercantil** commercial bank, merchant bank **Banco Mundial** World Bank **banco de negocios** merchant bank

banda nf band n, scale n **banda impositiva** tax bracket

bandeja nf pallet n

banquero, -era nm,f banker n **los banqueros suizos** the Gnomes of Zurich

barato adj (price) low adj, cheap adj

barco nm ship n **barco de carga** cargo ship

barrera nf barrier n **barrera arancelaria** tariff barrier, trade barrier, tariff wall **barrera comercial** trade barrier **barrera contra la inflación** hedge against inflation **barrera a la importación** import barrier

barrio nm barrios nmpl districts, suburbs **barrios residenciales de las afueras** outer suburbs

base nf base n, basis n **base de conocimientos** knowledge base **base de datos** data base **base de evaluación** basis of assessment

beneficiar vb benefit vb

beneficiario, -ria nm,f payee n, recipient n

beneficio nm benefit n, dividend n **beneficios, utilidades** (LAm) nm profits n, earnings n, proceeds n **beneficio extra** (formal) perquisite **beneficio ficticio** paper profit **beneficio inesperado** windfall profit **beneficio neto** net(t) profit **beneficio nulo** nil profit **beneficio no realizado** paper profit **beneficios contables/en li-**

bros, utilidades contables (LAm) book profit **beneficios de explotación, beneficios de operación** (LAm) operating profit **beneficios extraordinarios** extra profit **beneficios extrasalariales** fringe benefits
bianual adj biennial adj
bien nm **bienes** chattels npl, goods npl **bienes de capital** capital assets, capital goods **bienes duraderos** durable goods **bienes de equipo** capital goods **bienes ocultos** hidden assets **bienes raíces** real estate
bienestar nm welfare n
bienhechor, -ora nm,f benefactor n
bilateral, de doble mano; de doble vía (LAm) adj two-way adj
billete, pasaje; boleto; tiquete (LAm) nm ticket n **billete de abono, boleto de abono** (LAm) season ticket **billete de banco** banknote **billete de ida, pasaje sencillo; boleto sencillo** (LAm) (rail/flight) single/one-way ticket **billete de ida y vuelta** return ticket, round-trip ticket (US)
bimensual adj bimonthly adj
bloque, cuadra (LAm) nm, nf block n
bloquear, tapar (LAm) vb block vb, blockade vb
bloqueo nm blockade n
bodega nf stowage n, cellar n, hold n, warehouse (LAm) n
boicot nm boycott n
boicotear vb boycott vb
boletería nf (LAm) box office n
boletín nm bulletin n, journal n **boletín informativo** newsletter **boletín interno de la empresa** house journal/magazine
boleto nm coupon n, ticket (LAm) n
bolsa nf Stock Exchange **bolsa de empleo** Jobcentre, job shop **Bolsa de Nueva York** NYSE (New York Stock Exchange) **bolsa de valores** Stock Exchange, stock market
bombo nm hype n
bonificación nf bonus n, discount n, weighting n **bonificación recibida al concluir un seguro** terminal bonus
bonista nmf bondholder n
bono nm bond n, debenture n, voucher n **bono amortizable** redeemable bond **bono de fidelidad** fidelity bond **bono no garantizado** unsecured bond **bono sin intereses** fiat bond **bonos de financiación** funding bonds **bonos municipales** municipal bonds **bonos del Tesoro** gilts **bono de yen** yen bond
boom nm boom n **boom económico** economic boom

borrador nm draft n
botar vb (LAm) dismiss vb **botar del trabajo** dismiss from job, axe*
botín nm spoils npl
brecha nf gap n
brevedad nf brevity n **a su mayor brevedad posible** at your earliest convenience
británico adj British adj
bruto adj before tax adj, gross adj
buque nm ship n **en buque** ex ship **buque de carga** freighter **buque mercante** merchant ship
burocracia nf bureaucracy n, red tape n
burócrata nmf bureaucrat n
burocrático adj bureaucratic adj
buscar vb seek vb **buscar trabajo** look for work
cabeza nf head n **a la cabeza de** at the head of
cabina, casilla; caseta (LAm) nf booth n, cabin n **cabina de teléfonos** telephone box, telephone booth (US)
CAD (diseño asistido por ordenador) nm CAD (computer-aided or assisted design) abbr
cadena nf chain n **cadena hotelera** hotel chain **cadena de minoristas** retail chain **cadena de montaje** assembly line, production line **cadena de producción** production line **cadena de tiendas** chain of shops
caducado, vencido; perimido (LAm) adj out of date adj
caducar vb expire vb
caducidad nf expiry n, obsolescence n, termination n, expiration (US)
caer vb (market) weaken vb **caer en desuso** fall into abeyance **caer en picado** slump vb
caída nf (of economy) collapse n **caída bursátil** collapse on stock market **caída repentina** slump n
caído adj fallen adj **caído en desuso** obsolete
caja nf cash desk n **caja de ahorros** savings bank
cajero nm **cajero automático** automatic cash dispenser/machine, cashpoint
cajero, -era nm,f cashier n **cajero de banco** teller **cajero jefe** chief cashier
calculadora nf calculator n
calcular vb assess vb, calculate vb, estimate vb, measure vb **calcular el coste de un trabajo, calcular el costo de un trabajo** (LAm) cost a job

cálculo *nm* assessment *n*, calculation *n*, estimate *n*

calendario *nm* timescale *n*, calendar *n*

calidad *nf* quality *n* **de baja calidad shoddy* de calidad superior** high-grade **en mi calidad de presidente** in my capacity as chairman

calificación *nf* (LAm) qualification *n*, bond *n*

calificado *adj* (LAm) qualified *adj*

calificar *vb* label *vb*

cámara *nf* camera *n*, chamber *n* **Cámara de Comercio** Board of Trade, Chamber of Commerce **cámara de compensación** clearing house

cambiar *vb* (market) turn *vb*, (money) change *vb* **cambiar de domicilio** change address **cambiar impresiones** compare notes **cambiar radicalmente** reverse

cambio, vuelto; vueltas (LAm) *nm, nm; nfpl* (from purchase) change *n*, bureau de change *n*, foreign exchange dealings *npl*, shift *n*, swap *n*, turnabout *n* **a cambio** in return **cambio comprador** buying price **cambio favorable** favourable exchange **cambio de futuros** futures exchange **cambio de moneda extranjera** foreign exchange

cambista *nmf* exchange broker *n*, foreign exchange dealer *n*, money trader *n*

camino *nm* route *n*, way *n*

campaña *nf* campaign *n* **campaña dirigida a** targeted campaign **campaña de publicidad** advertising campaign **campaña publicitaria** advertising campaign, publicity campaign **campaña de reclutamiento** recruitment campaign **campaña de ventas** sales campaign

campo *nm* countryside *n* **campo editorial** publishing **campo de trabajo** working area

cancelación *nf* cancellation *n*

cancelar *vb* (contract) repudiate *vb*, liquidate *vb*, rescind *vb*, withdraw *vb*, cancel *vb*, write off *vb*

candidato, -ata *nm,f* (for job) candidate *n* nominee *n*

candidatura, postulación (LAm) *nf* nomination *n*

canje *nm* swap *n*

canjear *vb* swap *vb*

cantidad *nf* amount *n*, quantity *n*, volume *n*

capacidad *nf* ability *n*, volume *n* **capacidad de almacenaje** storage capacity **capacidad de almacenamiento** storage

capacity **capacidad excesiva** excess capacity **capacidad de ganar dinero** earning capacity/power **capacidad industrial** industrial capacity **capacidad de memoria** memory capacity **capacidad de negociación** negotiating skills **capacidad de pago** creditworthiness **capacidad de producción** manufacturing capacity **capacidad de rendimiento** earning capacity **capacidad no utilizada** idle capacity

capacitación *nf* training *n* **capacitación avanzada** advanced training

capacitado, calificado; capacitado (LAm) *adj* qualified *adj*, skilled (LAm) *adj*

capacitar *vb* (staff) train *vb*, authorize *vb*

capataz *nmf* foreman/forewoman *n*

capaz *adj* able *adj*, capable *adj* **capaz de realizar cálculos aritméticos elementales** numerate

cápita *nf* **per cápita** per capita, per head

capital *nm* capital *n* **capital certificado** registered capital **capital circulante** capital funds, trading capital, working capital **capital desembolsado** paid-up capital **capital disponible** capital assets **capitales de fuga** flight capital **capital de especulación** risk capital **capital de explotación** trading capital **capital fijo** fixed capital **capital inicial** initial capital **capital invertido** invested capital **capital a largo plazo** long-term capital **capital limitado** limited capital **capital líquido** liquid capital **capital nominal** nominal assets, registered capital **capital operativo** capital funds, working capital **capital de puesta en marcha** start-up capital **capital de riesgo** venture capital, risk capital **capital social** equity capital, share capital **capital de vendedor, -ora** vendor capital

capitalismo *nm* capitalism *n*

capitalista *nmf* backer *n*, capitalist *n*

capitalizar *vb* capitalize *vb*

captación *nf* gaining *n*, raising *n* **captación de datos** data capture

carácter *nm* character *n* **caracteres pequeños** small type **carácter numérico** numeric character

carestía *nf* scarcity *n*, high cost *n*

carga *nf* bulk cargo *n*, cargo *n*, freight *n*, load *n* (consignment) shipment *n*, charge *n* **carga aérea** air freight **carga a granel** bulk cargo **carga paletizada, mercaderías empaletizadas** (LAm) palletized freight **cargas fiscales** taxation

carga de trabajo workload **carga útil** (of vehicle) payload
cargamento *nm* cargo *n*
cargar *vb* (account) debit *vb*, charge *vb*, load *vb* **cargar algo** charge for sth **cargar algo a una cuenta** charge sth to an account **cargar un ordenador, cargar una computadora** (LAm) boot a computer
cargo *nm* debit *n*, office *n*, official *n* **altos cargos** top management **cargo de administrador** trusteeship
carguero *nm* cargo ship *n* **carguero de graneles** bulk carrier
caridad *nf* charity *n*
carné *nm* card *n*, permit *n* **carné de identidad** identity card
carnero, -era *nm,f* (LAm) (worker) scab* *n*
carpeta *nf* file *n*, folder *n*
carrera *nf* career *n*, course *n*
carretera *nf* road *n*, highway *n* **por carretera** by road
carta *nf* letter *n* **carta certificada, carta registrada; carta recomendada** (LAm) registered letter **carta de crédito** letter of credit **carta de crédito irrevocable** irrevocable letter of credit **carta de crédito revocable** revocable letter of credit **carta de recomendación** letter of introduction **carta de solicitud** letter of application **carta verde, permiso de residencia y trabajo** (LAm) green card
cartel *nm* cartel *n* (advertising) poster *n*
cartera *nf* briefcase *n*, portfolio *n*, wallet *n* **cartera de pedidos** order book **cartera de valores** holding, investment portfolio **cartera de valores en divisas** foreign exchange holdings **cartera de valores extranjeros** foreign holdings
casa *nf* establishment *n*, household *n* **casa de cambio** bureau de change **casa financiera** acceptance house **casa de la moneda** mint
casco *nm* hull *n*
casilla, caseta (LAm) *nf* box *n*, pigeonhole *n*, booth (LAm) *n* **casilla de la consigna automática, locker de la consigna** (LAm) left-luggage locker
caso *nm* case *n* **caso que sienta jurisprudencia** test case
categoría *nf* category *n*, quality *n* **de primera categoría** top-level
causar *vb* cause *vb* **causar daños graves** cause extensive damage
CE (Comunidad Europea) *abbr* EC (European Community) *abbr*
ceder *vb* yield *vb* **ceder en arriendo** lease

celebrar *vb* celebrate *vb* **celebrar una reunión** hold a meeting
cenit *nm* zenith *n*
censor, -ora *nm,f* auditor *n* **censor de cuentas interior** internal auditor
centralita *nf* telephone switchboard *n* **centralita de teléfonos, conmutador** (LAm) switchboard
centralización *nf* centralization *n*
centralizar *vb* centralize *vb*
centro *nm* centre *n*, center (US) *n* **centro de almacenaje y distribución** entrepôt **centro ciudad** town centre **centro comercial** business centre, shopping mall, shopping centre **centro de coste, centro de costo** (LAm) cost centre **centro financiero** business centre **centro financiero de Nueva York** Wall Street **centro de formación** training centre **centro informático** computer centre
cero *nm* nil *n*, zero *n* **bajo cero** below zero
cerrado *adj* closed *adj*
cerrar *vb* (informal) shut up shop *vb*, close *vb* **cerrar una cuenta** close an account **cerrar una empresa** close a business **cerrar un trato** call it a deal, clinch a deal, close a deal
certificado *nm* certificate *n* **certificado de empleo** certificate of employment **certificado de haber efectuado el despacho de aduana** clearance certificate **certificado de matrimonio** marriage certificate **certificado de origen** certificate of origin **certificado de propiedad** certificate of ownership **certificado de seguros** insurance certificate
certificar *vb* certificate *vb*, certify *vb*
cesante *adj* (LAm) unemployed *adj*, jobless *adj*
cesantía *nf* (LAm) unemployment *n*, strike *n*
cese *nm* (strike) stoppage, *n* redundancy *n*, shutdown *n*, termination *n*, termination of employment *n*
cesión *nf* assignment *n*, transfer *n* **cesión por el gobierno de la acción recaudatoria a un particular** particular farming of taxes
cesionario, -ria *nm,f* assignee *n*
cesta *nf* basket *n* **cesta de la compra** foodstuffs **cesta de monedas, canasta de divisas** (LAm) basket of currencies
chanchullo *nm* racket *n*
chantaje *nm* blackmail *n*
chatarra *nf* (metal) scrap *n*
checar *vb* (LAm) check *vb*
cheque *nm* cheque *n*, check (US) *n* **cheque**

abierto open cheque **cheque bancario** bank draft **cheque en blanco** blank cheque **cheque cruzado** crossed cheque **cheque no cubierto** dud cheque **cheque descubierto** bad cheque **cheque en divisas** exchange cheque **cheque sin fondos** bad cheque, dud cheque **cheque impagado** unpaid cheque **cheque negociable** negotiable cheque **cheque al portador** bearer cheque **cheque de tesorero** treasurer check (US) **cheque por valor de cien libras** a cheque for the amount of £100 **cheque de viajero/de viaje** traveller's cheque, traveler's check (US)

chequear vb (LAm) check vb

chequera nf cheque book n

chévere adj (LAm) great adj, brilliant adj, keen adj

ciclo nm cycle n **ciclo económico** economic cycle, trade cycle

cien nm hundred n **cien por cien** one hundred per cent

ciencias nfpl sciences npl **ciencias empresariales** business studies

ciento nm hundred n **por ciento** per cent

cierre nm seal n **cierre de una empresa** closure of a company **cierre patronal, paro patronal** (LAm) (of strikers) lockout

cif (coste, seguro y flete) abbr,nm c.i.f. (cost, insurance and freight) abbr

cifra nf figure n, sum n **cifra de facturación** turnover **cifras de ventas** sales figures

cinta nf tape n **cinta magnética** (DP) magnetic tape

circulación nf circulation n, movement n **en circulación** in circulation **circulación en la carretera, tránsito en la carretera** (LAm) road traffic

circular nf (letter) circular n

círculo n circle n

circunstancia nf circumstance n **circunstancias ajenas a nuestra voluntad** circumstances beyond our control **circunstancias imprevistas** unforeseen circumstances

circunvalar vb bypass vb

cita, hora (LAm) nf (to meet) engagement n, appointment n

clase nf kind n **de alta clase** high-class **clase preferente** (plane) business class

clasificación nf classification n, placing n **clasificación crediticia** credit rating

cláusula nf (in contract) clause n **cláusula de excepción** escape clause **cláusula de exclusión** exclusion clause **cláusula de**

incumplimiento neglect clause **cláusula de negligencia** negligence clause **cláusula de opción** option clause **cláusula de protección,** hedge clause (US) **cláusula de renuncia** waiver clause **cláusula de salvaguardia** escape clause

cliente, -nta nm,f buyer n, client n, customer n **cliente de la casa** regular customer **cliente habitual** regular customer

clientela nf clientele n, goodwill n, patronage n

climatizado adj air-conditioned adj

cobertura nf cover n **cobertura a plazo** forward cover **cobertura del seguro** insurance cover

cobrable adj chargeable adj

cobrar vb charge vb, receive vb **cobrar por algo** charge for sth **cobrar de más** overcharge **cobrar un cheque** cash a cheque **cobrar comisión** charge commission **cobrar una deuda** collect a debt **cobrar el sueldo** earn a living **cobrar honorarios** charge a fee **cobrar impuestos** levy taxes **cobrar interés** charge interest **cobrarle de menos a alguien** undercharge

cobro nm (of debt) recovery n, payment n **cobro por cancelación** cancellation charge **cobro a la entrega** COD (cash on delivery) abbr **cobro en metálico** encashment **cobro de morosos** debt collection **cobro al recibo de mercancías** cash on receipt of goods

codicioso adj acquisitive adj, greedy adj

código nm code nm **código de barras** bar code **código fiscal** tax code **código postal** post code, zip code (US) **código de práctica** code of practice

coeficiente nm coefficient n **con alto coeficiente de mano de obra** labour-intensive **coeficiente de expansión, tasa de expansión** (LAm) rate of expansion **coeficiente de gastos** expenditure rate

cohecho nm bribe n, bribery n

coima nf (LAm) bribe n

coimear vb (LAm) bribe vb

coincidir vb concur vb, tally vb **coincidir con** tally with vb

cola nf queue n **cola de comunicantes** hold queue, hold line (US)

colaborar vb collaborate vb

colega nmf associate n, colleague n

colgar, cortar (LAm) vb (telephone) hang up vb

colonia *nf* **colonias (LAm)** suburbs, housing complex

coloquio *nm* colloquium *n*

combinación *nf* combination *n* **combinación de medios de márketing** marketing mix **combinación de productos** product mix

comentario *nm* comment *n*, observation *n*

comercial *adj* commercial *adj*, marketable *adj*

comercializable, mercadeable (LAm) *adj* marketable *adj*

comercialización, mercadeo (LAm) *nf* merchandizing *n* **comercialización de futuros** futures marketing

comercializar *vb* market *vb*, merchandise *vb*

comerciante, feriante; puestero, -era (LAm) *nmf, nmf; nm,f* dealer *n*, merchant *n*, trader *n* **comerciante al por mayor** wholesaler

comerciar *vb* trade *vb* **comerciar con alguien** trade with sb **comerciar como (name)** trade as

comercio *nm* business *n*, commerce *n*, dealing *n*, trade *n*, trading (US) *n* **comercio de acciones** equity trading **comercio armamentístico** arms trade **comercio bilateral** bilateral trade **comercio de exportación** export trade **comercio exterior** foreign trade, overseas trade **comercio de futuros** futures trading **comercio internacional** international trade **comercio al por mayor** wholesale trade **comercio al por menor** retail outlet, retail trade **comercio minorista** retail trade **el comercio textil** (informal) the rag trade **comercio de ultramar** foreign trade, overseas trade

comestible 1. *adj* edible *adj* **2.** *nm* food *n*

cometer *vb* commit *vb* **cometer un error** make a mistake

comicios *nm* election *n*, general election *n*

comisión *nf* commission *n*, committee *n*, fee *n*, tribunal *n*, brokerage *n* **comisión asesora** advisory committee **Comisión de Bolsa y Valores** SEC (Securities and Exchange Commission) *abbr*, SIB (Securities and Investment Board) *abbr* **Comisión Consultiva Europea** European Advisory Committee **comisión de control** watchdog committee **comisión ejecutiva** executive committee **Comisión Europea** European Commission **comisión de fábricas** factory board **Comisión de Mono-**

polios y Fusiones Monopolies and Mergers Commission

comisionista *nmf* broker *n*, commission agent *n*, commission broker *n*

comité *nm* committee *n* **comité de empresa** works committee **comité de supervisión** supervisory board

compañero, -era *nm,f* companion *n* **compañero de trabajo** workmate

compañía *nf* company *n* **compañía asociada** sister company **compañía constituida legalmente** incorporated company (US) **compañía de crédito comercial** finance company **compañía fiduciaria** trust company **compañía limitada** limited company **compañía naviera** shipping line company **compañía en un paraíso fiscal** offshore company **compañía registrada** registered company **compañía de seguros** insurance company **compañía de transportes** haulage/road haulage/transport company **compañía de venta por correo** mail-order house

comparativo *adj* comparative *adj*

compartir *vb* share *vb* **compartir las responsabilidades** share the responsibilities

compatible *adj* compatible *adj*

compensación *nf* compensation *n*, quittance *n* **compensaciones por enfermedad** health benefits

compensar *vb* (cheque) clear *vb*, equalize *vb* **compensar por** compensate for

competencia *nf* competition *n*, expertise *n*, jurisdiction *n*, qualification *n*, terms of reference *npl* **competencia desleal** unfair competition **competencia encarnizada** cut-throat competition **competencia extranjera** foreign competition **competencia fuerte/intensa** tough competition **competencia internacional** international competition **competencia leal** fair competition **competencia de mercado** market competition

competidor, -ora *nm,f* competitor *n*

competir *vb* compete *vb* **competir con un/una rival** compete with a rival

competitividad *nf* competitiveness *n*

competitivo *adj* competitive *adj* (price) keen *adj*

complejo 1. *adj* complex *adj* **2.** *nm* **complejo habitacional/de viviendas, colonia (LAm)** housing complex, housing estate, housing tenement (US) **complejo**

de viviendas subvencionadas housing project
complemento *nm* allowance *n*
completamente *adv* wholly *adv*
complicado *adj* complex *adj*
compra *nf* acquisition *n*, buy-out *n*, purchase *n* **una buena compra** a good buy **compra de cupos** quota buying **compra ficticia** fictitious purchase **compra a plazos** hire purchase **compras hechas sin salir del hogar** home shopping **compra de tierras** land purchase
comprador, -ora *nm,f* buyer *n*, vendee *n* **comprador de vivienda** home buyer
comprar *vb* purchase *vb*, bribe *vb* **comprar algo caro** buy sth at a high price **comprar algo a crédito** buy sth on credit **comprar en grandes cantidades** buy in bulk **comprar a granel** buy in bulk **comprarle su parte a** buy out **comprar algo al por mayor** buy sth wholesale **comprar algo a plazos** buy sth by instalments **comprar algo de segunda mano** buy sth second hand
compraventa *nf* buying and selling *n*
comprensión *nf* understanding *n*
comprobación *nf* proof *n*
comprobante *nm* voucher *n*
comprobar, chequear; checar (LAm) *vb* check *vb*
comprometer *vb* commit *vb*
comprometerse *vb* give one's word *vb*, undertake *vb*
compromiso *nm* (to meet) appointment *n*, engagement *n*, commitment *n*, obligation *n*, undertaking *n*
computadora, computador (LAm) *nf, nm* computer *n*
común *adj* common *adj* **en común** jointly *prep*
comunicación *nf* communication *n*
comunicado *nm* bulletin *n*, communication *n* **comunicado a la prensa** press release
comunicar *vb* inform *vb*, transmit *vb* **comunicar la reacción** give feedback **comunicarse con alguien** (phone) get through to sb
comunidad *nf* community *n* **Comunidad Europea del Carbón y del Acero** ECSC (European Coal and Steel Community) *abbr* **Comunidad Europea (CE)** European Community
conceder *vb* grant *vb* **conceder una desgravación** grant a rebate **conceder en**

franquicia franchise **conceder indemnización** pay compensation **conceder un permiso** license, furlough (US) **conceder un préstamo** grant a loan
concepto *nm* concept *n*, idea *n* **bajo ningún concepto** under no circumstances
concertar *vb* arrange *vb*, plan *vb* **concertar una cita, pedir una cita** (LAm) make an appointment
concesión *nf* franchise *n* (patent) grant *n* **concesión de franquicias** franchising
concesionario, -ria *nm,f* franchisee *n*, licensee *n*, authorized dealer *n*
concluir *vb* wind up *vb*, end *vb*
conclusión *nf* winding-up *n*, end *n*
concurrir *vb* concur *vb*
concurso, licitación (LAm) *nm*, *nf* tender *n*
condición *nf* condition *n* **condiciones de compra** conditions of purchase **condiciones de crédito** credit terms **condiciones de pago** conditions of payment **condiciones de trabajo** working conditions **condiciones de venta** conditions of sale **condiciones de vida** living conditions
conducta *nf* conduct *n* **conducta del consumidor** consumer habits **mala conducta** misconduct
conducto, ducto (LAm) *nm* pipeline *n*
conectar *vb* (phone) put sb through to sb (machine) turn on *vb*
conexión *nf* connection *n* **en conexión directa con el ordenador central** on--line *adj* **conexiones comerciales** (LAm) business contacts
confederación *nf* confederation *n* **Confederación de Sindicatos** Trades Union Congress
conferencia *nf* conference *n* **conferencia personal** person-to-person call
conferir *vb* confer *vb*
confiable *adj* (LAm) reliable *adj*
confianza *nf* confidence *n* **de la máxima confianza** gilt-edged
confidencial *adj* confidential *adj*
confirmación *nf* confirmation *n*
confirmar *vb* confirm *vb* **sin confirmar** unconfirmed
confiscación *nf* forfeit *n*, forfeiture *n*, repossession *n* **confiscación de acciones** forfeit of shares
confiscar *vb* impound *vb*, repossess *vb*
conflicto, diferendo (LAm) *nm* dispute *n* **conflicto colectivo** industrial dispute

conflicto laboral industrial dispute, labour dispute
conforme adj consistent adj, satisfied adj
conforme a in accordance with
congelación nf (on prices, wages) freeze n **congelación salarial** wage(s) freeze
congelar vb (prices, wages) freeze vb, peg vb
conglomerado nm conglomerate n
congreso nm conference n, congress n
conjunto 1. adj joint adj 2. nm unit n
conocer vb meet vb, know vb **conocer a alguien** make the acquaintance of sb **conocer algo a fondo** have a thorough knowledge of sth
conocido 1. adj well-known adj 2. nm,f **conocido, -ida de negocios** business acquaintance **conocidos de negocios, conexiones comerciales; palancas** (LAm) business contacts
conocimiento nm knowledge n **conocimiento de embarque** bill of lading **conocimiento de embarque de exportación** export bill of lading **conocimientos** expertise, knowledge **conocimientos básicos** working knowledge **conocimientos y experiencia** know-how **con conocimientos de informática** computer literate
consecución nf accomplishment n, achievement n
consecuencia nf consequence n **consecuencias** outcome
conseguir vb (capital, loan) raise vb, accomplish vb, achieve vb, gain vb, obtain vb, win vb **conseguir buen precio** get value for one's money **conseguir crédito** obtain credit
consejero, -era nm,f adviser/advisor n, director n
consejo nm advice n, council n **consejo de administración** board of directors **consejo de administración fiduciaria** (bank) trustee department **Consejo Británico** British Council **Consejo de Europa** Council of Europe **consejo de la fábrica** factory board **consejo de obreros** works council **consejo práctico** (suggestion) tip
consentimiento nm agreement n, consent n
consentir vb consent vb
conservar vb retain vb
consideración nf (for contract) consideration n
consigna nf left luggage n, left luggage office n, slogan n

consignación nf consignment n, shipment n
consolidación nf consolidation n
consolidar vb consolidate vb
consorcio nm consortium n, syndicate n
construcción nf construction industry n, building n **construcción naval** shipbuilding
cónsul nmf consul n
consulado nm consulate n
consultar vb consult vb, look up vb
consultivo adj advisory adj
consultor, -ora nm,f consultant n **consultor de empresas** management consultant
consultoría nf consultancy n, consulting (US) n
consumidor, -ora nm,f consumer n **consumidor final** end consumer
consumismo nm consumerism n
consumo nm consumption n **consumo global** world consumption
contabilidad nf accountancy n, book-keeping n **contabilidad comercial trimestral** quarterly trade accounts **contabilidad financiera** financial accounting **contabilidad general** general accounting **contabilidad gerencial** management accounting
contable nmf accountant n, book-keeper n **contable colegiado, -ada, contador, -ora público, -ica** (LAm) chartered accountant
contactar vb contact vb **contactar con** contact
contacto nm **contactos** connections, contacts **contactos comerciales, conexiones comerciales** (LAm) business contacts, business connections
contado adj few adj, numbered adj **al contado** for cash, in cash
contador, medidor (LAm) nm meter n
contar vb count vb, relate vb
contenedor nm container n
contener, postergar (LAm) vb (not release) hold back vb
contestación nf answer n **en contestación a su carta de** in reply to your letter of...
contestador nm answering machine n **contestador automático** answering machine **contestador telefónico** Ansaphone (R)
contestar vb answer vb
contrabandear vb smuggle vb
contracción nf contraction n
contraerse vb shrink vb
contrario adj contrary adj, opposite adj

contrario a la ética profesional unprofessional
contraste *nm* contrast *n*, hallmark *n* **en contraste con** in contrast to
contratación *nf* (to a position) appointment *n*, recruitment *n* **contratación de empleados/de personal** employee recruitment
contratante *adj* contracting *adj* **las partes contratantes** the contracting parties
contratar *vb* employ *vb*, hire *vb*, recruit *vb*, retain *vb*
contratista *nmf* builder *n*, contractor *n*, entrepreneur *n* **contratista de la construcción/de obras** building contractor **contratista de transporte por carretera** haulage contractor
contrato *nm* contract *n* **contrato de alquiler, contrato de arriendo** (LAm) hire contract **contrato en firme** formal contract **contrato de futuros** futures contract **contrato hipotecario** mortgage deed **contrato a plazo fijo** forward contract **contrato de préstamo** loan agreement **contrato de seguros** insurance contract **contrato-tipo** standard agreement **contrato de trabajo** employment contract
contravenir *vb* contravene *vb*
contribución *nf* contribution *n* **contribuciones municipales, tasas** (LAm) (tax) rates **contribución territorial rústica** land tax
contribuir *vb* contribute *vb*, subscribe *vb*
contribuyente *nmf* taxpayer *n*
control *nm* (customs) inspection *n* **control de aduana** customs check **control de calidad** quality control **control de crédito** credit control **control de divisas** exchange control **control de existencias** stock control, inventory control (US) **control financiero** financial control **control de finanzas** financial control **control de gastos** expense control **control de importaciones** import control **control de producción** production control **control público de existencias, Dirección General Impositiva; Impuestos Internos** (LAm) inventory control
controlador, -ora *nm,f* controller *n* **controlador aéreo** air traffic controller
convalidar *vb* validate *vb*
convenido *adj* agreed *adj*
convenio *nm* agreement *n*, covenant *n*, treaty *n* **convenio colectivo** collective agreement **convenio de compensación**

de cambio exchange clearing agreement **convenio internacional** international agreement **convenio sobre los precios mínimos de venta al público** fair-trade agreement **convenio salarial** wage agreement, wage(s) settlement
convenir *vb* agree *vb*
conversación *nf* conversation *n* **conversaciones comerciales** trade talks **conversación sobre ventas** sales talk
conversión *nf* conversion *n* **conversión al sistema métrico** metrication
convidar *vb* invite *vb*, offer *vb*
convocar *vb* call *vb*, convene *vb* **convocar una reunión** call/convene a meeting
cooperativa *nf* collective *n*, cooperative *n*
copia *nf* copy *n* **copia de la factura** duplicate invoice
copiar *vb* (photocopy) copy *vb*
copropiedad *nf* joint ownership *n*, timeshare *n*
corona *nf* crown *n* **corona danesa** (Danish) krone **corona noruega** (Norwegian) krone **corona sueca** (Swedish) krona
corporación *nf* corporation *n*, guild *n*
corporativo *adj* corporate *adj*
corredor, -ora *nm,f* broker *n* salesperson, agent **corredor de Bolsa, corredor** (LAm) floor broker, stockbroker **corredor marítimo** shipping broker **corredor de parquet** floor broker **corredor de seguros** insurance agent, insurance broker
corregir *vb* amend *vb*, correct *vb*
correo *nmf* courier *n*, mail *n*, post *n* **correo aéreo** airmail **correo certificado, correo recomendado** (LAm) registered mail **correo certificado con acuse de recibo** recorded delivery **correo electrónico** electronic mail, email **por servicio de correo** by courier service
correr *vb* run *vb*
correspondencia *nf* correspondence *n*
corresponder *vb* correspond *vb*, concern *vb* **nos corresponde** the onus is on us to...
corretaje *nm* brokerage *n*
corriente *adj* going *adj* **muy al corriente, muy interiorizado** (LAm) well-informed
corrupción *nf* corruption *n*
cortar *vb* cut *vb*, (phone) hang up (LAm) *vb*
corte *nf* court *n*
corto *adj* short *adj* **corto plazo** short term
coser *vb* sew *vb* **coser a máquina** machine sew
cosignatario, -ria *nm,f* cosignatory *n*
coste, costo (LAm) *nm* cost *n* **coste**

adicional extra cost **coste de capital** capital cost **coste de explotación** operating cost, running cost **coste indirecto** indirect cost **coste marginal** marginal cost **coste neto** net(t) cost **coste original** original cost **costes de administración** administrative costs **costes corrientes, costos de operación** (LAm) running costs **costes de manipulación** handling charges **costes de explotación** operating expenditure, operating expenses **costes fijos** fixed costs **costes fiscales** fiscal charges **costes judiciales** legal charge **costes de la mano de obra** labour costs **costes de mantenimiento** maintenance costs **costes de reparación** costs of repair **costes de transporte** carriage costs, forwarding charges **costes variables** variable costs **coste total** full cost **coste total de los salarios** wage(s) bill **coste de transporte** carrying cost **coste unitario, costo por unidad; costo unitario** (LAm) unit cost **coste de vida** cost of living

cotitular *nmf* joint holder *n*

cotización *nf* price *n*, quotation *n* **cotización de apertura** opening price **cotizaciones de la bolsa** stock exchange prices **cotizaciones a la Seguridad Social, aportes a la seguridad social** (LAm) social security contributions

coyuntura *nf* trend *n*, point in time *n*

creación *nf* establishment *n*, creation *n* **creación de empleo** job creation

crecer *vb* thrive *vb*, grow *vb*, increase *vb*

crecimiento *nm* growth *n* (in unemployment) rise *n* **crecimiento cero** zero growth **crecimiento económico** economic growth **crecimiento regido por las exportaciones** export-led growth

crédito *nm* cash advance *n*, credit *n*, goodwill *n*, loan *n* **crédito abierto** open credit **crédito en condiciones desventajosas** hard loan **crédito congelado** frozen credits **crédito al consumidor** consumer credit **crédito a la exportación** export credit **crédito extranjero** foreign loan **crédito fijo** fixed credit **crédito sin garantía** unsecured credit **crédito ilimitado** unlimited credit **crédito a largo plazo** long-term credit **crédito personal** personal loan **crédito puente** bridging loan, bridge loan (US)

crianza *nf* farming *n*, rearing *n*

crimen *nm* crime *n* **crimen organizado** racketeering

crisis *nf* (economic) depression *n* **crisis económica** economic crisis, financial crisis

criterio *nm* criterion *n*

criticar *vb* find fault with *vb* (disparage) knock *vb*

cronometraje *nm* timing *n*

crudo *adj* (unprocessed) raw *adj*, crude *adj*

cuadra *nf* (LAm) block *n*

cuadrar *vb* tally *vb*, tally up *vb*

cuadro *nm* table *n*, chart *n* **cuadros** leaders **cuadros medios** middle management

cualificación, calificación (LAm) *nf* qualification *n* **cualificaciones necesarias** necessary qualifications **cualificación profesional** professional qualification

cualificado, calificado; capacitado (LAm) *adj* qualified *adj* (worker) skilled *adj*

cualitativo *adj* qualitative *adj*

cuantitativo *adj* quantitative *adj*

cuanto *adv* as much as *adv* **en cuanto a** with regard to... **cuanto antes** a.s.a.p (as soon as possible) *abbr*

cuasicontrato *nm* quasi-contract *n*

cuasingresos *nmpl* quasi-income *n*

cuenta, adición; rubro (LAm) *nf, nf; nm* bill *n* tally *n* **cuenta de ahorros** deposit account **cuenta bancaria** bank account **cuenta bloqueada** blocked account **cuenta de caja de ahorros** savings account **cuenta corriente** current account **cuenta de crédito** charge account **cuenta de ejercicio** trading account **cuenta de explotación** trading account **cuenta de gastos de representación** expense account **cuenta nueva** new account **cuenta en participación** joint account **cuenta de pérdidas y ganancias** operating statement, profit and loss account **por cuenta propia** freelance **cuenta rebasada** overdrawn account **por cuenta y riesgo del comprador** at the buyer's risk **las cuentas** the books **cuentas a cobrar** accounts receivable **cuentas definitivas** final accounts **cuentas a pagar** accounts payable

cuestión *nf* matter *n*, question *n* **cuestión principal** key question

cuestionario *nm* questionnaire *n* **cuestionario para realizar investigaciones de mercado** market research questionnaire

culpa *nf* blame *n*, fault *n* **culpa concurrente** contributory negligence **culpa grave** gross negligence

cultivo *nm* farming *n* **cultivo comercial** cash crop

culto *adj* knowledgeable *adj*, educated *adj*
cumplir *vb* accomplish *vb*, carry out *vb*
cumplir sus compromisos meet one's
obligations **cumplir formalidades** observe formalities **cumplir con las leyes**
comply with legislation **cumplir su palabra** keep one's word **cumplir el reglamento** comply with the rules
cuota *nf* instalment *n*, quota *n*, share *n*,
effect *n*, payment *n*, toll *n* **cuota de
comisión** commission fee **cuota fija, tasa
de interés fija** (LAm) flat rate **cuota
inicial, pie** (LAm) down payment **cuota
de licencia** licence fee **cuota de mercado**
market share **cuotas fijas** standing
charges
cupo *nm* quota *n* **cupo arancelario** tariff
quota **cupo de importación** import quota
cupo de ventas sales quota
cupón *nm* coupon *n*
currículum *nm* curriculum vitae *n* **currículum vitae (CV)** curriculum vitae (CV),
résumé (US)
cursar *vb* send *vb*, study *vb*
cursillo *nm* short course *n* **cursillo de
actualización** training course
cursiva *nf* italic type *n*
curso *nm* process *n*, course *n*, direction *n*
curso de reciclaje, plan de recapacitación
(LAm) retraining programme, retraining
program (US)
curva *nf* curve *n* **curva de la experiencia**
experience curve **curva de rendimiento**
yield curve
dañar *vb* damage *vb*
daño *nm* damage *n* **daños por accidente**
accidental damage **daños materiales**
damage to property **daños sufridos por
mercancías durante el transporte** damage to goods in transit
dar *vb* give *vb* **dar cuentas de** account for
dar instrucciones brief **dar interés** bear
interest **dar orden de no pagar** cancel an
order **dar su palabra** give one's word **dar
por perdido** (debts) write off **dar por
terminado un asunto** (informal) shut up
shop **dar la vuelta a, voltear; dar vuelta**
(LAm) turn over
dato *nm* fact *n* **datos** data, information
datos de prueba test data **datos tabulados** tabulated data
deber 1. *nm* obligation *n* **2.** *vb* owe *vb*
debido *adj* appropriate *adj*, due *adj* **debido aviso** due warning
debido a *adv* due to *adv* **debido a
circunstancias imprevistas** due to un-

foreseen circumstances **debido a un
error** due to an oversight
debilitarse *vb* (market) weaken *vb*
débito *nm* debit *n*
decidirse *vb* make a resolution *vb*
declaración *nf* statement *n* **declaración de
aduana** customs declaration **declaración
jurada** affidavit **declaración de tonelaje**
bill of tonnage
declarar *vb* declare *vb* **sin declarar**
(goods) undeclared **declararse en
huelga, ir al paro; declararse en paro**
(LAm) strike **declarar siniestro total**
(vehicle) write off
declive *nm* decline *n* **declive económico**
economic decline
dedicar *vb* dedicate *vb* **dedicarse al
negocio de** (informal) be in the trade
deducción *nf* deduction *n* **deducción
impositiva** tax allowance
deducible *adj* deductible *adj*
deducir *vb* deduct *vb*
defecto *nm* defect *n*, fault *n* **sin defecto**
zero defect **defecto grave** serious fault
defecto menor minor fault **defecto
oculto** hidden defect
defectuoso *adj* defective *adj*
defender *vb* defend *vb* **defenderse bastante bien en algo** have a working
knowledge of sth
defensor, -ora *nm,f* defender *n* **defensor
del pueblo** ombudsman
deficiencia *nf* deficiency *n*
deficiente *adj* deficient *adj*,
unsatisfactory *adj*
déficit *nm* deficit *n* **déficit de la balanza de
pagos** balance of payments deficit **déficit
comercial** trade gap **déficit presupuestario, déficit presupuestal** (LAm) budgetary deficit
deflación *nf* deflation *n*
deflacionista *adj* deflationary *adj*
DEG (derechos especiales de giro) *abbr*
SDRs (special drawing rights) *abbr*
dejar *vb* abandon *vb*, lend *vb* **dejar de** quit
dejar atrás (resign from) leave **dejar
flotar** (currency) float **dejar pasar** overlook
delegación *nf* delegation *n* **delegación de
poderes** delegation
delegado, -ada *nm,f* delegate *n* **delegado
sindical** shop steward, union representative
delegar *vb* delegate *vb*, farm out *vb*
delito *nm* offence *n*, offense (US) *n*
demanda *nf* legal action *n*, demand *n*

demanda de aumento salarial wage claim **demanda de consumo** consumer demand **demanda máxima** peak demand **con demanda que supera a la oferta** oversubscribed **haber mucha demanda** be in hot demand
demandante *nmf* claimant *n*
democracia *nf* democracy *n* **democracia industrial** industrial democracy
demografía *nf* demography *n*
demora *nf* delay *n*, holdup (LAm) *n*
demorar *vb* delay *vb*
departamento *nm* department *n* **departamento de comercialización** marketing department **Departamento de Comercio y Exportación** Board of Trade **departamento de control de prácticas comerciales** Trading Standards Office (US) **Departamento de Estado** Federal Bureau (US) **departamento de exportación** export department **departamento de importación** import department **departamento de márketing** marketing department **Departamento Nacional de Investigación Económica** National Bureau of Economic Research (US) **departamento de personal** personnel department **departamento de reclamaciones** claims department, complaints department **Departamento del Tesoro** the Treasury Department (US)
dependiente, -nta, corredor, -ora; empleado, -ada de tienda (LAm) *nm,f* salesperson *n*, shop assistant *n*
depositar *vb* deposit *vb*
depositario, -ria *nm,f* depository *n*
depósito, bodega (LAm) *nm*, *nf* entrepôt *n*, warehouse *n*, warehousing *n*, deposit (down payment) *n* **en depósito aduanero** in bond **depósito aduanero, bodega aduanera** (LAm) bonded warehouse, customs warehouse **depósito de contenedores** container depot **depósito a largo plazo** long deposit
depreciación *nf* depreciation *n*, write-off *n*
depreciar *vb* write down *vb*
depreciarse *vb* depreciate *vb*, lose value *vb*
depresión *nf* slump *n*
derecha *nf* (politics) right *n*
derecho *nm* (customs) duty *n* law *n*, right *n* **el derecho a algo** the right of sth **derecho civil** civil law **derecho consuetudinario** common law **derecho contractual** law of contract **el derecho a hacer algo** the right to do sth **derecho de importación** import duty **derecho internacional** international

law **derecho laboral** employment law, labour law **derecho mercantil** commercial law **derecho de paso** right of way **derecho penal** criminal law **derecho público** public law **derecho a recurrir** right of recourse **derechos sobre el activo** equity **derechos adquiridos** vested rights **derechos de aduana** customs charges **derechos de amarre** mooring rights **derechos de autor** copyright **derechos de dársena** harbour dues **derechos exclusivos** sole rights **derechos de muelle** quayage **derechos portuarios** harbour dues, harbour fees **derechos de reproducción** copyright **derecho de suscripción de nuevas acciones** warrant **derecho de voto** voting right
deriva *nf* drift *n* **deriva de ingresos** earnings drift
derivado *nm* by-product *n*
derogación *nf* abolition *n*
derrochar *vb* squander *vb*
desaceleración *nf* slowdown *n* **desaceleración económica** economic slowdown
desacelerar *vb* slow down *vb*
desagraviar *vb* make amends *vb*
desahucio *nm* eviction *n*
desarrollar *vb* (research, project) progress *vb*, develop *vb*
desarrollo *nm* expansion *n*, growth *n*, development *n* **desarrollo económico** economic development/growth **desarrollo profesional** career development
descansar *vb* take a break *vb*
descargar *vb* unload *vb*
descargo *nm* quittance *n*
descendente *adj* downward *adj*
descenso *nm* decrease *n*
descompuesto *adj* (LAm) out-of-action *adj*
descomunal *adj* king-size(d) *adj*
descontado *adj* discounted *adj*, reduced *adj*
descripción *nf* description *n* **descripción del puesto de trabajo** job description
descuento *nm* deduction *n*, discount *n*, rebate *n* **con descuento** at a discount **descuento por grandes cantidades** quantity discount **descuento por pago al contado** cash discount **descuento por volumen** volume discount
descuido *nm* oversight *n*
desechable *adj* (not for reuse) disposable *adj*
desechos *nm* waste *n*, spoilage *n* **desechos industriales** industrial waste

desembalar, desempacar (LAm) *vb* unpack *vb*

desembolsar *vb* disburse *vb*

desembolso *nm* expenditure *n* **desembolsos** outgoings

desempleado, cesante (LAm) *adj* jobless *adj*, redundant *adj*, unemployed *adj* **los desempleados, los cesantes** (LAm) the jobless

desempleo, cesantía (LAm) *nm, nf* unemployment *n* **desempleo masivo, cesantía general** (LAm) mass unemployment

desequilibrio *nm* imbalance *n* **desequilibrio demográfico** population gap

desfalco *nm* embezzlement *n*

desgaste *nm* wastage *n*

desglosar *vb* itemize *vb*

desglose *nm* breakdown *n*, itemization *n* **desglose de estadísticas** (of figures) breakdown

desgravable *adj* deductible *adj*, tax--deductible *adj*

desgravación *nf* deduction *n*, exemption *n*, rebate *n* **desgravación fiscal** tax allowance

desgravar *vb* deduct *vb*

deshacer *vb* unpack *vb*, dissolve *vb*

deshacerse *vb* break up *vb* **deshacerse de** unload

desintegración *nf* breakup *n*

desintegrar *vb* break up *vb*, split *vb*

desocupado *adj* idle *adj*, vacant *adj* **los desocupados, los cesantes** (LAm) the jobless

despachar *vb* (goods) dispatch *vb* **sin despachar** (customs) uncleared **despachar algo por aduana** clear sth through customs

despacho *nm* office *n* **despacho de aduana** customs office **despacho de billetes, boletería** (LAm) ticket office

despedir, botar (LAm) *vb* (employee) dismiss *vb*, axe* *vb*, sack *vb*, ax *vb*, fire (US) *vb* **despedir a alguien por reducción de plantilla** make sb redundant **despedirse de alguien** take leave of sb **despedir temporalmente** (workers) lay off

desperdicio *nm* wastage *n*, waste *n*

despido *nm* redundancy *n*, termination of employment *n* **despido injusto** unfair dismissal, wrongful dismissal

despilfarrador *adj* spendthrift *adj*

despilfarrar *vb* squander *vb*, waste *vb*

desplazamiento *nm* shift *n*

desplome *nm* (of economy) collapse *n*

despreocupado *adj* negligent *adj*

destinar *vb* assign *vb* **destinar fondos** fund *vb*

destinatario, -ria *nm,f* addressee *n*, consignee *n*, recipient *n*, sendee *n*

destrozar *vb* wreck *vb*

detallar *vb* itemize *vb*

detener *vb* (delay) hold up *vb*, arrest *vb* **detener el pago de un cheque** stop a cheque

determinar *vb* govern *vb*, determine *vb*

deuda *nf* borrowing *n*, debt *n* **deuda consolidada** funded debt **deuda fiscal** tax liability **deuda incobrable** bad debt **deuda nacional** national debt **deuda pendiente** outstanding debt **deudas a largo plazo** fixed liabilities

deudor, -ora *nm,f* debtor *n* **deudor hipotecario** mortgagor

devaluación *nf* devaluation *n*

devengar *vb* earn *vb*, yield *vb* **que no devenga interés** non-interest-bearing **devengar interés, intereses** bear interest

devolver *vb* refund *vb*, repay *vb*, send back *vb* **devolver un cheque** refer a cheque (to drawer) **devolver la llamada, devolver el llamado** (LAm) (on phone) call back *vb*

día *nm* day *n* **al día, moderno** (LAm) up-to-date **día festivo, día feriado; fiesta patria** (LAm) bank holiday **día laborable** workday (US) **día libre** day off work **día de liquidación** (stock exchange) Account day

diagrama *nm* diagram *n* **diagrama de flujos** flow chart

diario *nm* newspaper *n*, daily newspaper *n* **diario hablado** news bulletin

dictar *vb* dictate *vb* **dictar un mandato judicial** issue a writ

dieta *nf* allowance *n* **dieta para gastos de alojamiento** accommodation allowance

difamación *nf* libel *n*

diferendo *nm* (LAm) dispute *n*

diferido *adj* (tax) deferred *adj*

dificultad *nf* difficulty *n* **dificultad financiera** financial difficulty

digital *adj* digital *adj*

digno *adj* worthy *adj* **digno de notarse** noteworthy

diluir *vb* water down *vb*

dimisión *nf* resignation *n*

dimitir *vb* leave *vb*, resign *vb* **dimitir el cargo** resign from office

dinámica *nf* dynamics *npl*

dinámico adj dynamic adj, high--powered adj
dineral, platal; lanón (LAm) nm (money) bundle n, packet n
dinero, plata (LAm) nm, nfcash n, money n **dinero caliente** hot money **dinero caro** dear money **dinero de curso forzoso** fiat money **dinero en efectivo, plata** (LAm) cash **dinero especulativo** hot money **dinero fraccionario** fractional money **dinero en mano** spot cash **dinero en metálico** hard cash **dinero público** public money **dinero a la vista** call money
Dios nm God n **a la buena de Dios, a la sanfasón** (LAm) hit-or-miss
diputado, -ada nm,f Member of Parliament (MP) (GB) n
dirección nf administration n, fronting n, leadership n (of business) operation n **alta dirección** senior management, top management **Dirección General Impositiva** (LAm) Inland Revenue **sin dirección** zero address **dirección comercial** business address, business management, sales management **dirección financiera** financial management **dirección general** general management, management, regional office **dirección hotelera** hotel management **dirección de información** information management **dirección lineal** line management **dirección por objetivos** management by objectives **dirección de oficina** office management **dirección particular** home address **dirección de personal** personnel management **dirección portuaria** harbour authorities **dirección privada** home address **dirección registrada** registered address **mala dirección** mismanagement
directamente adv directly adv, first--hand adv
directivo, -iva nm,f director n
directo adj direct adj, non-stop adj
director, -ora nm,f director n, executive n, manager n, supervisor n **director adjunto** associate director, deputy director **director de banco** bank manager **director de campo** field manager **director de contabilidad** head accountant **director ejecutivo** managing director **director de fábrica** plant manager, works manager **director de finanzas de la empresa** company treasurer **director general** chief executive, general manager **director gerente** managing director **director de márketing, mercadeo** (LAm) marketing

director **director obrero** worker-director **director de planta** plant manager **director regional** area manager **director de sucursal** branch manager **director técnico** technical director
dirigir vb (department) head vb, administer vb, be head of vb, manage vb **dirigir un hotel** run a hotel **dirigirse a** address, head for
disco nm disk n **disco duro** hard disk **disco flexible** floppy disk **disco magnético** magnetic disk
discrepancia nf variance n, disagreement n
diseñado adj designed adj **una máquina bien/mal diseñada** a machine of good/bad design
diseñador, -ora nm,f (commercial) designer n
diseñar vb design vb
diseño nm design n **diseño asistido por ordenador (CAD), diseño asistido por computadora** (LAm) computer-aided design (CAD) **diseño de cuestionarios** questionnaire design
disminución nf abatement n, decrease n, depletion n, reduction n, slowdown n
disminuir vb abate vb, decrease vb
disparar vb (gun) fire vb
dispensable adj non-essential adj
disponer vb arrange vb, provide vb, have available vb
disposición nf (stipulation) provision n **de acuerdo con las disposiciones** according to the regulations **disposiciones aduaneras** customs regulations **disposiciones de liquidación** winding-up arrangements
disputa, diferendo (LAm) nf, nm dispute n
disquete nm disk n
distancia nf distance n **a distancia** long--range
distribución nf distribution n **distribución de noche** overnight delivery
distribuidor, -ora nm,f distributor n **distribuidor autorizado** authorized dealer
distribuir vb (payments) spread vb, distribute vb
distrito nm district n **distrito postal** postal area
diversificación nf diversification n
diversificarse vb diversify vb
diverso adj wide-ranging adj
dividendo nm dividend n **dividendo de fin de año** year-end dividend
dividir vb split vb, divide vb
divisa nf (foreign) currency n **divisa débil** soft currency **divisa de reserva** reserve

currency **divisas** foreign currency, foreign exchange **divisas forzosas** forced currency **divisas fuertes** hard currency
división *nf* (of company) division *n* **división del mercado** market segmentation **división del trabajo** division of labour **división triple** three-way split **división por zonas** zoning
divulgar *vb* broadcast, *vb* (document) circulate *vb*
doble *adj* double *adj*, two-way *adj* **de doble mano/de doble vía** (LAm) two-way
documento *nm* document *n* **documento de trabajo** working paper
dólar, verde (LAm) *nm* buck* (US) *n* **el dólar de Hong Kong está vinculado al dólar norteamericano** the HK dollar is pegged to the US dollar
domiciliación *nf* bank payment *n*, bank details *npl*
domicilio *nm* home *n* **domicilio social** HO (Head Office), headquarters, registered address, registered office
dominar *vb* govern *vb* **dominar los principios básicos de algo** have a working knowledge of sth
donación *nf* bequest *n*, donation *n*
dotación *nf* endowment *n* **dotación de personal** staffing
ducto *nm* (LAm) pipeline *n*
dueño, -eña *nm,f* owner *n*, proprietor *n* **dueño de casa** householder **dueño de hacer lo que quiera** free agent
duplicado *nm* duplicate *n*
echar *vb* fire *vb*, throw *vb* **echarse a perder** go to waste **echar por tierra** wreck **echar del trabajo, botar del trabajo** (LAm) sack, fire* (US)
econometría *nf* econometrics *n*
economía *nf* (system) economy *n* economics *n*, savings *npl* **economía avanzada** advanced economy **economía global** global economy **economía libre** free economy **economía de mercado** free market economy, market economy **economía de mercado libre** free market economy **economía mixta** mixed economy **economía nacional** national economy **economía nueva** young economy **economía planificada** planned economy **economías de escala** economies of scale **economía subdesarrollada** underdeveloped economy **economía sumergida, economía informal; economía paralela** (LAm) black economy **eco-**

nomía en vías de desarrollo developing economy
económico *adj* economical *adj*, financial *adj*, economic *adj*, (price) low *adj*
economista *nmf* economist *n*
ecu (European Currency Unit) *nm* ECU (European Currency Unit) *abbr*
editorial *nf* publishing house *n*
efectivo *nm* cash *n*, hard cash *n*
efecto *nm* effect *n*, toll *n* **efecto bancario** (financial) draft **efecto indirecto** spin-off **efectos financieros** financial effects **efectos negociables** commercial paper **efecto a la vista** sight draft
eficaz *adj* efficient *adj*
eficiencia *nf* efficiency *n*
eficiente *adj* efficient *adj*
EFTA (la) *nf* (abbr) EFTA (European Free Trade Association) *abbr*
egresado, -ada *nm,f* (LAm) graduate *n*
ejecución *nf* enforcement *n*, foreclosure *n* **ejecución de un juicio hipotecario** foreclosure
ejecutar *vb* (policy) enforce *vb*, carry out *vb*
ejecutivo, -iva *nm,f* executive *n*
ejemplo *nm* example *n*, sample *n*
ejercer *vb* exercise *vb*, practice *vb*
ejercicio *nm* exercise *n*, (financial) year *n* **ejercicio comercial** trading year **ejercicio financiero** financial year **ejercicio fiscal** fiscal year, tax year
elaboración *nf* making *n*, preparation *n*
elaborar *vb* process *vb* **elaborar un informe, hacer un reporte** (LAm) draw up a report **elaborar el presupuesto** draw up a budget
elasticidad *nf* elasticity *n* **elasticidad de demanda** elasticity of demand **elasticidad de ingresos** income elasticity **elasticidad de producción** elasticity of production
elección *nf* election *n*, option *n* **elecciones generales** general election **elecciones municipales** local election
electrónico *adj* electronic *adj*
elevar *vb* raise *vb*
eliminación *nf* elimination *n*
elogioso *adj* complimentary *adj*
embajada *nf* embassy *n*
embalaje *nm* package *n*, packaging *n*
embalar *vb* pack *vb* **embalar algo** box sth up
embarcarse *vb* go aboard *vb*
embargar *vb* impound *vb*

embargo *nm* embargo *n* **embargo co-mercial** trade embargo
embolsar *vb* net(t) *vb*
embotellamiento *nm* bottleneck *n*
emergencia *nf* emergency *n*
emigración *nf* emigration *n*
emisión *nf* broadcast *n*, flotation *n* **emisión de derechos** rights issue **emisión fiduciaria** fiduciary issue **emisión de nuevas acciones** share issue, stock issue (US)
emitir *vb* (notes) issue *vb* broadcast *vb*, transmit *vb* **emitir una factura** issue an invoice
empleado, -ada *nm,f* clerk *n*, employee *n* **empleado de tienda** (LAm) shop salesperson **empleado de banco, bancario** (LAm) bank clerk **empleado de oficina** clerical worker, white-collar worker **empleados** staff
emplear *vb* employ *vb*, spend *vb*, utilize *vb*
empleo *nm* employment *n*, utilization *n* **empleo eventual, trabajo temporario** (LAm) temporary employment **empleo fijo** permanent employment **empleo remunerado** gainful employment
emprender *vb* undertake *vb*
empresa *nf* (project) enterprise *n* business *n*, company *n*, corporation *n*, undertaking *n* **empresa que comercia con otra** trading partner **empresa conjunta** collaborative venture, joint venture **empresa constructora** builder, building firm **empresa de creación reciente** new business **empresa donde los trabajadores no tienen obligación de afiliarse** open shop **empresa que emplea exclusivamente a trabajadores sindicados** closed shop **empresa envasadora** packing house (US) **empresa estatal** government entreprise, state-owned entreprise **empresa exterior** foreign company **empresa extraterritorial** offshore company **empresa familiar** family business, family corporation **empresa ficticia** phoney* company **empresa filial** branch company, subsidiary **empresa ilimitada** unlimited company **empresa líder del mercado** market leader **empresa líder del sector** market leader **empresa matriz** parent company **empresa mediana** medium--sized firm **empresa multinacional** multinational corporation **empresa de primera clase** blue-chip company **empresa privada** private enterprise **empresa de propiedad pública** state-owned enterprise

empresa pública government enterprise **empresa rival** competing company **empresa de tamaño mediano** medium-sized firm **empresa de transporte por carretera** haulage company, freight company (US) **empresa de transportes** carrier, transport company **empresa de transportes urgentes** express carrier **empresa de utilidad pública** public utility **las grandes empresas** big business
empresarial *adj* corporate *adj*, entrepreneurial *adj*
empresario, -ria *nm,f* employer *n*, entrepreneur *n*
encabezamiento, acápite (LAm) *nm* heading *n*
encabezar *vb* be head of *vb*
encargado, -ada *nm,f* foreman/forewoman *n* **encargado de compras** buyer
encargar *vb* farm out *vb*, place an order *vb* **encargar a alguien con algo** charge sb with sth
encargarse *vb* undertake *vb* **encargarse de** (deal) handle
encargo, comisión (LAm) *nm, nf* commission *n*, job *n*, request *n*
encender *vb* light up *vb*, switch on *vb*
enchufe *nm* **enchufes, conexiones comerciales; palancas** (LAm) business contacts
encierro *nm* sit-in protest *n* **encierro en señal de protesta** (strike) sit-in
encomendar *vb* charge *vb*, entrust *vb*
encontrar *vb* find *vb* **encontrarse con** meet
encuentro *nm* meeting *n*
encuesta *nf* survey *n* **encuesta familiar** household survey
endeudado *adj* indebted *adj*
endeudamiento *nm* debt *n* **endeudamiento de una sociedad** corporate debt
endeudarse *vb* get into debt *vb*
endosar *vb* (cheque) endorse *vb*
enfermedad *nf* illness *n* **enfermedad profesional** occupational disease
enfermo, -rma *nm,f* patient *n* **enfermo fingido** malingerer
enlace *nm* link *n* **enlace sindical** shop steward
enmendar *vb* amend *vb*
enmienda *nf* amendment *n*
ensayo *nm* test *n* **ensayo y error** trial and error
enser *nm* **enseres** equipment, fittings

enseres domésticos domestic goods, household goods
entablar *vb* begin *vb*, institute *vb* **entablar juicio hipotecario** foreclose **entablar negociaciones** begin negotiations **entablar un pleito** take legal action
entender *vb* hear *vb*, understand *vb* **entenderse con alguien** relate to sb
entendimiento *nm* understanding *n*
entidad *nf* institution *n* **entidad caritativa** charitable trust **entidad crediticia** lender **entidad financiera** financial company, financial institution
entrada, pie (LAm) *nf, nm* deposit *n*, down payment *n* **entrada gratuita/libre** free entry **entrada para mercancías exentas de derechos de aduana, entrada para mercaderías exentas de derechos de aduana** (LAm) entry for free goods **entrada en vigor, entrada a vigor** (LAm) entry into force
entrar *vb* enter *vb* **entrar en** access **entrar a** access **entrar en dársena** dock **entrar en déficit** be in the red **entrar en liquidación voluntaria** go into voluntary liquidation
entrega *nf* delivery *n* **entrega contra reembolso** cash on delivery (COD) **entrega a domicilio** home delivery **entrega futura** future delivery **entrega general** general delivery (US) **entrega gratuita/incluida en el precio** free delivery **entrega insuficiente** short delivery **entrega urgente** express delivery
entregar *vb* (goods) deliver *vb*, file *vb*, hand over *vb* **entregar por servicio de mensajero** deliver by courier
entrevista *nf* interview *n*
entrevistar *vb* interview *vb*, hold an interview *vb*
envasar *vb* pack *vb*
envase *nm* package *n*, packaging *n*
enviar *vb* (goods) dispatch *vb*, forward *vb*, send *vb* **enviar por fax** fax
envío *nm* consignment *n*, forwarding *n*, remittance *n* **envío parcial** part shipment
época *nf* season *n*, period *n*
equilibrar *vb* balance *vb* **equilibrar el presupuesto** balance the budget
equilibrio *nm* equilibrium *n*
equipamiento *nm* equipment *n*
equipar *vb* equip *vb*
equiparación *nf* comparison *n* **equiparación de cargas** equalization of burdens
equipo *nm* computer hardware *n*, equipment *n*, kit *n* **equipo de investiga-**

ción research team **equipo de oficina** office equipment **equipo de trabajo** working party **equipo de vídeo** video facilities
equivocación *nf* mistake *n*
equivocarse *vb* make a mistake *vb*
ergonomía *nf* ergonomics *n*
error *nm* mistake *n* **error de cálculo** miscalculation **error de copia** clerical error **error tipográfico** typing error
escala *nf* scale *n* **escala móvil** sliding scale **a escala nacional** nationwide **sin escalas** non-stop **escala salarial** salary/wage scale **escala de tiempo** timescale **a gran escala** large-scale
escalada *nf* (prices) escalation *n*, increase *n*
escalera *nf* staircase *n* **escalera mecánica** escalator
escalonar *vb* graduate *vb*, (holidays) stagger *vb*
escasez *nf* deficiency *n*, lack *n*, scarcity *n*, shortage *n*
escindirse *vb* split *vb*
esconder *vb* hide *vb*, hoard *vb*
escribir *vb* write *vb* **escribir a máquina, tipear** (LAm) type *vb*
escrito *adj* written *adj* **escrito a mano** handwritten *adj*
escritura *nf* (law) deed *n* **escritura de propiedad** title deed **escritura de transferencia** deed of transfer **escritura de venta** deed of sale
escudo *nm* escudo *n*
esfuerzo *nm* effort *n* **esfuerzos** labour, effort, labor (US)
eslogan *nm* slogan *n*
espacio *nm* room *n*, space *n* **espacio disponible en un muelle** quayage **espacio para maniobrar** room for manoeuvre
especialidad *nf* speciality *n*
especialista *nm,f* consultant *n*, specialist *n* **especialista en idiomas** language specialist
especializado, capacitado (LAm) *adj* (worker) skilled *adj*
especializar *vb* specialize *vb*
especificación *nf* specification *n*
especulador, -dora *nm,f* speculator *n*
especular *vb* profiteer *vb*, speculate *vb* **especular al alza** (stock exchange) bull *vb*
esperar *vb* (wait) hang on *vb* (on phone) hold on *vb* **esperando para hablar** (on phone) on hold
espiral *nm* spiral *n* **espiral inflacionista** inflationary spiral

espónsor *nmf* sponsor *n*

estabilidad *nf* stability *n* **estabilidad financiera** financial stability

estable *adj* (economy) stable *adj*

establecer *vb* establish *vb* **establecer un fideicomiso** set up a trust

establecimiento *nm* establishment *n*, institution *n*

estación *nf* season *n* **estación de autobuses, estación de micros/omnibuses/colectivos** (LAm) bus station

estacional *adj* seasonal *adj*

estadística *nf* statistic *n* **estadísticas** statistics **estadísticas de la balanza comercial** trade figures **estadísticas consolidadas** consolidated figures

estado *nm* government *n*, state *n* **estado asistencial/benefactor** welfare state **estado de cuenta** bank balance, statement of account **estado de cuentas** bank statement **estado financiero** financial statement

estafa *nf* fraud *n*, racket *n*, swindle* *n*

estafador, -ora *nm,f* swindler* *n*, racketeer *n*

estafar *vb* defraud *vb*

estafeta *nf* sub post office *n*

estancamiento *nm* stagnation *n*

estandarización *nf* standardization *n*

estar *vb* be *vb* **estar de acuerdo** agree **estar a la cabeza de** (department) head **estar desempleado, estar en cesantía** (LAm) be out of work **estar al día** (events) keep up with **estar dispuesto a dar referencias sobre** act as referee **estar encargado** be in charge **estar encomendado de algo** hold sth in trust **estar exento de IVA** be zero-rated for VAT **estar insolvente** be bankrupt **estar necesitado de** be in need **estar en números rojos** be in the red **estar en paro, estar en cesantía** (LAm) be out of work **estar en plantilla, estar en planilla** (LAm) be on the payroll **estar pluriempleado** moonlight*

estatuto *nm* statute *n*

esterlina *nf* sterling *n*

estimar *vb* estimate *vb*

estimular *vb* stimulate *vb* **estimular la producción** boost production

estipulación *nf* requirement *n* **de acuerdo con sus estipulaciones** in accordance with your requirements

estoc *nm* (goods) stock *n*, inventory (US) *n* **en estoc** in stock

estraperlo *nm* black market *n*

estrategia *nf* strategy *n* **estrategia de**

crecimiento growth strategy **estrategia de desarrollo** development strategy **estrategia económica** economic strategy **estrategia de exportación** export strategy **estrategia financiera** financial strategy **estrategia de inversión** investment strategy

estratégico *adj* strategic *adj*

estrés *nm* stress *n* **estrés profesional** executive stress

estropear *vb* damage *vb*

estructura *nf* structure *n* **estructura financiera** financial structure

estudiar, revisar (LAm) *vb* examine *vb*, study *vb*

estudio *nm* research *n*, study *n*, workshop *n* **estudio económico** economic survey **estudio de mercado** consumer survey, market research, market research survey **estudios sobre el terreno** field work **estudio del trabajo** work study **estudio de viabilidad** feasibility study

etapa *nf* stage *n* **por etapas** in stages

etiqueta *nf* label *n* **etiqueta del precio** price ticket

etiquetar *vb* label *vb*

eurobono *nm* eurobond *n*

eurocapital *nm* eurocapital *n*

eurocheque *nm* eurocheque *n*

eurocracia *nf* eurocracy *n*

eurócrata *nmf* eurocrat *n*

eurocrédito *nm* eurocredit *n*

eurodiputado, -ada Member of the European Parliament (MEP) *n*

eurodivisa *nf* eurocurrency *n*

eurodólar *nm* eurodollar *n*

euroescéptico *adj* eurosceptic *n*

eurofondos *nmpl* eurofunds *npl*

eurofusión *nf* euromerger *n*

euromercado *nm* euromarket *n*

euromoneda *nf* euromoney *n*

europeo *adj* European *adj*

evadir *vb* avoid *vb*, evade *vb*

evaluación, avalúo (LAm) *nf, nm* appraisal *n*, assessment *n*, evaluation *n* **evaluación de puestos de trabajo** job analysis **evaluación del rendimiento** performance appraisal

evaluador, -dora *nm,f* referee *n*

evaluar *vb* assess *vb*

evasión *nf* evasion *n* **evasión fiscal/de impuestos** tax avoidance/evasion

evitar *vb* avoid *vb*

exactitud *nf* accuracy *n*

exacto *adj* accurate *adj*

exagerar *vb* exaggerate *vb* **exagerar los méritos de** oversell

examen, revisación (LAm) *nm, nf* examination *n*

examinar *vb* examine *vb*, inspect *vb*

excedencia, licencia (LAm) *nf* leave of absence *n*

excedente *nm* surplus *n* **excedente de financiación** financing surplus **excedente de importaciones** import surplus

excesivo *adj* exorbitant *adj*, redundant *adj*

exceso *nm* surplus *n* **exceso de equipaje** excess luggage **exceso de personal** overmanning **exceso de peso** excess weight **exceso de reservas** excess reserves

excluir *vb* exclude *vb*

exención *nf* exemption *n*, waiver *n* **exención fiscal concedida a una nueva empresa** tax holiday

exento *adj* exempt *adj* **exento de impuestos** tax-exempt, tax-free, zero rate/ rating

exhibición *nf* (of goods) display *n* (exhibition) show *n*

exhibir *vb* display *vb*, exhibit *vb*

exigir *vb* call for *vb*, demand *vb*, insist on *vb* **exige el contrato que** it is a requirement of the contract that... **exigir el pago inmediato de un préstamo** (loan) call in

existencia *nf* existence *n*, stock *n* **existencias** (goods) stock, inventory (US) **existencias acabadas** finished stock **con las existencias agotadas** out of stock **de existencias disponibles** ex stock **existencias pendientes** outstanding stock **existencias de reserva** reserve stock

éxito *nm* achievement *n*, success *n*

exoneración *nf* exemption *n*

expandir *vb* expand *vb*

expansión *nf* expansion *n*, growth *n* **expansión del comercio** expansion of trade **expansión económica** economic expansion **expansión industrial** industrial expansion **expansión del mercado** market growth **expansión urbana descontrolada** urban sprawl **en fuerte expansión** booming

expectativa *nf* expectation *n* **expectativas del consumidor** consumer expectations

expedición, flete de mercancías (LAm) *nf, nm* forwarding *n*, dispatch *n*

expedidor, -ora *nm,f* dispatcher *n*, shipper *n*

expedir *vb* (tickets) issue *vb* **expedir un recibo** issue a receipt

expeditar *vb* expedite *vb*

experiencia *nf* experience *n* **con experiencia** experienced **experiencia laboral** work experience

experimentar *vb* experience *vb*

experto, -rta *nm,f* expert *n*

expiración *nf* expiry *n*, expiration (US) *n*

explicar *vb* explain *vb* **explicarse claramente** make oneself clear

explotación *nf* exploitation *n*, operation *n*

explotado *adj* overworked *adj*

explotador, -ora *nm,f* shark* *n*

explotar *vb* exploit *vb*, operate *vb* **explotar recursos** tap resources

exponer *vb* display *vb*, exhibit *vb*

exportación *nf* export *n* **exportación de capitales** export of capital **exportaciones de capital** capital exports **exportaciones invisibles** invisible exports **exportaciones mundiales** world exports **exportaciones visibles** visible exports

exportador, -ora *nm,f* exporter *n*

exportar *vb* export *vb*

exposición *nf* (of goods) display *n* exhibition *n* **exposición universal** world fair

expresar *vb* express *vb* **expresar una objeción** make/raise an objection

expropiación *nf* expropriation *n*

expropiar *vb* expropriate *vb*

extender *vb* (cheques/shares) issue *vb* **extender un cheque** make out a cheque **extender un recibo** issue a receipt **extender un contrato** extend a contract

exterior *adj* external *adj*, foreign *adj*, overseas *adj*

externo *adj* external *adj*

extorsión *nf* extortion *n*

extra *adj* extra *adj*

extracción *nf* extraction *n*

extragrande *adj* king-size(d) *adj*

extranjero *adj* foreign *adj*, overseas *adj*

f.a.b. (franco a bordo) *abbr* FOB (free on board) *abbr*

fábrica *nf* works *n*, factory *n* **fábrica piloto** pilot plant

fabricación *nf* manufacture *n*, production *n* **de buena fabricación** well-made **fabricación asistida por ordenador (CAM)**, **fabricación asistida por computadora** (LAm) computer-aided manufacture (CAM) **fabricación en cadena** flow line production, flow

production **fabricación en serie** mass production
fabricado *adj* made *adj*, produced *adj*
fabricado en Francia made in France
fabricante *nmf* manufacturer *n*, producer *n*
fabricar *vb* manufacture *vb*, produce *vb*
fácil *adj* easy *adj* **fácil acceso** accessibility **fácil de utilizar** user-friendly
facilidad *nf* facility *n*
facsímil *nm* facsimile (fax) *n*
factible *adj* feasible *adj*, workable *adj*
factor *nm* factor *n* **factor limitativo** limiting factor **factor de producción** factor of production
factura *nf* bill *n*, invoice *n* **factura definitiva** final invoice **factura negociable** negotiable bill **factura sin saldar** unpaid bill **factura de venta** bill of sale
facturación *nf* invoicing *n*, turnover *n*, check-in *n* **facturación de activo fijo** fixed asset turnover
facturar, voltear; dar vuelta (LAm) *vb* turn over *vb*
faena *nf* task *n*
fallar *vb* (negotiations) fail *vb*
fallo *nm* failure *n* **fallo de poca importancia** minor fault
falsificación *nf* counterfeit *n*, falsification *n*, forgery *n* **falsificación de cuentas** falsification of accounts
falsificar *vb* counterfeit *vb*
falso *adj* fictitious *adj*, phoney* *adj*
falta *nf* default *n*, fault *n*, lack *n*, shortage *n* **falta de actividad** (laxity) slackness *n* **a falta de datos** in the absence of information **falta de entrega** non-delivery **a falta de información** in the absence of information **falta de inversión** lack of investment
fama *nf* reputation *n*
fanático, -ica *nm,f* fanatic *n*, supporter *n*
favor *nm* favour *n*
fax *nm* facsimile (fax) *n*
fe *nf* faith *n* **de buena fe** bona fide
fecha *nf* date *n* **sin fecha** not dated **fecha de caducidad** best-before date, expiry date, termination date **fecha de entrega** delivery date **fecha de expedición** date of dispatch **fecha objetivo** target date **fecha tope** time limit **fecha de vencimiento** expiry date, expiration (US)
federación *nf* federation *n*
federal *adj* federal *adj*
feria *nf* (exhibition) show *n* **feria de muestras** trade fair
feriante *nm,f* (LAm) operator *n*

ferrocarril *nm* railway *n*, railroad (US) *n*
fiabilidad *nf* reliability *n*
fiable *adj* (LAm) reliable *adj*
fiacún, -una *nm,f* (LAm) shirker *n*
fianza *nf* bail *n*, caution money *n*, collateral *n* **fianza fiduciaria** fiduciary bond
fichar *vb* sign *vb* **fichar a la entrada al trabajo, checar tarjeta al entrar al trabajo** (LAm) clock in **fichar a la salida del trabajo, checar tarjeta al salir del trabajo** (LAm) clock out
ficticio *adj* fictitious *adj*
fidedigno, fiable; confiable (LAm) *adj* reliable *adj*
fideicomisario, -ria *nm,f* trustee *n*
fideicomiso *nm* trusteeship *n*
fidelidad *nf* accuracy *n*, fidelity *n* **fidelidad a un establecimiento** customer loyalty
fiesta *nf* holiday *n*, festival *n* **fiesta nacional, día feriado; fiesta patria** (LAm) bank holiday (GB)
figura *nf* figure *n*
fijar *vb* fix *vb* **fijar el precio** fix the price **fijarse una meta** set a target
fijo *adj* built-in *adj*, fixed *adj*
filial *nf* subsidiary company **filial de entera propiedad** wholly-owned subsidiary
fin *nm* end *n*, purpose *n* **fin de año fiscal** fye (fiscal year end) *abbr* **sin fines de lucro** non-profitmaking
final 1. *adj* terminal *adj* 2. *nm* end *n*
financiación *nf* financing *n*, funding *n* **financiación de acciones** equity financing **financiación de déficit** deficit financing **financiación de valores** equity financing
financiar *vb* finance *vb*, fund *vb*
financiero *adj* financial *adj*
financiero, -era *nm,f* financier *n*
finanzas *nfpl* finance *n* **las altas finanzas** high finance
fingido *adj* phoney* *adj*
firma *nf* signature *n*
firmante *nmf* signatory *n* **los firmantes del contrato** the signatories to the contract
firmar *vb* sign *vb* **firmar un cheque** sign a cheque **firmar un contrato** sign a contract
fisco, Dirección General Impositiva; Impuestos Internos (LAm) *nm, nf; nmpl* the Inland Revenue, The Internal Revenue Service (IRS) (US)
fletador, -ora *nm,f* freighter *n*
flete, flete de mercaderías (LAm) *nm* freight *n*, forwarding *n*
flexibilidad *nf* (of prices) flexibility *n*

flexibilizar *vb* (market) open up *vb* (restrictions) relax *vb*
flojonazo, -aza *nm,f* (LAm) shirker *n*
florín *nm* guilder *n*
fluctuación *nf* fluctuation *n* **fluctuaciones de ventas** fluctuation in sales
fluctuante *adj* (prices) volatile *adj*
fluctuar *vb* fluctuate *vb* (market) turn *vb*
fluido *adj* fluid *adj*
flujo *nm* flow *n* **flujo de caja** cash flow **flujo de caja descontado** discounted cash flow (DCF) **flujo de caja negativo** negative cash flow **flujo de fondos** funds flow **flujo de ingresos** flow of income
folleto *nm* leaflet *n* **folleto informativo** prospectus **folleto publicitario** brochure, prospectus
fomentar *vb* boost *vb*, promote *vb* **fomentar la demanda** boost demand
fondo *nm* fund *n* **en el fondo** at the bottom **fondo de amortización** redemption fund **fondo de comercio, llave** (LAm) goodwill **fondo de custodia** trust fund **fondo de emergencia** emergency fund **Fondo Europeo de Cooperación Monetaria (FECM)** European Monetary Cooperation Fund (EMCF) **Fondo Europeo de Desarrollo (FED)** European Development Fund (EDF) **Fondo Europeo de Desarrollo Regional (FEDR)** European Regional Development Fund (ERDF) **fondo de fideicomiso** trust fund **fondo de inversión mobiliaria, costo por unidad; costo unitario** (LAm) unit trust **Fondo Monetario Internacional (FMI)** International Monetary Fund (IMF) **fondo de pensiones** pension fund **fondo de seguros** insurance fund **fondos para invertir** capital funds **fondos mutuos, costo por unidad; costo unitario** (LAm) unit trust, mutual fund (US) **Fondo Social Europeo (FSE)** European Social Fund (ESF) **fondos públicos** public funds
forma *nf* form *n*, means *npl*, (printed) form (LAm) *n* **forma de pago** method of payment
formación *nf* instruction *n*, training *n* **formación de capital** capital formation **formación de directivos** management training **formación de empleados** employee training
formal *adj* businesslike *adj*, formal *adj*, reliable *adj*, responsible *adj*
formalidad *nf* reliability *n* **formalidades aduaneras** customs clearance **formali-**
dades aduaneras/legales customs/legal formalities
formar, capacitar (LAm) *vb* (staff) train *vb*, constitute *vb*
formulario, impreso de aplicación (LAm) *nm* form *n*, application form *n* **formulario de pedido** order form
fortuna *nf* fortune *n*
fotocopia *nf* photocopy *n*
fotocopiadora *nf* photocopier *n*, Xerox (R) *n*
fotocopiar *vb* (photocopy) copy *vb* photocopy *vb*, xerox *vb*
fracasar *vb* (attempts) fail *vb*
fracaso *nm* failure *n*, write-off *n*
fracción *nf* fraction *n*
fraccionamiento *nm* split division *n*
fraccionario *adj* fractional *adj*
frágil *adj* fragile *adj*, handle with care *vb*
franco 1. *adj* free *adj*, frank *adj* **franco a bordo** free on board (FOB) **franco a domicilio** carriage paid, franco domicile **franco en fábrica** ex factory/works **franco en muelle** FAS (free alongside ship) *abbr*, free on quay **franco de porte, franco de flete** (LAm) carriage paid, free of freight **franco de precio** franco price **2.** *nm* franc *n* **franco belga** Belgian franc **franco francés** French franc **franco suizo** Swiss franc
franquear *vb* frank *vb*, exempt *vb*
franqueo *nm* postage *n* **franqueo pagado** Freepost (R) (GB) *n*
franquicia *nf* franchise *n*, franchise outlet *n*
fraude *nm* fraud *n* **fraude fiscal** tax evasion
fraudulento *adj* fraudulent *adj*
frecuencia *nf* frequency *n*
frenar *vb* (inflation) halt *vb*
frenarse *vb* slow down *vb*
frontera *nf* frontier *n*
fuente *nf* (of a product) origin *n* source *n*
fuerte *adj* (competition) keen *adj* well--made *adj*, strong *adj*
fuerza *nf* power *n* **con fuerza jurídica** legally binding **fuerza laboral** workforce **fuerzas del mercado** market forces
fuga *nf* escape *n*, flight *n* **fugas de existencias** stock shrinkage
función *nf* (role) function *n* **funciones ejecutivas** executive duties
funcionamiento *nm* (of machine) operation *n*
funcionario, -ria *nm,f* civil servant *n*, official *n* **funcionario de aduana** customs officer

fundación *nf* (of company) formation *n* **fundación benéfica** charitable trust
fundador, -ora *nm,f* founder *n*
fundamental *adj* main *adj*, basic *adj*
fundar *vb* found *vb* **fundar una empresa** found a company
fusión *nf* amalgamation *n*, merger *n* **fusión horizontal** horizontal integration
fusionarse *vb* amalgamate *vb*, merge *vb*
futuro *nm* future commodity **futuros futures**
gama *nf* (of products) range *n* **gama de productos** product line
ganado *adj* earned *adj*, gained *adj*
ganancia, utilidad (LAm) *nf* profit *n*, benefit *n* **ganancias** earnings, proceeds **ganancias y pérdidas** profit and loss **una parte de las ganancias** a share in the profits
ganar *vb* earn *vb*, gain *vb*, win *vb* **ganarse apoyo** win support **ganarse la vida** make a living
ganga, pichincha (LAm) *nf* bargain *n*
garante, garantía (LAm) *nmf* backer *n*, guarantor *n*
garantía *nf* caution money *n*, collateral *n*, guarantee *n*, pledge *n*, warranty *n*, backer (LAm) *n* **bajo garantía** under warranty **garantía de calidad** quality guarantee **garantía colateral** collateral security
garantizar *vb* warrant *vb*
gas *nm* gas *n* **gas natural** natural gas
gastar *vb* spend *vb*
gasto *nm* cost *n*, expenditure *n*, expense *n* **gasto complementario, costo adicional** (LAm) extra cost **gasto indirecto, costo indirecto** (LAm) indirect cost **gasto público** state expenditure **gastos** expenditure, outgoings, spending **gastos de administración, costes de administración** (LAm) administrative costs **gastos bancarios** bank charges **gastos en capital** capital expenditure **gastos de capital** capital outlay **gastos de envío** delivery charges **gastos de estiba** stowage **gastos de explotación, costos de operación** (LAm) business expenses, operating costs **gastos de fábrica, costos de fábrica** (LAm) factory costs **gastos generales** overheads **gastos generales de fabricación** factory overheads **gastos del hogar** household expenditure **gastos indirectos** indirect expenses, overhead costs **gastos menores** incidental expenses **gastos de representación** entertainment expenses

gastos de tramitación, costos de manipulación (LAm) handling charges **gastos de viaje** travelling expenses, travel expenses (US) **gastos de transporte** carriage charges
GATT (Acuerdo General sobre Aranceles Aduaneros y Comercio) *nm* GATT (General Agreement on Tariffs and Trade) *abbr*
generación *nf* generation *n* **generación de ingresos** income generation
generar *vb* generate *vb* **generar ingresos** generate income
género *nm* **géneros** merchandise **géneros futuros** future goods
generosidad *nf* generosity *n*
geografía *nf* geography *n* **geografía económica** economic geography
gerencia *nf* management *n* **gerencia de personal** personnel management
gerente *nmf* manager *n* **gerente regional** area manager
gestión *nf* (of business) operation *n* **gestión de deudas de otras compañías con descuento** (of debts) factoring **gestión de empresas** business management **gestión financiera** financial management **gestión ministerial, ministerio; secretaría** (LAm) ministry **gestión de recursos humanos (GRH)** human resource management (HRM) **gestión de riesgos** risk management **gestión de tareas** task management **gestión del tiempo** time management **gestión total de calidad** TQM (Total Quality Management) *abbr* **gestión de transacciones** transaction management **gestión de ventas** sales management
gestionar *vb* address *vb*, negotiate (LAm) *vb*, manage *vb*
girar *vb* (cheque) draw *vb* **girar en descubierto** overdraw **girar en descubierto una cuenta** overdraw on an account
giro *nm* (financial) draft *n* remittance *n*, turnabout *n* **giro bancario** bank draft **giro positivo** upturn **giro postal** money order
global *adj* global *adj*, net(t) *adj*, worldwide *adj*
globalización *nf* globalization *n*
gobernar *vb* govern *vb*
gobierno *nm* government *n*
gordo *nm* jackpot *n*
grado *nm* level *n*, grade *n* **de alto grado** high-grade **grado de rendimiento** earning capacity, earning power
graduar *vb* graduate *vb*

gráfico *nm* chart *n*, graph *n* **gráfico de barras** bar chart **gráfico sectorial** pie chart **gráficos de ordenador** computer graphics
grande, gran *adj* large *adj*, great *adj* **Gran Bretaña, La Gran Bretaña** (LAm) Great Britain
gratificación *nf* gratuity *n*, perk *n* **gratificación por fin de servicio** golden handshake, golden parachute **gratificación por méritos** merit payment
gratis *adv* free of charge *adv*
gratuito *adj* free of charge *adj*
gravar *vb* (tax) levy *vb* **gravar con un impuesto** impose a tax
gremio *nm* guild *n*, syndicate (LAm) *n*
grueso *adj* thick *adj*
grupo *nm* group *n*, (of goods) batch *n* **grupo de países** group of countries **grupos socioeconómicos** socio-economic categories
guardamuebles *nm* depository *n*, furniture storage *n*
guardar *vb* keep *vb*, store *vb* **guardarse** (goods) keep *vb* **guardarse dinero** (money) keep back *vb*
guardián, -ana *nm,f* (fig.) watchdog *n*
guerra *nf* war *n* **guerra comercial** trade war **guerra de precios** price war
guía *nf* handbook *n* **guía comercial** trade directory **guía de fabricantes y comerciantes** trade directory **guía telefónica, directorio telefónico** (LAm) telephone directory **guía de turismo** courier, tourist guide
h. *abbr* (hour) h *abbr*
habilidad *nf* ability *n*, skill *n*
habitación *nf* room *n* **habitación libre** vacancy
hablar *vb* speak *vb*, talk *vb* **hablar mal de** (disparage) knock **hablar de negocios** talk business **hablar en serio** talk business **hablar del trabajo** (informal) talk shop
hacendado, -ada *nm,f* (LAm) landlord *n*
hacer *vb* make *vb*, do *vb*, wage *vb* **hace un dineral** he/she mints money **hacemos referencia a nuestra carta de** we refer to our letter of... **hacer aportes** (LAm) contribute **hacer la caja** cash up **hacer una campaña** run/wage a campaign **hacer caso** take notice **hacer circular** (document) circulate **hacer la competencia** compete **hacer cuadrar las cuentas** balance the books **hacer la cuenta** tally up **hacer un curso de reconversión,**

hacer un curso de recapacitación (LAm) retrain **hacer dinero** make money **hacer factoring** (debts) factor **hacer una fortuna** make a fortune **hacer frente a sus obligaciones** meet one's obligations **hacer un gran avance** make a breakthrough **hacer huelga, ir al paro; declararse en paro** (LAm) strike *vb* **hacer huelga de celo, trabajar a reglamento** (LAm) work to rule **hacer impresión** (credit card) take an imprint **hacerle un favor a alguien** do sb a favour **hacerle propaganda a, hacerle réclame a** (LAm) advertise **hacer una oferta, licitar** (LAm) bid **hacer un pedido** place an order **hacer planes** make plans **hacer progresos** make headway **hacer público** (policy) issue **hacer reformas en** refurbish **hacer una reserva, hacer una reservación** (LAm) make a reservation **hacer responsable a alguien** hold sb liable/responsible **hacerse con** acquire **hacerse buena reputación** build a reputation **hacerse cargo de** take charge of sth **hacerse con clientes** win customers **hacerse conocer** build a reputation **hacerse rico** make a fortune **hacerse un seguro** take out insurance **hacer transbordo** (transport) transfer **hacer uso de algo** make use of sth **hacer una visita** visit
hacia *prep* towards *prep* **hacia abajo** downward **hacia arriba** upward
Hacienda, Dirección General Impositiva; Impuestos Internos (LAm) *nf, nf; nmpl* the Inland Revenue, The Internal Revenue Service (IRS) (US), tax office **Hacienda Pública (la)** the Treasury
hecho *adj* made *adj*, done *adj* **hecho a mano** handmade **hechos ciertos** known facts **los hechos puros y duros** the hard facts
heredar *vb* inherit *vb*
herencia *nf* inheritance *n* **herencia fiduciaria** trust estate
hermético *adj* (fig.) watertight *adj*
hidroelectricidad *nf* hydroelectricity *n*
hierro *nm* iron *n* **hierro en lingotes** pig iron
hiperinflación *nf* hyperinflation *n*
hipermercado *nm* hypermarket *n*
hipoteca *nf* mortgage *n*
hipótesis *nf* hypothesis *n*
historial *nm* record *n* **historial de empleo, historia profesional** (LAm) employment/work history
hogar *nm* household *n*

hoja, forma (LAm) *nf* (document) form *n*
hoja de cálculo spreadsheet **hoja de instrucciones** instruction sheet **hoja de solicitud, impreso de aplicación** (LAm) application form
homenaje *nm* testimonial *n*
homólogo, -oga *nm,f* opposite number *n*
honor *nm* honour *n* **de honor** honorary
honorario 1. *adj* honorary *adj* **2.** *nm* fees *npl* **honorarios por asesoría** consultancy fees, consulting fees (US)
hora *nf* hour *n*, appointment (LAm) *n* **por hora** hourly, per hour **a la hora** per hour **hora cero** zero hour **hora de cierre** closing time **hora extra(s), sobretiempo** (LAm) overtime **hora de Greenwich** GMT (Greenwich Mean Time) *abbr* **hora punta, hora pico** (LAm) rush hour **horas de oficina** business hours, office hours **horas punta** peak period, busy hours (US) **horas de trabajo** business hours **a última hora** at short notice
horario *nm* schedule *n*, timetable *n* **fuera del horario de trabajo** after hours **horario de atención al público** opening times **horario bancario** banking hours **horario fijo** fixed hours **horario flexible** flexitime, flextime (US) **horario normal de venta al público** normal trading hours **horario de oficina** business hours, office hours **horario de trabajo** working hours
hostelería *nf* hotel industry/trade *n*
hotel *nm* hotel *n* **hotel de cinco estrellas** five-star hotel
huelga, paro (LAm) *nf, nm* industrial action *n*, strike *n*, strike action *n* **huelga de advertencia** token strike **huelga no autorizada** unofficial strike **huelga autorizada por el sindicato, paro oficial** (LAm) official strike **huelga general, paro general** (LAm) general strike **huelga ilegal** unofficial strike **huelga oficial, paro oficial** (LAm) official strike **huelga pasiva, trabajo a reglamento** (LAm) (strike) go--slow **huelga salvaje, paro incontrolado; paro imprevisto** (LAm) wildcat strike
huelguista, trabajador, -ora en paro (LAm) *nmf, nm,f* striker *n*
huso *nm* **huso horario** time zone
identificación *nf* identification *n* **identificación por marca** family branding
idioma *nm* language *n* **idioma de trabajo** working language
igualar *vb* equalize *vb*
igualdad *nf* equality *n*, parity *n* **igualdad salarial** equal pay

ilegal *adj* illegal *adj*
imagen *nf* image *n* **imagen de marca** brand image **imagen pública de la empresa** corporate image
impago *nm* non-payment *n*
impedir, tapar (LAm) *vb* block *vb*, forestall *vb*
imponer *vb* (tax) levy *vb* **imponer un embargo** impose an embargo **imponer un límite a algo** put a ceiling on sth
importación *nf* import *n*, importation *n* **importaciones** imports **importaciones invisibles** invisible imports
importador, -ora *nm,f* importer *n*
importancia *nf* importance *n*
importante *adj* leading *adj*, weighty *adj* **más importante** major
importar *vb* (be of importance to) concern *vb* import *vb*
importe *nm* amount *n* **importe neto** net(t) amount **importe a pagar** outstanding amount **importe a pagar todavía** unpaid balance
imposición *nf* (of tax) imposition *n*, deposit *n*, taxation *n* **imposición del 0% del IVA** zero rate/rating for VAT **imposición de sociedades** corporate taxation
impreso, forma (LAm) *nm, nf* (document) form *n* **impreso de aplicación** (LAm) application form **impreso de reclamación** claim form
imprudencia *nf* imprudence *n* **imprudencia temeraria** gross negligence
impuesto *nm* tax *n* **antes de deducir impuestos** before tax **después de deducir impuestos** after tax **impuesto sobre beneficios extraordinarios** excess profit(s) tax **impuesto directo** direct tax **impuesto elevadísimo** supertax **impuesto a la exportación** export tax **impuesto indirecto** indirect tax **impuesto de lujo** luxury tax **impuesto sobre el patrimonio** wealth tax **impuesto sobre la(s) plusvalía(s)** capital gains tax **impuesto sobre la propiedad residencial** house duty (US) **impuesto sobre la renta, impuesto a los réditos** (LAm) income tax **impuesto sobre la renta a cuota fija, impuesto a los réditos a cuota fija** (LAm) flat-rate income tax **impuesto sobre la renta personal** income tax **impuestos sobre gastos** expenditure taxes **Impuestos Internos** (LAm) Inland Revenue **impuestos locales** local taxes **impuesto de sociedades** corporation tax **impuesto territorial** land tax **impuesto de transferencia** transfer duty

impuesto sobre transferencias transfer tax **impuesto sobre el valor agregado/ añadido (IVA)** value-added tax, sales tax (US) **impuesto sobre la venta** excise duty **impuesto sobre las ventas al detalle** retail sales tax **impuesto sobre el volumen de ventas y negocios** turnover tax **incluidos impuestos y gastos en entrega** inclusive of tax and delivery costs **van incluidos los impuestos** taxes are included
impulso *nm* boost *n*
inactivo *adj* idle *adj*
inadecuado *adj* inadequate *adj*, inappropriate *adj*
incentivo *nm* incentive *n* (formal) perquisite *n* **incentivos** fringe benefits **incentivos financieros** financial incentive
inclinar *vb* lean *vb*, incline *vb*
incompetente *adj* inadequate *adj*, inefficient *adj*
incondicional *adj* unconditional *adj*
inconveniente **1.** *adj* inconvenient *adj* **2.** *nm* inconvenience *n*
inconvertible *adj* non-convertible *adj*
incorporado *adj* built-in *adj*
incrementar *vb* (value) enhance *vb* (prices, taxes) increase *vb* (price, interest rate) raise *vb* **incrementar aranceles** raise tariffs **incrementar las ventas** boost sales
incremento *nm* (in inflation) rise *n* **incremento salarial** pay rise, wage increase
incumbir *vb* concern *vb*, be incumbent *vb* **nos incumbe...** the onus is on us to...
incumplimiento *nm* neglect *n* **incumplimiento de contrato** breach of contract
incumplir *vb* default *vb*
incurrir *vb* incur *vb* **incurrir en** (expenses) incur
indemnidad *nf* indemnity *n*
indemnización *nf* compensation *n*, recompense *n*, reparation *n* **indemnización por despido** golden handshake, golden parachute, severance pay
indemnizar *vb* indemnify *vb* **indemnizar por** compensate for
indicar *vb* indicate *vb*, specify *vb*
índice *nm* index *n* **índice de acciones** share index **índice del coste de la vida, índice del costo de la vida** (LAm) cost of living index **índice de cotización de acciones** Thirty-Share Index **índice de cotización bursátil del 'Financial Times'** FT Index (Financial Times Index) **índice de crecimiento** growth index **índice Dow**

Jones Dow-Jones average (US) **índice ponderado** weighted index **índice de precios** price index **índice de rotación de existencias** turnover rate
indicio *nm* indication *n*, sign *n*
indirecto *adj* indirect *adj*
industria *nf* industry *n* **industria del acero** steel industry **industria aeroespacial** aerospace industry **industria de asistencia médica** health care industry **industria del automóvil** automobile/motor industry **industria automovilística** motor industry **industria clave** key industry **industria de la construcción** building/ construction industry **industria de construcción de viviendas** housing industry **industria familiar** family industry **industria farmacéutica** pharmaceutical industry **industria hotelera** hotel industry/trade **industria minera** mining industry **industria nacional** home industry **industria pesada** heavy industry **industria petrolera** oil/petroleum industry **industria del plástico** plastics industry **industria química** chemical industry **industria de servicios** service industry **industria textil** textile industry **la industria del turismo** the tourist trade **la industria del vestido** (informal) the rag trade
industrial *adj* industrial *adj*
industrialización *nf* industrialization *n* **de reciente industrialización** newly-- industrialised
ineficiente *adj* inefficient *adj*
inesperado *adj* unexpected *adj*
inestabilidad *nf* instability *n*
inestable *adj* (prices) volatile *adj*
infalible *adj* (fig.) watertight *adj*
inferior *adj* (goods) inferior *adj*
inflación *nf* inflation *n* **inflación de demanda por cambio de estructura** bottleneck inflation **inflación galopante** galloping inflation **inflación nominal** nominal inflation **inflación provocada por la demanda excesiva** excess demand inflation
inflacionista *adj* inflationary *adj*
influencia *nf* patronage *n*, influence *n*
información *nf* data *npl*, feedback *n*, information *n*, information desk *n* **información clasificada como secreta** classified information **información concreta** hard news/information **información confidencial acerca del mercado** market tip

informado adj knowledgeable adj
informar vb brief vb, inform vb, notify vb
informática nf information technology (IT) n
informe nm briefing n, reference n, report n **informe de calidad** quality report **informe sobre la calidad** quality report **informe financiero** financial report
infracapitalizado adj undercapitalized adj
infracción nf contravention n, offence n, offense (US) n
infraestructura nf infrastructure n **infraestructura económica** economic infrastructure
infrasegurado adj underinsured adj
infrautilizado adj underemployed adj
infravalorar vb undervalue vb
infringir vb contravene vb
infructuoso adj unprofitable adj
ingeniería nf engineering n **ingeniería de caminos** civil engineering **ingeniería civil** civil engineering **ingeniería eléctrica** electrical engineering **ingeniería marina** marine engineering **ingeniería mecánica** mechanical engineering **ingeniería de precisión** precision engineering
ingresar vb deposit vb **ingresar algo en una cuenta** credit sth to an account
ingreso nm entry n, payment into n **de altos ingresos** high-income **ingreso fiscal** fiscal receipt **ingreso real** real wages **ingresos** earnings, income, financial means, revenue, takings **ingresos básicos** basic income **ingresos brutos** gross income **ingresos disponibles** disposable income **ingresos de explotación, ingresos de operación** (LAm) operating income **ingresos de los factores** factor income **ingresos familiares** family income **ingresos fijos** fixed income **ingresos franqueados** franked income **ingresos gravables** taxable income **ingresos marginales** marginal revenue **ingresos netos** net(t) earnings/income **ingresos de publicidad** advertising revenue
iniciado, -ada nm,f insider n
iniciar vb initiate vb **iniciar una moda** set a trend
iniciativa nf (project) enterprise n **iniciativa del gobierno** government enterprise **iniciativa privada** private enterprise
inicio nm start-up n
inmovilizado nm fixed assets npl
inmovilizar vb (capital) tie up vb
inoportuno adj inconvenient adj

inquilino, -ina nm,f lessee n, occupant n, tenant n
insatisfactorio adj unsatisfactory adj
insistir vb insist vb **insistir en** insist on vb
insolvencia nf bankruptcy n, insolvency n
insolvente adj bankrupt adj, insolvent adj
inspeccionar vb inspect vb **inspeccionar algo, chequear; checar** (LAm) make a check on sth
inspector, -ora nm,f inspector n **inspector de fábrica** factory inspector
instalación nf facility n, installation n **instalaciones** amenities **instalaciones fijas y accesorios** fixtures and fittings **instalaciones portuarias** harbour facilities
instalar vb establish vb, instal(l) vb
institución nf institution n **institución crediticia** credit institution
instituto nm institute n
instrucción nf instruction n, statement n
insuficiente adj deficient adj, inadequate adj
integración nf integration n **integración económica** economic integration **integración vertical** vertical integration
integrar vb amalgamate vb
intensificarse vb escalate vb
intensivo adj intensive adj **intensivo en capital** capital-intensive
intento nm bid n
intercambiar vb swap vb
intercambio nm swap n
intercesión nf intervention n
interconectar vb network vb
interés nm appeal n, interest n, takeup n **sin interés** ex interest, interest-free **interés acumulado** accrued interest **interés bruto** gross interest **interés compuesto** compound interest **intereses en títulos** equity interests **interés fijo** fixed interest **interés nacional** national interest **interés neto** net(t) interest **interés personal** vested interest **interés de tipo flotante, interés de tasa flotante** (LAm) floating rate interest **interés trimestral** quarterly interest
interesar vb appeal vb (be of importance to) concern vb
interino, provisorio (LAm) adj interim adj
interior adj inland adj, inner adj
intermediario, -ria nm,f jobber n, middleman n
intermedio adj interim adj, intermediary adj, median adj
internacional adj international adj
interrelación nf interface n

interurbano *adj* long-distance *adj*
intervención *nf* intervention *n* **intervención del estado** state intervention
intervenir *vb* intervene *vb*
interventor, -ora *nm,f* auditor *n*, inspector *n* **interventor de cuentas** auditor
intransferible *adj* non-transferable *adj*
introducir *vb* (product) launch *vb*, introduce *vb* **introducir legislación** introduce legislation
inutilizable, descompuesto (LAm) *adj* out of action *adv/prep*
invendible *adj* unmarketable *adj*, unsaleable *adj*
invendido *adj* unsold *adj*
inventario *nm* inventory *n* **inventario por cierre de ejercicio** year-end inventory **inventario de existencias** stocktaking
inversión *nf* investment *n*, stake *n* **inversión bruta** gross investment **inversión de capital** capital expenditure **inversión cotizada** quoted investment **inversión de empresa** corporate investment **inversiones** investment **inversión exterior** foreign investment **inversión financiera** financial investment **inversión neta** net(t) investment
inversionista *nmf* investor *n*
inversor, -ora *nmf* investor *n*, stakeholder *n*
invertir *vb* (money) invest *vb*, reverse *vb*
investidura *nf* installation *n*, investment *n*
investigación *nf* enquiry *n*, research *n* **investigación de campo** field investigation, field research **investigación sobre el consumo** consumer research **investigación y desarrollo (I&D)** research and development (R&D) **investigación de mercado** market research, market research survey
invisible *adj* invisible *adj*
invitación *nf* invitation *n*
invitado, -ada *nm,f* visitor *n*
invitar *vb* invite *vb* **invitar a un cliente** entertain a client
ir *vb* go *vb* **ir por buen camino** be on the right track **ir camino de** head for **ir contracorriente** buck a trend **ir al extranjero** go abroad **ir recortando** (stocks) run down **irse** leave **irse al extranjero** go abroad **ir tirando** tick over
irrecuperable *adj* (loss) irrecoverable *adj*
irrevocable *adj* irrevocable *adj*
isla *nf* island *n* **Islas Británicas** British Isles
itinerario *nm* itinerary *n*

IVA (impuesto al valor agregado, impuesto sobre el valor añadido) *abbr,nm* VAT (value added tax) *abbr*
jefe, -efa *nm,f* boss *n*, manager *n* **jefe de contabilidad** chief accountant **jefe de departamento** head of department **jefe ejecutivo** chief executive **jefe de finanzas** chief financial officer **jefe de gobierno** head of government **jefe de línea** line manager **jefe de taller** works manager
jerarquía *nf* (corporate) hierarchy *n* **jerarquía de datos** data hierarchy **jerarquía de dirección** executive hierarchy **jerarquía de necesidades** hierarchy of needs
jingle *nm* jingle *n* **jingle publicitario** advertising jingle
jornada *nf* day's work *n* **a jornada completa** full-time **a jornada reducida** part--time
jubilación *nf* retirement *n*, retirement pension *n* **jubilación anticipada** early retirement
jubilarse *vb* retire *vb*
judicial *adj* judicial *adj*
jugar *vb* play *vb* **jugar al mercado** play the market
juicio *nm* opinion *n*, lawsuit *n*
junta *nf* board *n* **junta anual** AGM (Annual General Meeting) *abbr* **junta de dirección** board meeting **junta directiva** board of directors **junta extraordinaria** extraordinary meeting **junta general ordinaria** ordinary general meeting
jurado *nm* jury *n*
jurisdicción *nf* jurisdiction *n*
justificar *vb* account for *vb*, warrant *vb*
justo *adj* fair *adj*
kilo *nm* kilogram *n*, kg *abbr*
kilometraje *nm* kilometres travelled *npl*
kilómetro *nm* kilometre *n*, km *abbr*, kilometer (US) *n*
kilovatio *nm* kilowatt *n*, kW *abbr*
kilovatio-hora kWh *abbr*
Km *abbr* kilometre *n*, km *abbr*, kilometer (US)
labor *nf* labour *n*, work *n* **labor de asesoría** consultancy work, consulting work (US)
laboral *adj* occupational *adj*
lamentar *vb* regret *vb* **lamentamos informarle que** we regret to inform you that...
lanón *nm* (LAm) bundle (of money) *n*
lanzamiento *nm* eviction *n* **lanzamiento de un producto** product launch
lanzar *vb* (product) bring out *vb*,

introduce *vb*, launch *vb* **lanzarse al mercado** hit the market

latifundista *nmf* landowner *n*

LBO (compra apalancada de empresas) *abbr,nf* LBO (leveraged buy-out) *abbr*

legado *nm* bequest *n*, endowment *n*, inheritance *n*, legacy *n*

legajo *nm* bundle *n*

legal *adj* legal *adj*

legalización *nf* probate *n*, legalisation *n*

legar *vb* bequeath *vb*

legislación *nf* legislation *n*

legislar *vb* legislate *vb*

legitimidad *nf* validity *n*

legítimo *adj* aboveboard *adj*, valid *adj*

lengua *nf* language *n*

lenguaje *nm* language *n* **lenguaje de ordenador, lenguaje de computadora** (LAm) computer language

letra *nf* letter *n* **letra de cambio** bill of exchange **letra grande** large type **letra al propio cargo** promissory note **letras descontadas** bills discounted **letra a la vista** sight draft

levantar *vb* raise *vb*, lift *vb* **levantar un embargo** lift an embargo **levantarse** adjourn, rise

ley *nf* law *n*, statute *n* **leyes sobre la herencia** inheritance laws **Ley Presupuestaria** Finance Act, finance bill **ley sobre la propiedad intelectual** copyright law **ley que regula la descripción comercial de productos** Trade Descriptions Act **ley de rendimientos decrecientes** law of diminishing returns **ley de sociedades anónimas** company law

liar *vb* bundle up *vb*

libelo *nm* libel *n*

liberal *adj* **las profesiones liberales** the professions

libertad *nf* freedom *n* **libertad de elección** freedom of choice

libra *nf* (weight) pound *n* **libra esterlina** pound sterling, sterling **libra verde** green pound

librar *vb* wage *vb*, save *vb*, (cheque) draw *vb*

libre *adj* exempt *adj*, vacant *adj* **libre competencia** free competition **libre de derechos de aduana** (goods) duty-free **libre de impuestos** duty-free, tax-free

librecambio *nm* free trade *n*

librería *nf* bookshop *n*, bookstore (US) *n*

librero, -era *nm,f* bookseller *n*

libreta *nf* notebook *n*

libro *nm* book *n* **libro de instrucciones** instruction book **libro mayor** ledger **libro mayor de compras** bought ledger **libro mayor de la fábrica** factory ledger **libro mayor de ventas** sales ledger **libro de pedidos** order book

licencia *nf* franchise *n*, leave *n*, leave of absence (LAm) *n*, licence *n*, furlough (US) *n*, permit *n* **licencia por enfermedad** sick leave **licencia por maternidad** maternity leave **licencia de obras** building permit

licenciado, -ada, egresado, -ada (LAm) *nm,f* (of university) graduate *n*

licenciatario, -ria *nm,f* franchisee *n*

licitación *nf* bid *n*, tender (LAm) *n*, tendering *n*

licitador, -ora *nm,f* (LAm) tenderer *n*

licitar *vb* bid *vb*, lodge a tender *vb* **licitar para un contrato** tender for a contract

liderazgo *nm* leadership *n*

limitado *adj* limited *adj*

limitar *vb* restrict *vb* **limitar el tipo de interés, limitar la tasa de interés** (LAm) cap the interest rate

límite *nm* (on prices) ceiling *n*, limit *n*, restriction *n* **fuera de los límites** out of bounds **límite de crédito** credit limit

limpio *adj* fair *adj*, clean *adj*

línea *nf* (of products) range *n* **línea aérea** airline, carrier **línea (de cambio) de fecha** International Date Line **línea directa** hot line **de línea dura** hard-line **línea de fuego** hot seat **línea de montaje** assembly line

liquidación *nf* clearance sale *n*, liquidation *n*, winding-up *n* **liquidación de activo** asset stripping, realization of assets **liquidación por cierre** closing-down sale, closing-out sale (US) **liquidación judicial** winding-up order

liquidar *vb* liquidate *vb*, redeem *vb*, sell off *vb*, wind up *vb* **liquidar una cuenta** settle an account **liquidar una factura** pay a bill, settle an invoice **liquidar una reclamación** settle a claim

liquidez *nf* liquidity *n*

líquido *adj* fluid *adj*, liquid *adj*

lista *nf* index *n*, list *n*, register *n*, schedule *n* **lista de correos, poste restante** (LAm) poste restante **lista de destinatarios** mailing list **lista de espera** hold queue, waiting list, hold line (US)

listo *adj* ready *adj*, clever *adj* **listo para entrega** ready for despatch

litigante *nmf* litigant *n*

litigar *vb* litigate *vb*

litigio *nm* litigation *n*
llamada, llamado (LAm) *nf, nm* call *n*
llamada a cobro revertido, llamado por cobrar (LAm) reverse-charge call, collect call (US) **llamadas telefónicas gratuitas** Freefone (R) (GB) **llamada telefónica, llamado telefónico** (LAm) telephone call
llamamiento *nm* appeal *n*, call *n*
llamar *vb* call *vb* **llamar a** invite **llamar a alguien para la entrevista** invite sb to interview
llegar *vb* arrive *vb* **llegar a un acuerdo** come to an accommodation, call it a deal, make a treaty **llegar a un acuerdo sobre** (agreement, policy) thrash out **llegar a un acuerdo mutuo / llegar a un arreglo, transar** (LAm) reach a compromise **llegar al conocimiento de alguien** come to the notice of sb
llevar *vb* (premises) occupy *vb* **que lleva mucho tiempo** time-consuming **llevar a cabo** carry out **llevar la contabilidad** keep the books **llevar un negocio** operate a business **llevar un tren de vida que los ingresos no permiten** live beyond one's means
local 1. *adj* local *adj* 2. *nm* premises *npl* **local comercial** business premises **local de una oficina** office premises
lógica *nf* rationale *n*
logística *nf* logistics *n*
lograr *vb* achieve *vb*, mediate *vb*, win *vb* **lograr un objetivo** reach an objective
logro *nm* accomplishment *n*, achievement *n*
lonja *nf* mart *n*
lote *nm* (of goods) batch *n* (at auction) lot *n*
lucrativo *adj* lucrative *adj*
lugar *nm* place *n* **lugar de la conferencia** conference venue **lugar de trabajo** workplace
lujo *nm* luxury *n*
macroeconomía *nf* macroeconomics *n*
madurar *vb* (business, economy) mature *vb*
mafioso,-osa *nm,f* racketeer *n*
magistratura *nf* magistracy *n* **Magistratura del Trabajo** industrial tribunal
magnate *nmf* magnate *n*, tycoon *n* **magnate de la prensa** press baron
malgastar *vb* waste *vb*
maltratar *vb* abuse *vb*
maltrato *nm* mishandling *n*
malversación *nf* embezzlement *n*, misappropriation *n*
malversador, -ora *nm,f* embezzler *n*

malversar *vb* embezzle *vb*
mandamiento *nm* order *n*, warrant *n* **mandamiento judicial** injunction, writ
mandar *vb* forward *vb*, send *vb*, order *vb* **mandar por correo** post
mandato *nm* term of office **mandato de pago** warrant for payment
mando *nm* command *n* **mando intermedio** middle manager **mandos intermedios** middle management
manejar *vb* **gestionar** (deal) handle *vb*, manage *vb* **manejar dinero** (money) handle
manejo *nm* (of machine) operation *n* **manejo de datos** data handling
mano *nf* hand *n* **a mano** handy **mano de obra** labour, manpower, labor (US) **mano de obra empleada a base de contrato** contract labour **entre manos** in hand **de primera mano** first-hand
mantener *vb* maintain *vb* **mantener bajos los precios** (prices) keep down
mantenimiento *nm* maintenance *n*, retention *n*
manual 1. *adj* manual *adj* 2. *nm* handbook *n*
manufacturar *vb* manufacture *vb*
manutención *nf* maintenance *n*
maqueta *nf* working model *n*
máquina *nf* machine *n* **máquina de escribir** typewriter **máquina expendedora automática** vending machine **máquina franqueadora** franking machine
maquinaria *nf* machinery *n*, plant *n*
marca *nf* brand *n*, trademark *n* **marca de calidad**, kite mark (US) **marca comercial** brand name **marca de contraste** hallmark **de marca registrada** proprietary brand **marca registrada** proprietary brand, registered trade name, registered trademark
marcar *vb* mark *vb*
marcha *nf* progress *n*
marchar *vb* walk *vb*, function *vb*, (machine) work *vb*
marcharse *vb* leave *vb*
marco *nm* framework *n*, (deutsche) mark *n* **marco alemán** Deutsche Mark **marco de oportunidad** window of opportunity
margen *nm* margin *n* **margen de beneficio** markup, profit margin **margen bruto** gross margin **margen comercial** trading margin **margen competitivo** competitive edge **margen reducido** narrow margin
marginal *adj* marginal *adj*

marina *nf* navy *n* **marina mercante** merchant marine, merchant navy
marino *adj* marine *adj*
marítimo *adj* marine *adj*
márketing, mercadeo (LAm) *nm* marketing *n* **márketing global** global marketing **márketing de masas, mercadeo de masas** (LAm) mass marketing
materia *nf* **materias** matter, materials **materias primas** raw materials
material *nm* material *n* **materiales de construcción** building materials **material sobrante** waste products
matriz, talón (LAm) *nf*, *nm* counterfoil *n*
mayor *adj* main *adj*, major *adj*, senior *adj* **al por mayor** at/by wholesale **la mayor parte de** the bulk of
mayoría *nf* majority *n* **mayoría suficiente** working majority
mayorista *nmf* wholesaler *n* **mayorista de pago al contado** cash and carry
mayoritariamente *adv* in the majority *prep*
MBA (Máster en Administración de Empresas) *abbr* MBA (Master of Business Administration) *abbr*
mecánico *adj* mechanical *adj*
mecanismo *nm* machinery *n*, works *npl* **mecanismo de paridades** exchange rate mechanism (ERM) **mecanismo de tasas de cambio** exchange rate mechanism (ERM)
mecanógrafo, -afa *nm,f* typist *n*
mecenazgo *nm* sponsorship *n*
media *nf* average *n* **media general** general average **media hora** half-an-hour **media pensión** half-board
mediación *nf* mediation *n*
mediador, -ora *nm,f* mediator *n*
mediano *adj* medium *adj* **mediano plazo** medium term
mediante *prep* by means of *prep* **mediante negociaciones** by negotiation
mediar *vb* mediate *vb*
médico 1. *adj* medical *adj* 2. *nm* doctor *n*
medida *nf* measure *n* **medida financiera** financial measure **medidas antiinflacionarias** anti-inflationary measures **medida de seguridad** safety measure **medidas financieras** financial measures **medidas fiscales** fiscal measures **medidas de reconversión** rationalization measures
medidor *nm* (LAm) meter *n*
medio 1. *adj* (average) mean *adj* median *adj*, medium *adj* **medio plazo** medium term **medio sueldo** half-pay 2. *nm* means *npl*, mode *n* **medio de pub-**

licidad advertising medium **medio publicitario** advertising medium **medios ability to pay, means, resources** **medios de comunicación** media **medios de comunicación de masas** mass media
medir *vb* measure *vb*
megaocteto *nm* megabyte *n*
mejor *adj* better *adj*, best *adj* **mejor de la gama** top-of-the-range
mejora *nf* amendment *n*, upturn *n* **mejora salarial** wage increase
mejorar *vb* improve *vb*, pick up *vb*, upgrade *vb*
membrete *nm* letterhead *n*
memorándum *nm* memo *n*, memorandum *n*
memoria *nf* (DP) memory *n* **memoria anual** annual report **memoria de lectura ROM** (read only memory) **memoria RAM** (DP) RAM (random access memory)
mencionado *adj* mentioned *adj* **arriba mencionado** above-mentioned
menor *adj* junior *adj*, minor *adj*
mensaje, mandado (LAm) *nm* message *n* **mensaje publicitario, aviso; réclame** (LAm) advertisement
mensajero, -era *nm,f* courier *n*, messenger *n*
mensual *adj* monthly *adj*
mercadeable *adj* marketable *adj*
mercadeo *nm* (LAm) merchandising *n*, marketing *n*
mercaderías *nfpl* freight *n*
mercado *nm* market *n*, mart *n* **de mercado** going **mercado alcista** bull market, buoyant market **mercado amplio** broad market **mercado bajista** bear market **mercado de bonos** bond market **mercado de capitales** capital market **Mercado Común** Common Market **mercado de divisas** foreign exchange market, exchange market **mercado de entrega spot** spot market **mercado de la eurodivisa** eurocurrency market **mercado exterior** foreign/overseas market **mercado de factores (de producción)** factor market **mercado favorable a los compradores** buyer's market **mercado favorable al vendedor** seller's market **mercado financiero** financial/money market **mercado firme** firm market **mercado fluido** fluid market **mercado de futuros** forward/futures market **el mercado se ha desfondado, los precios han caído en picada** (LAm) the bottom has fallen out of the market **mercado inactivo** flat market

mercado inestable fluid market mercado inmobiliario property market, real estate market (US) mercado libre free/open market mercado marginal fringe market mercado al por mayor wholesale market mercado al por menor retail market mercado monetario money market mercado mundial global/world market mercado nacional/interior domestic/home market mercado negro black market mercado de oferta buyer's market mercado de opciones de compra y venta de acciones options market mercado de oro gold market de mercado popular (product) down-market mercado previsto target market mercado reducido narrow market de mercado selecto (product) up-market mercado subsidiario secondary market mercado con tendencia a la baja falling market mercado con tendencia a subir bull market mercado terminal terminal market mercado de trabajo labour market mercado turístico the tourist trade mercado de valores stock market mercado de valores de primera clase gilt-edged market
mercancía nf mercancías, mercaderías (LAm) goods, wares mercancías abandonadas abandoned goods mercancías en curso goods in process mercancías de exportación export goods mercancías a granel bulk goods mercancías a prueba goods on approval mercancías en tránsito transit goods mercancías de venta fácil, mercaderías de venta rápida (LAm) fast-selling goods
mercantil adj commercial adj, mercantile adj
merecer vb be worth vb
merecido adj earned adj, deserved adj bien merecido hard-earned
mes nm month n del pasado mes ultimo adj, adv
meta nf target n
metal nm metal n
método nm organization n, method n método contable para valorar existencias LIFO (last in first out) abbr método de producción production method métodos de contabilidad accounting conventions
métrico adj metric adj
metro nm metre n, meter (US) metro cuadrado square metre metro cúbico cubic metre
metrópoli(s) nf metropolis n

microeconomía nf microeconomics n
microficha nf microfiche n
micrófono nm microphone n micrófono oculto, peste (LAm) (listening device) bug
microordenador, microcomputador,-ora (LAm) nm, nm,f microcomputer n
microprocesador nm microprocessor n
miembro nmf member n miembro de un jurado juror miembro vitalicio life member
mil nm thousand n mil libras esterlinas (1000) K, pounds
milla nf mile n milla marina nautical mile
millón nm million n
millonario, -ria nm,f millionaire n
mina nf mine n mina de carbón coal mine
mineral nm mineral n
minería nf mining n
mínimo adj fractional adj, minimal adj minimum adj mínima parte fraction
ministerio, secretaría (LAm) nm, nf government department n, ministry n el Ministerio de Hacienda the Treasury Department (US) Ministerio de Salud Ministry of Health Ministerio de Transporte, Secretaría de Transporte (LAm) Ministry of Transport
ministro, -tra nm,f minister n ministro, -tra de Economía y Hacienda Chancellor of the Exchequer (GB)
minoría nf minority n en minoría in the minority
minusvalía nf capital loss n
mirar vb look (at) vb
misión nf assignment n
mitad nf half n mitad de precio half-price
mítin nm meeting n
mobiliario nm furnishings npl, fittings npl mobiliario de oficina office equipment
moda nf trend n moda actual current trend
modelo nmf (person) model n
módem nm modem n
moderación nf moderation n moderación salarial wage restraint moderación voluntaria en las reivindicaciones salariales voluntary wage restraint
moderado adj moderate adj
moderar vb moderate vb
modernización nf modernization n
modernizar vb modernize vb
moderno adj modern adj, up-to-date (LAm) adj
modo nm mode n
módulo nm module n, unit n

molestia *nf* **molestias** inconvenience, *n*, nuisance *n*
moneda *nf* currency *n*, coin *n* **moneda clave** key currency **moneda convertible** convertible currency, hard currency **moneda no convertible** soft currency **moneda de curso legal** legal currency, legal tender **moneda extranjera** foreign currency, foreign exchange **moneda fuerte** hard currency **moneda de oro** gold coin **monedas, sencillo; feria; menudo** (LAm) (coins) loose/small change **moneda verde** green currency
monetario *adj* monetary *adj*
monetarismo *nm* monetarism *n*
monopolio *nm* monopoly *n*
montar *vb* establish *vb* (company) set up *vb* **montar un negocio** set up in business, found a company
montón *nm* load *n*
morder *vb* (LAm) bribe *vb*
mordida *nf* (LAm) bribe *n*, sweetener *n*
mostrador *nm* counter *n*, desk *n* **mostrador de transbordos** (transport) transfer desk
motivo *nm* design *n* **motivo de queja** grievance
movilizar *vb* mobilize *vb* **movilizar fondos** raise capital
movimiento *nm* movement *n* **movimiento de capital** funds flow **movimiento libre de mercancías, movimiento libre de mercaderías** (LAm) free movement of goods **movimientos de capitales** capital turnover **mucho movimiento (en la bolsa)** heavy trading
muelle *nm* (for berthing) dock *n* quay *n* **en el muelle** ex quay, ex wharf
muestra *nf* exhibition *n*, sample *n* **muestra de oferta** trial offer
muestreo *nm* sampling *n* **muestreo de cuotas** quota sampling
multa *nf* forfeit *n*, fine *n*, penalty *n*
multilateral *adj* multilateral *adj*
multinacional *adj* multinational *adj*
multiplicar *vb* multiply *vb*
multipropiedad *nf* timeshare *n*
multiuso *adj* multipurpose *adj*
mundial *adj* global *adj*, worldwide *adj*
mundo *nm* world *n* **el mundo de la banca** banking circles **el mundo comercial** the commercial world **el mundo editorial** publishing **el Tercer Mundo** the Third World
municipal *adj* local *adj*
municipio *nm* town council *n*, town hall *n*

mutuamente *adv* mutually *adv*
mutuo *adj* mutual *adj*, reciprocal *adj*
nación *nf* nation *n* **Naciones Unidas (la ONU)** United Nations
nacional *adj* inland *adj*, national *adj*
nacionalidad *nf* nationality *n*
nacionalización *nf* nationalization *n*
nacionalizar *vb* nationalize *vb*
necesario *adj* necessary *adj*
necesidad *nf* (goods) necessity *n*, requirement *n* **necesidades materiales** material needs
negar *vb* withhold *vb*, deny *vb* **negarse a aceptar** (goods) reject **negarse a pagar, rehusar pagar** (LAm) refuse payment **negarse a pagar una reclamación** refuse a claim
negativa, plante (LAm) *nf*, *nm* refusal *n*
negligencia *nf* malpractice *n*, neglect *n*, negligence *n*
negligente *adj* negligent *adj*
negociable *adj* negotiable *adj*
negociación *nf* negotiation *n*, transaction *n* **en negociación** under negotiation **negociación colectiva** collective bargaining **negociaciones arancelarias** tariff negotiations **negociaciones comerciales** trade talks **negociaciones salariales** wage negotiations
negociador, -ora *nm,f* negotiator *n*
negociante *nmf* merchant *n*
negociar *vb* bargain *vb*, negotiate *vb*, trade *vb*
negocio *nm* deal *n* **negocio difícil** hard bargain **negocio ilícito** racketeering **negocio en marcha** going concern **negocio en participación** collaborative venture, joint venture **negocio en plena marcha** going concern **negocios** business
negrita *nf* bold type *n*
neto *adj* net(t) *adj*, after tax *adv*
neutral *adj* neutral *adj*
nivel *nm* level *n* **de dos niveles** two-tier **nivel de calidad** quality standard **nivel de cobertura** extent of cover **nivel de desempleo, nivel de cesantía** (LAm) level of unemployment **nivel de empleo** level of employment **nivel de inflación** level of inflation **nivel de precios** level of prices **nivel de producción** flow line production **nivel en el que la tasa de impuestos cambia** tax threshold **nivel de vida** standard of living
no *det* no *det*, not *adv* **no aceptación** non-acceptance **no se admiten agentes** no agents wanted **no aprobar** negative

(US) no asegurable uninsurable **no asistencia** non-attendance **no colgar, no cortar** (LAm) (phone) hang on **no corresponde** N/A (not applicable) **no cubierto por entero** undersubscribed **no dar a conocer un documento** withhold a document **no discriminatorio** non-discriminatory **no disponemos de los medios para...** we do not have the means to... **no disponible** not available **no finalización** non-completion **no intervención** non-intervention **no negociable** non-negotiable **no perder el hilo de los sucesos** (events) keep up with **no pertinente** not applicable **no podemos correr el riesgo** we cannot afford (to take) the risk **no me puedo permitir el lujo de comprar una nueva impresora** I can't afford to buy a new printer **no rehabilitado** (bankrupt) undischarged **no rentable** non-profitmaking, unprofitable **no retornable** non-returnable **no tener fondos** (cheque) bounce* **no tener más remedio que** resort to **no terminación** non-completion
noción *nf* notion *n* **nociones elementales de cálculo aritmético** numeracy
nombramiento *nm* (to a position) appointment *n*, nomination *n*
nombrar, postular (LAm) *vb* assign *vb*, nominate *vb* **nombrar a alguien a un consejo/una comisión, postular a alguien a un consejo/una comisión** (LAm) nominate sb to a board/committee **nombrar a alguien a un puesto** appoint sb to a position
nombre *nm* name *n* **de nombre** by name **en el nombre de** in the name of **nombre y apellidos** full name
nómina, planilla (LAm) *nf* payroll *n*
nominal *adj* nominal *adj*
norma *nf* norm *n* **norma de calidad** quality standard **normas comerciales** trading standards
normal *adj* standard *adj*
normalización *nf* standardization *n*
normalizar *vb* standardize *vb*
nota *nf* memo *n*, note *n*, message *n* **nota de cobertura, póliza provisoria** (LAm) cover note **nota de crédito** credit note **nota de débito** debit note **nota de entrega** delivery note **nota de envío** dispatch note, forwarding note **nota de expedición, nota de flete** (LAm) dispatch note, forwarding note
notable *adj* noteworthy *adj*

notario, -ria *nm,f* notary *n*
noticia, reporte (LAm) *nf* report *n* **noticias** news **buenas noticias** good news **malas noticias** bad news **noticias financieras** financial news
notificación *nf* advice *n*, notification *n*
notificar *vb* inform *vb*, notify *vb* **notificar de algo** give notice of sth
nuevo *adj* new *adj* **nueva tecnología** new technology **nuevos negocios** new business
nulo *adj* useless *adj*, void *adj* **nulo y sin valor** null and void
numérico *adj* numerical *adj* **numérico-alfabético** alpha-numeric
número *nm* copy *n*, number *n* **número de cuenta** account number **número equivocado** (phone) wrong number **número de pedido** order number **número de referencia** box number, reference number **número de serie** serial number **número de teléfono** telephone number
obedecer *vb* obey *vb*
objeción *nf* objection *n*
objetivo *nm* objective *n*, target *n* **objetivo económico** economic objective **objetivo de producción** production target **objetivo de ventas** sales target
obligación *nf* bond *n*, commitment *n*, debenture *n*, obligation *n* **obligación conjunta** joint obligation **obligación desvalorizada** junk bond **obligaciones contractuales** contractual obligations **obligaciones garantizadas por los activos de la compañía** debenture capital, debenture stock (US) **obligación del Estado** government bond **obligación de fidelidad** fidelity bond **obligación no hipotecaria** debenture bond **obligación registrada** registered bond
obligatoriedad *nf* compulsoriness *n*
obligatorio *adj* binding *adj*, obligatory *adj*
obra *nf* building site *n*, work *n* **obras** works **obras de beneficencia** charity
obrero, -era *nm,f* blue-collar worker, guest worker, labourer, manual worker **obrero no calificado, obrero no calificado; peón** (LAm) unskilled worker **obrero cualificado** skilled worker **obrero especializado** skilled worker **obrero manual, peón** (LAm) manual worker **obreros sindicados** organized labour **obreros** shopfloor
observación *nf* comment *n*, observation *n* **en observación** under observation
observar *vb* observe *vb*
obsolescencia *nf* obsolescence *n* **obso-**

lescencia planificada built-in/planned obsolescence
obstaculizar, tapar (LAm) vb block vb
obtener vb achieve vb, acquire vb, gain vb, net(t) vb obtener beneficios make a profit
ocasionar vb cause vb
octeto nm byte n
ocupación nf employment n, occupation n, tenure n
ocupacional adj occupational adj
ocupado adj busy adj
ocupante nmf occupant n, occupier n
ocupar vb (premises) occupy vb ocupar un cargo hold office
oferente nmf offeror n
oferta, licitación (LAm) nf bargain n, bid n, supply n, offer n, tender n, tendering n oferta combinada package deal oferta y demanda supply and demand oferta por escrito offer in writing oferta final closing bid oferta en firme firm offer oferta por liquidación, oferta por realización (LAm) clearance offer oferta monetaria money supply oferta de pago en efectivo cash offer oferta provisional, oferta provisoria (LAm) tentative offer oferta pública de adquisición (OPA) tender offer oferta de rebaja bargain offer oferta no solicitada unsolicited offer oferta sujeta a confirmación offer subject to confirmation oferta superior higher bid oferta de trabajo job offer oferta válida hasta... offer valid until...
oficial adj formal adj, official adj
oficina nf office n le remitimos a nuestra oficina central we refer you to our head office oficina de administración fiduciaria (bank) trustee department oficina de cambio bureau de change oficina central HO (head office), headquarters, parent company oficina de correos, correo (LAm) post office oficina de empleo employment agency, Jobcentre (GB), job shop oficina de importación import office oficina de información information desk/office oficina de objetos perdidos lost-property office oficina regional regional office
oficinista nmf clerical worker n, clerk n, white-collar worker n
oficio nm profession n, trade n de oficio by trade
ofrecer, licitar (LAm) vb bid vb ofrecer más outbid
oído adj heard adj de oídas by hearsay
oleada nf (of mergers, takeovers) wave n

oligopolio nm oligopoly n
omisión nf default n, omission n
opción nf option n opción de anular option to cancel opción de compra option to buy opción de compra/venta de acciones a cierto precio para el futuro, beneficios de operación (LAm) share option, stock option (US)
operación nf transaction n operación comercial business transaction operación al contado cash transaction operaciones en bolsa dealing, trading (US) operaciones de cambio foreign exchange dealings, foreign exchange trading (US) operaciones de exportación export operations operaciones de iniciado insider dealing, insider trading (US) operación financiera financial operation operación en el mercado de valores equity transaction operación de trueque barter transaction
operador, -ora, feriante; puestero, -era (LAm) nm,f, nmf; nm,f operator n, trader n operador de cambios exchange broker, foreign exchange dealer, money trader operador de teclado computer operator
operario, -ria nm,f operator n
oponerse vb object vb
oportunidad nf opportunity n oportunidad comercial market opportunity oportunidades de mercado market opportunities
oportuno adj convenient adj
optar vb opt vb
optativo adj optional adj
orden nm order n, rank n orden nf injunction n, instruction n orden del día agenda órdenes brief, orders orden jerárquico line management orden judicial writ orden permanente de pago banker's order, standing order de primer orden (investment) first-rate
ordenador, computador,-ora (LAm) nm, nm,f computer n ordenador central (DP) mainframe ordenador personal (PC) personal computer (PC) ordenador portátil laptop computer, portable computer
ordenar, sindicalizar (LAm) vb organize vb, order vb
organigrama nm flow chart organigrama de flujo flow chart
organismo nm organism n, body n organismo gubernamental government body
organización nf organization n organización estatal government body organización funcional functional organization

organización internacional international organization **organización patronal** employers' federation
organizar, sindicalizar (LAm) *vb* organize *vb* **organizar una conferencia** organize/arrange a conference
órgano *nm* organ *n*
orientación *nf* direction *n*, guidance *n* **orientación profesional, orientación vocacional** (LAm) careers advice
origen *nm* source *n*
oro *nm* gold *n* **oro en lingotes** gold bullion **oro y plata en lingotes** bullion
otorgar *vb* grant *vb* **otorgar crédito** extend credit
PAC (Política Agrícola Común) *nf* CAP (Common Agricultural Policy) *abbr*
pacto *nm* covenant *n*, agreement *n*
paga *nf* pay *n*, wage *n* **paga doble** double time **paga de vacaciones, sueldo gozado durante la licencia** (LAm) holiday pay
pagadero *adj* payable *adj* **pagadero por adelantado** payable in advance
pagado *adj* paid *adj*
pagar *vb* remunerate *vb*, repay *vb* (account) settle *vb* **pagar de más** overpay **sin pagar** (cheque) uncleared **pagar de menos** underpay **pagar por adelantado** pay in advance **pagar con cheque** pay by cheque **pagar al contado** pay in cash **pagar una cuenta** pay a bill **pagar la cuenta y marcharse** (of hotel) check out **pagar una cuota** pay a fee **pagar en efectivo** pay in cash **pagar una factura** pay/settle an invoice **pagar interés** pay interest **pagar a la orden de...** pay to the order of... **pagar por un servicio** pay for a service **pagar con tarjeta de crédito** pay by credit card
pagaré *n* banknote *n*, debenture *n*, promissory note *n* **pagaré de favor** accommodation bill **pagaré del Tesoro** Treasury bill, open note (US)
página *nf* page *n* **las páginas amarillas** the Yellow pages (R) (GB)
pago *nm* payment *n*, redemption *n* **pago por adelantado** prepayment **pago anticipado** advance payment, cash before delivery, prepayment **pago de compensación** clearing payment **pago al contado** cash payment, spot cash **pago a cuenta** payment on account **pago en efectivo** cash payment **pago en exceso** overpayment **pago ex-gratia** ex gratia payment **pago al hacer el pedido** cash before delivery, cash with order **pago**

inicial, pie (LAm) down payment **pago insuficiente** underpayment **pago íntegro** full payment **pago de intereses de una deuda** debt service **pago parcial** part payment **pagos por etapas** staged payments **pago simbólico** token payment **pagos de transferencia** transfer payments **pago total** full payment
país *nm* country *n* **país comerciante** trading nation **país que comercia con otro** trading partner **país desarrollado** developed country **país importador** importing country **país de origen** country of origin, home country **país productor de petróleo** oil state **país anfitrión** host country **país subdesarrollado** underdeveloped country **país del Tercer Mundo** third-world country **país en vías de desarrollo** developing country
palabra *nf* word *n* **palabra clave** (computer) keyword **palabra por palabra** verbatim **palabras por minuto** wpm (words per minute)
palanca *nf* lever *n* **palancas** (LAm) business contacts, influence
paleta *nf* pallet *n*
panorama *nm* prospect *n*
pantalla *nf* screen *n* **pantalla de visualización** visual display unit (VDU)
papel *nm* document *n* (role) function *n* **papel comercial** commercial paper **papel con membrete** headed notepaper, letterhead **papel moneda** paper currency **papel de primera clase** first-class paper
papeleo *nm* paperwork *n*, red tape *n*
paquete *nm* bundle *n*, package *n*, packet *n* **paquete accional autónomo** stake **paquete de software** software package
par *nf* par *n* **por debajo de la par** below par **por encima de la par** above par, at a premium
parado, cesante (LAm) *adj* unemployed *adj*, redundant *adj*
paralización *nf* shutdown *n*
parar *vb* (inflation) halt *vb*
parecer *vb* seem *vb* **parecerle mal a** find fault with
paridad, tasa de cambio (LAm) *nf* parity *n*, exchange rate *n*
parlamento *nm* parliament *n* **Parlamento Europeo** European Parliament
paro, cesantía (LAm) *nm*, *nf* strike *n*, unemployment *n*, stoppage *n* **en paro, cesante** (LAm) jobless **paro generalizado, cesantía general** (LAm) mass

unemployment **paro patronal (LAm)** lockout

parte *nf* block *n*, half *n* **parte contratada** covenantee **parte contratante** covenantor

participación *nf* holding *n*, interest *n*, share *n*, stake *n* **participación mayoritaria** majority holding **participación en el mercado** market share **participación minoritaria** minority holding **participación obrera** worker participation **participación de los trabajadores en la gestión** worker participation

participar *vb* compete *vb*, intervene *vb* **participar en** take part in

partida *nf* batch *n*, entry *n* **de partida doble** (bookkeeping) double-entry

partidario, -ria *nm,f* backer *n*

partir *vb* split *vb* **partir por la mitad** halve

pasaje *nm* ticket *n*, passengers *npl* **pasaje sencillo, boleto sencillo (LAm)** (rail/flight) single/one-way ticket **pasaje de ida y vuelta** return ticket, round-trip ticket (US)

pasajero, -era *nm,f* passenger *n*, traveller *n*, traveler (US) **pasajero en tránsito** (transport) transit passenger

pasar *vb* hand over *vb*, spend *vb* **pasar a** (call) transfer **pasar por alto** overlook **pasar a buscar** call for **pasar a cuenta nueva** carry forward, carry over **pasar por encima** bypass **pasar a máquina, tipear (LAm)** key in, type **pasar la pelota** pass the buck* **pasar la prueba** stand the test

pasivo *nm* debit *n*, liabilities *npl* **pasivo circulante** current liabilities **pasivo a largo plazo** fixed liability

paso *nm* step *n*, pass *n*

pastor, -ora *nm,f* minister *n*

patentado *adj* patented *adj*, proprietary *adj*

patente *nf* patent *n*

patrimonio *nm* wealth *n* **patrimonio nacional** national wealth **patrimonio neto** equity

patrocinador, -ora *nm,f* sponsor *n*

patrocinio *nm* patronage *n*, sponsorship *n*

patrón, -ona *nm,f* boss *n*, employer *n* **patrón oro** gold standard

pauta *nf* indication *n* **pautas de consumo** spending patterns

peaje *nm* (road) toll *n*

pedido *nm* request *n*, demand *n*, order *n*, appeal (LAm) *n*, legal action (LAm) *n* **pedido de pago** request for payment **pedido efectuado por correo** mail order **pedido fijo** standing order **pedido suple-**

mentario repeat order **pedido urgente** rush order

pedir *vb* apply for *vb*, call for *vb* **pedir crédito** request a loan **pedir indemnización** claim compensation **pedir prestado** borrow **pedir una referencia** take up a reference

peligro *nm* hazard *n*, risk *n* **peligro inevitable** natural hazard **peligro para la salud** health hazard

peligroso *adj* hazardous *adj*

penetración *nf* penetration *n* **penetración en el mercado** market penetration

pensión *nf* annuity *n*, pension *n*, retirement pension **pensión de jubilación** retirement pension **pensión proporcional al sueldo** earnings-related pension

pequeño *adj* minor *adj*, small *adj* **pequeño hurto** pilferage

perder *vb* (custom) lose *vb* **perder el derecho a** forfeit **perder valor** depreciate, lose value

pérdida *nf* forfeiture *n*, loss *n*, wastage *n*, waste *n* **pérdida bruta** gross loss **pérdida de ejercicio** trading loss **pérdida de empleo** loss of job **pérdida financiera** financial loss **pérdida de ingresos** loss of earnings **pérdida neta** clear loss, net(t) loss **pérdida sobre el papel** paper loss **pérdidas de estoc** stock shrinkage **pérdida de tiempo** waste of time **pérdida de valor** depreciation

perdido *adj* lost *adj*, missed *adj* **perdido en tránsito** lost in transit

periférico *adj* peripheral *adj*

perimido *adj* (LAm) out of date *adj*

periódico *nm* daily paper *n*, newspaper *n* **periódico de formato grande** broadsheet

periodismo *nm* journalism *n*

período *nm* period *n* **período de aviso** notice period **período de contabilidad** accounting period **período de gestación** lead time **período de gracia** period of grace **período de mayor afluencia** peak period **período de prueba** trial period **período de reflexión** cooling-off period **período de servicio** tour of duty **período de vigencia del tipo de interés, período de vigencia de la tasa de interés (LAm)** interest period

perito *adj* expert *adj*

permiso *nm* leave *n*, leave of absence *n*, licence *n*, permit *n*, furlough (US) *n* **permiso de exportación** export licence **permiso de importación** import licence **permiso de obras** building permit **per-**

miso de residencia y trabajo (LAm) green card **permiso de trabajo** work permit
permitir vb allow vb, furlough (US), vb
permutar vb barter vb
perro nm dog n **perro guardián** (fig) watchdog
persona nf person n **por persona** per capita, per head **persona en aprendizaje** trainee **persona clave** key person **persona que concede un permiso o una licencia** licensor **persona que da referencias sobre otra** referee **persona mencionada** named person **persona que otorga la concesión** franchisor **persona que trabaja por libre** freelance, freelancer
personal 1. adj personal adj, vested adj
2. nm manpower n, staff n, workforce n **con demasiado personal** overmanned **personal administrativo** office staff **personal de campo** field personnel **personal cualificado, personal calificado** (LAm) qualified personnel **personal directivo** executive personnel
perspectiva nf prospect n **perspectivas comerciales** business outlook **perspectivas futuras** future prospects
pertinente adj relevant adj
pesar vb weigh vb **pesar ventajas y desventajas** weigh the pros and cons
peseta nf peseta n
peso nm load n, tonnage n, weight n **peso bruto** gross weight **peso muerto** dead weight **peso neto** net(t) weight **pesos y medidas** weights and measures
petición, pedido (LAm) nf, nm demand n, request n **petición final** final demand **petición de informe sobre el crédito** credit enquiry **petición de informes** enquiry
petrodólar nm petrodollar n
PIB (Producto Interior Bruto) nm GDP (Gross Domestic Product) abbr
pichincha nf (LAm) bargain n
pico nm peak n
pie nm foot n, deposit (LAm) n **al pie de la letra** verbatim
pieza nf (of a machine) part n **pieza de recambio, refacción** (LAm) (for machine) spare part
pinchar vb burst vb **pinchar el teléfono, intervenir un llamado** (LAm) bug a call
piquete nm picket n
piratería nf (at sea) piracy n **piratería de programa informático** software piracy
pista nf track n **pista de máxima velocidad** fast track

plan nm (agreement) arrangement n **plan de campaña** plan of campaign **Plan Europeo de Recuperación** European Recovery Plan **plan de inversiones** investment programme, investment program (US) **plan de pensiones** pension scheme **plan piramidal** pyramid scheme **plan provisional, plan provisorio** (LAm) tentative plan **plan de reactivación** recovery scheme **plan de trabajo** work schedule
planear vb design vb, plan vb
planificación nf planning n **planificación económica** economic planning **planificación económica estatal** centralised economic planning **planificación estatal** central planning **planificación financiera** financial planning **planificación a largo plazo** long-term planning **planificación regional** regional planning **planificación de servicios** facility planning
planificar vb plan vbr, design vb
planilla nf (LAm) payroll n
planta nf plant n **planta de almacenaje frigorífico** cold storage plant **planta piloto** pilot plant
plante nm (LAm) refusal n
plantilla, planilla (LAm) nf payroll n, staff n, workforce n **plantilla sindicada** closed shop
plata nf silver n, cash (LAm) n
platal nm (money LAm) fortune n, bundle n
plaza nf square n, place n, job n
plazo, cuota (LAm) nm, nf instalment n, payment n, time limit, n, installment (US) n **a largo plazo** long-haul, long-range, long-term **largo plazo** long term **plazo de entrega** delivery time, lead time **plazo de preaviso** term of notice **plazo de tiempo** time frame
pleito nm legal action n, lawsuit n
plenario adj (assembly, session) plenary adj
pleno adj full adj **plena responsabilidad** full liability **pleno empleo** full employment
plus nm bonus n **plus según rendimiento** performance-related bonus
plusvalía nf capital gain n
PNB (Producto Nacional Bruto) nm GNP (Gross National Product) abbr
población nf population n **población activa** working population
poco adv & adj hardly adv, little adj
poder nm power n **poder adquisitivo** buying power, purchasing power **po-**

deres (power) proxy **poder notarial** power of attorney
polígono *nm* area *n*, zone *n* **polígono industrial** industrial trading estate
política *nf* politics *n*, policy *n* **Política Agrícola Común** Common Agricultural Policy (CAP) **política arriesgada** brinkmanship **política de comercio de reciprocidad arancelaria** fair-trade policy **política económica** economic policy **política de la empresa** company policy **política financiera** financial policy **política fiscal** fiscal policy **política del gobierno** government policy **política monetaria** monetary policy **política monetaria expansiva** easy-money policy **política nacional** domestic policy **política de precios** pricing policy **política presupuestaria, política presupuestal** (LAm) budgetary policy **política de reducción de plantilla** LIFO (last in first out) **política salarial** wage policy
político *adj* political *adj*
polivalente *adj* multipurpose *adj*
póliza *nf* policy *n* **la póliza cubre los riesgos siguientes** the policy covers the following risks **póliza dotal** endowment policy **póliza provisional, póliza provisoria** (LAm) cover note **póliza de seguros** insurance certificate, insurance policy
ponencia *nf* presentation *n*, proposal *n* **ponencia de primera categoría** first-class paper
poner *vb* (manage) run *vb* (company) set up **poner en circulación** issue **poner con** (call) transfer **poner fecha adelantada, diferir** (LAm) postdate **poner una fecha anterior a un cheque** backdate a cheque **poner fin prematuro a un proyecto** kill a project **poner en marcha, prender** (LAm) (machine) turn on **poner un negocio** set up in business **poner una objeción** make/raise an objection **poner a prueba** carry out trials, try out **poner restricciones** impose restrictions **ponerse en contacto con** contact **poner un servicio** (manage) run **poner un télex** (message) telex **¿me pone con...?, comuníqueme con...** (LAm) (phone) could you connect me to...?
porcentaje *nm* percentage *n*
portacontenedores *nm* container ship *n*
portador, -ora *nm,f* bearer *n*, holder *n*, payee *n*
portátil *adj* portable *adj*
portavoz, vocero, -era (LAm) *nmf, nm,f* spokesperson *n*

porte *nm* carriage *n* **porte debido** carriage forward **porte incluido** carriage included **porte pagado** carriage paid **portes a pagar** carriage forward
poseedor, -ora *nm,f* bearer *n*
poseer *vb* own *vb* **poseer valores en cartera** have holdings
posesión *nf* tenure *n*
posibilidad *nf* feasibility *n*, opportunity *n*, option *n*, prospect *n* **posibilidades** potential **posibilidades de ventas** sales potential
posible *adj* feasible *adj* **lo antes posible** a.s.a.p (as soon as possible)
posición, ubicación (LAm) *nf* location *n*, position *n*, post *n*
posponer *vb* defer *vb*, postpone *vb*
póster *nm* (advertising) poster *n*
postergar *vb* postpone *vb*
postor, -ora, licitador,-ora (LAm) *nm,f* tenderer *n*
postulación *nf* (LAm) nomination *n*
postulado, -ada *nm,f* (LAm) nominee *n*
postular *vb* (LAm) assign *vb*
potencia *nf* power *n*
potencial *nm* potential *n*
potenciar *vb* (product) promote *vb* **potenciar la demanda** boost demand **potenciar al máximo** maximise **potenciar la producción** increase output
potentado, -ada *nm,f* magnate *n*
potente *adj* powerful *adj* **muy potente** high-powered
práctica *nf* practice *n* **mala práctica** malpractice **prácticas** work experience **prácticas comerciales leales** fair trading **prácticas restrictivas** restrictive practices **práctica de vender a precio mínimo al público** fair-trade practice
practicar *vb* practise *vb* **practicar el pluriempleo** moonlight*
práctico *adj* businesslike *adj*, convenient *adj*, handy *adj*
preaviso *nm* advance notice *n*
precio *nm* price *n*, tariff *n* **bien de precio** (price) reasonable **nuestro precio incluye la entrega** our price includes delivery **de precio alto** high-priced **precio más bajo** bottom price **precio de catálogo** list price **precio al cierre** closing price **precio de compra** buying price, purchase price **precio de coste, precio de costo** (LAm) cost price **precio a cuota fija** flat-rate tariff **precio al detallista** trade price **precio de entrega inmediata** spot price, spot rate **precio en fábrica** factory price **precio de**

los factores de producción factor price **precio favorable** favourable price **precio fijo** fixed price, hard price **precio en firme** firm price **precio flexible** flexible price **precio franco fábrica** factory price **precio de futuros** futures price **precio de ganga, precio rematado** (LAm) knockdown price **precio máximo** maximum price **precio al por mayor** wholesale price **precio de mercado** market price **precio mínimo, precio rematado** (LAm) knockdown price **precio mínimo al que pueden venderse en la UE** threshold price **precio neto** net(t) price **precio de ocasión** bargain price **precio de oferta** tender price **precio real** real price **precio de referencia** bench mark price **los precios citados incluyen...** the prices quoted are inclusive **precios fijos** fixed charges **precio simbólico** nominal price **precios de punta** top prices **precios con tendencia a la baja** falling prices **precio de transferencia** transfer price **precio umbral** threshold price **precio por unidad** unit price **precio de venta al público** retail price **el precio de la vivienda** house prices

precioso adj valuable adj
precisar vb specify vb
precisión nf accuracy n
preciso adj accurate adj, necessary adj
predecir vb forecast vb
predicción nf forecast n
predominio nm predominance n
preferencia nf priority n, right of way n **preferencia comunitaria** community preference
preferencial adj preferential adj
prefijo nm STD code n
pregunta nf enquiry n, question n **pregunta clave** key question
preguntar vb enquire vb, ask vb
prenda nf guarantee n, pledge n
prender vb (LAm) turn on vb
preparación nf preparation n **preparación básica** basic training
preparar vb prepare vb **preparar una campaña** run a campaign **preparar el presupuesto** draw up a budget
presenciar vb witness vb
presentación nf fronting n, packaging n, presentation n, introduction n
presentar vb bring forward vb, file vb (motion, paper) table vb **presentar la carta de denuncia** hand in one's resignation **presentar una demanda de**

indemnización claim for damages **presentar una factura** (invoice) bill **presentar en forma de tabla** (data) tabulate **presentar un informe, reportear** (LAm) submit/present a report **presentar una oferta, licitar** (LAm) lodge a tender **presentar una queja** make a complaint **presentar una reclamación** claim for damages, put in a claim **presentarse** (at airport) check in **presentar una solicitud** put in a claim
presidente, -nta nm,f chief executive (of company), president n
presidir vb take the chair **presidir una reunión** chair a meeting
prestación nf allowance n **prestación estatal a la familia, asignación familiar** (LAm) family allowance
prestamista nmf lender n
préstamo nm cash advance n, borrowing n, loan n **préstamo de ahorro-vivienda** home loan **préstamo bancario** bank loan **préstamo estatal** government loan **préstamo exterior pagadero en moneda fuerte** hard loan **préstamo extranjero** foreign loan **préstamo financiero** financial loan **préstamo garantizado** secured loan **préstamo garantizado por obligaciones** debenture loan **préstamo hipotecario** mortgage, mortgage loan **préstamo inmovilizado** tied loan **préstamo puente** bridging loan, bridge loan (US) **préstamos** borrowing
prestar vb lend vb **prestar atención** take notice
prestigio nm kudos n, prestige n
presupuestar vb budget for vb
presupuesto nm budget n (price) quotation n **presupuesto de costes, presupuesto de costos** (LAm) estimate of costs **presupuesto fijo** fixed budget **presupuesto flexible** flexible budget **presupuesto de gastos, presupuesto de costos** (LAm) estimate of costs **presupuesto de gastos de capital** capital budget **presupuesto promocional** promotional budget **presupuesto de publicidad** advertising budget **presupuesto publicitario** promotional budget
prevenir vb forestall vb **prevenir a alguien contra algo** warn sb against doing sth
previo adj prior adj, previous adj **sin previo aviso** without warning
previsión nf forecast n, forecasting n

previsión económica economic forecast **previsión de ventas** sales forecast
prima nf bonus n, premium n **prima por ausencia de siniestralidad** no-claims bonus **prima de enganche** golden hello **prima de seguros, cuota de seguros** (LAm) insurance premium
primera adj first rate **primera clase** first class **primer, -era cliente, -nta** first customer **primera hipoteca** first mortgage **primera letra de cambio** first bill of exchange **primeras entradas, primeras salidas** FIFO (first in first out)
principal adj leading adj, main adj, major adj, senior adj
principio nm principle n, beginning n
prioridad nf priority n **prioridad absoluta** top priority
privatización nf privatization n
privatizar vb denationalize vb, privatize vb
pro nm pro n **pros y contras** pros and cons
probado adj well-tried adj
probar vb sample vb, try out vb
procedencia nf sourcing n, origin n
proceder vb proceed vb **proceder en contra de** take legal action
procedimiento nm process n **procedimiento para presentar reclamaciones** claims procedure
procesador nm processor n **procesador de palabras** word processor
procesamiento nm processing n **procesamiento de datos** data processing **procesamiento por lotes** (DP) batch processing **procesamiento de textos** word processing
proceso nm lawsuit n, process n **proceso de datos** data handling, data processing, information processing **proceso electrónico de datos (EDP)** electronic data processing
producción nf manufacture n, output n, production n **producción bruta** gross output
producir vb net(t) vb, produce vb **que produce intereses** interest-bearing **producir en exceso** overproduce
productividad nf productivity n
productivo adj productive adj
producto nm product n **producto básico** basic commodity **producto interior bruto (PIB)** gross domestic product (GDP) **producto líder** leading product **producto nacional bruto (PNB)** gross national product (GNP) **producto nuevo** new product **producto primario** primary product **producto principal** leading product **producto principal de la marca** brand leader **productos** goods, produce **productos acabados** final products, finished goods **productos básicos** staple commodities **productos de desecho** waste products **productos finales** final products **productos gratuitos, mercaderías gratuitas** (LAm) free goods **productos a prueba, mercaderías a prueba** (LAm) goods on approval **productos químicos** chemical products
profesión nf career n, occupation n, profession n **de profesión** by trade
programa nm (DP) program n, programme n schedule n, timescale n, timetable n **programa de asistencia al exterior** foreign aid programme **programa económico** economic plan **programa informático** computer program, software **programa de obras públicas** public works programme (GB) **programa de ordenador, programa de computadora** (LAm) computer program **programa de participación en los beneficios** profit-sharing scheme **programa piloto** pilot scheme **programa de reciclaje, plan de recapacitación** (LAm) retraining programme, retraining program (US) **programa de recuperación** recovery scheme
programación nf (DP) programming n
programador, -ora nm,f (DP) programmer n **programador de ordenadores, programador** (LAm) computer programmer
programar vb schedule vb
progreso nm progress n
prohibido adj out of bounds adv, forbidden adj
prolongado adj long-term adj
prolongar vb prolong vb
promedio nm average n, mean n **promedio aritmético** arithmetical mean **promedio ponderado** weighted average
promesa nf pledge n, promise n
promoción nf (of product) promotion n **promoción de las exportaciones** export marketing
promocionar vb (product) promote vb
promotor, -ora nm,f developer n **promotor de construcciones** property developer **promotor inmobiliario** property developer **promotor de ventas** merchandizer
pronosticar vb forecast vb
pronto adv promptly adv, soon adv

propensión *nf* liability *n*, tendency *n*
propenso *adj* liable *adj*, inclined *adj*
propiedad *nf* holding *n*, ownership *n*,
property *n* **co-propiedad** joint ownership
propiedad colectiva workers' collective
propiedades property **propiedad inmobiliaria** real estate **propiedad privada**
private property
propietario, -ria *nm,f* landlord *n*, owner *n*,
proprietor *n* **propietario absentista** absentee landlord **propietario ocupante de
una vivienda** owner-occupier **propietario
de una vivienda** home owner
propina *nf* gratuity *n*, tip *n*
proponer, postular (LAm) *vb* nominate *vb*
proporcionalmente *adv* pro rata *adv*
proporcionar *vb* (supply) provide *vb*
proporcionar algo a alguien issue sb with
sth
propósito *nm* (decision) resolution *n*,
purpose *n*
prorrata *nf* pro rata *n* **a prorrata** pro rata
prorrateo *n* pro rata *n*
prórroga *nf* (of contract) extension *n*
prosperar *vb* boom *vb*, thrive *vb*
prosperidad *nf* prosperity *n* **prosperidad
industrial** industrial health
próspero *adj* booming *adj*, prosperous *adj*
proteccionismo *nm* protectionism *n*
proteccionista *adj* protectionist *adj*
protestar *vb* complain *vb*, make a
complaint *vb* **protestar por algo** complain about sth
provecho *nm* benefit *n*, mileage *n*, profit *n*
proveedor, -ora *nm,f* supplier *n* **proveedor principal** main supplier
proveer *vb* provide *vb*, equip *vb*, supply *vb*
proveer en exceso oversupply *vb*
provisión *nf* (stipulation) provision *n*
provisional, temporario; provisorio
(LAm) *adj* interim *adj*, temporary *adj*
provisorio *adj* (LAm) interim *adj*,
temporary *adj*
proyectar *vb* design *vb*, plan *vb*,
schedule *vb*
proyecto *nm* project *n* **proyecto de contrato** draft contract **proyecto relativo a la
vivienda** housing scheme
prueba *nf* test *n* **a prueba** on approval
prueba sobre el terreno field test
publicar *vb* (policy) issue *vb*, publish *vb*
publicidad *nf* publicity *n*
publicitario *adj* promotional *adj*
público *adj* public *adj*
puente *nm* bridge *n* **puente aéreo** shuttle
puerto *nm* harbour *n*, port *n* **puerto de**

entrada port of entry **puerto franco** free
port, free trade area
puestero, -era *nm,f* (LAm) dealer *n*
puesto *nm* (job) post *n*, booth *n*
puesto *nm*, **casilla** *nf*, (LAm) booth *n*
pujar *vb* push *vb*, bid *vb*
punto *nm* item *n* **punto crítico** break-even
point **punto máximo** peak **punto
muerto** stalemate **punto de venta** point
of sale, sales outlet
quebrar *vb* go out of business *vb*, go to
the wall *vb*
quedar *vb* stay *vb*, remain *vb* **quedarse
con dinero** (money) keep back
queja *nf* complaint *n*, grievance *n*
quejar *vb* complain *vb* **quejarse de algo**
complain about sth
quiebra *nf* bankruptcy *n*, failure *n* (of
company) collapse *n*
quincenal *adj* biweekly *adj*
quórum *nm* quorum *n* **con quórum**
quorate **quórum de acreedores** quorum
of creditors
racionalización *nf* rationalization *n*
racionalizar *vb* rationalize *vb*
RAM *nf* (DP) RAM (random access
memory) *abbr*
rama *nf* branch *n*
ramo *nm* branch *n* **ramo profesional** line
of business
rango *nm* rank *n* **de alto rango** high--
ranking
rápido *adj* prompt *adj*, fast *adj*
ratificación *nf* confirmation *n*,
ratification *n*
ratificar *vb* ratify *vb*
ratio *nm* ratio *n* **ratio de facturación, ratio
de renovación** turnover ratio
razón *nf* reason *n* **razón social** trade name
razonable *adj* (price) reasonable *adj*
reacción *nf* feedback *n* **reacción negativa**
negative feedback
reactivación *nf* (economic) recovery *n*,
reflation *n*, upswing *n*
readjudicar *vb* (funds) reallocate *vb*
real *adj* actual *adj*, real *adj*, royal *adj*
realidad *nf* actuality *n*, reality *n*
realizar *vb* accomplish *vb*, carry out *vb*
(profit) realize *vb* **realizar ensayos** carry
out trials **realizar ganancias excesivas**
profiteer
reanudar *vb* (policy, contract) renew *vb*
reasegurar *vb* reinsure *vb*
reaseguro *nm* reinsurance *n*
reasignación *nf* (of funds) reallocation *n*
rebaja *nf* markdown *n*, reduction *n*

rebajado adj reduced adj **a un precio muy rebajado** at a greatly reduced price
rebajar vb (prices) bring down vb, mark down vb, reduce vb, cut vb, (employee) demote vb **rebajar algo a mitad de precio** reduce sth by half
rebasar vb overdraw vb **rebasar una cuenta** overdraw on an account
recadista nmf messenger n
recalentamiento nm (of economy) overheating n
recargar vb mark up vb, overcharge vb
recargo nm additional charge n, markup n, premium n **recargo del impuesto sobre la renta** surtax
recaudación nf takings npl **recaudación neta** net(t) proceeds
recaudado adj collected adj
recaudar vb (tax) levy vb **recaudar fondos** raise money
recepcionista nmf desk clerk n, receptionist n
receptor, -ora nm,f recipient n **receptor de la oferta** offeree
recesión nf (economic) depression n, recession n
rechazar vb negative (US), (goods) reject vb, (contract) repudiate vb, (offer) turn down vb **rechazar un cheque** bounce* a cheque **rechazar mercancías** refuse goods
rechazo, plante (LAm) nm refusal n
recibir vb receive vb **recibir a un cliente** entertain a client
reciclable adj (materials) reclaimable adj recyclable adj
reciclaje nm recycling n **reciclaje profesional** retraining
reciclar vb recycle vb
reciente adj recent adj **recién contratado** newly-appointed
recíproco adj reciprocal adj
reclamación, reclamo (LAm) nf, nm complaint n **reclamación de impuestos** tax claim
reclamar vb demand vb, make a complaint vb **reclamar por daños y perjuicios** (legal) claim damages
réclame nm (LAm) advertisement n
reclamo nm (LAm) complaint n
reclutar vb recruit vb
recobrar vb repossess vb
recogida nf collection n
recomendación nf recommendation n, testimonial n
recompensa nf payment n, recompense n,

compensation n **recompensa de directivos** executive compensation
reconocimiento nm recognition n **reconocimiento de deuda** acknowledgement of debt
recontratación nf reappointment n
reconversión nf rationalization n, retraining n
reconvertir vb restructure vb, rationalise vb
recordatorio nm reminder n
recorrido nm route n, trip n **de corto recorrido** short-haul **de largo recorrido** long-distance, long-haul
recortar vb (reduce) cut vb, (price) knock down vb, axe* vb, shrink vb, ax (US) (spending) squeeze vb (investment) trim vb **recortar gastos** axe* expenditure
recorte nm reduction n
recuerdo nm (DP) memory n
recuperación nf repossession n **recuperación de datos** information retrieval **recuperación de documentos** document retrieval
recuperar vb recover vb, recuperate vb **recuperar dinero a alguien** recover money from sb **recuperarse** (improve) pick up
recurrir vb have recourse vb, resort vb **recurrir a** (have recourse) resort to
recurso nm **recursos** ability to pay, means, resources **recursos financieros** financial means/resources **recursos humanos** human resources, manpower **recursos naturales** natural resources
red nf net n, network n **red bancaria** banking network **red de comunicaciones** communication network **red de distribución** distribution network **red de ordenadores, red de computadores** (LAm) computer network
redacción nf wording n, writing-up n
redactar vb write up vb, draft vb **redactar un contrato** draw up a contract **redactar un informe, hacer un reporte** (LAm) draw up a report
redimir vb redeem vb
redistribución nf (of funds) reallocation n
redistribuir vb (funds) reallocate vb
rédito nm earnings yield n
reducción nf abatement n, depletion n, markdown n, reduction n **reducción de costes** cost-cutting, cost trimming **reducción de gastos, reducción de costos** (LAm) cost-cutting **reducción en los impuestos** tax cut
reducir, rematar (LAm) vb (prices) bring

down *vb*, knock down *vb*, mark down *vb*, reduce *vb* **reducir al mínimo** (stocks) run low **reducir al mínimo las pérdidas** minimise losses **reducir a la mitad** halve **reducir la plantilla** (workforce) trim
reelección *nf* re-election *n*
reelegir *vb* re-elect *vb*
reembolsable *adj* refundable *adj* (deposit) returnable *adj*
reembolsar *vb* refund *vb*, reimburse *vb*, repay *vb*
reembolso *nm* rebate *n*, refund *n*, reimbursement *n* (of loan) repayment *n* **sin reembolso** ex repayment
reemplazar *vb* replace *vb*
reexpedir *vb* (mail) redirect *vb*
referencia *nf* reference *n* **con referencia a** re, with reference to **referencia de crédito** credit reference
referéndum *nm* referendum *n*
referir *vb* refer *vb* **por lo que se refiere a** regarding
reflación *nf* reflation *n*
reflacionario *adj* reflationary *adj*
reforma *nf* reform *n* **reforma agraria** land reform **reforma arancelaria** tariff reform **reforma monetaria** currency reform
reforzar *vb* consolidate *vb* **reforzar la moral** boost morale
refrendar *vb* countersign *vb*
regalar *vb* give *vb*, (as gift) present *vb*
regalo *nm* giveaway *n*, gift *n*
regatear *vb* bargain *vb*
región *nf* region *n*
registrar *vb* register *vb* **registrarse** (to hotel) check in *vb*
registro *nm* register *n*, tally *n* **registro de antecedentes, historial** (LAm) track record **registro catastral** land register **registro de fábricas** factory ledger
reglamento *nm* regulation *n*
regulación *nf* regulation *n*
rehusar *vb* refuse *vb*
reimportación *nf* reimportation *n*
reimportar *vb* reimport *vb*
reintegrar *vb* refund *vb*
reintegro *nm* refund *n* **reintegro de fondos, retiro de fondos** (LAm) withdrawal of funds
reinvertir *vb* (profits) plough back *vb*, plow back (US), *vb*
reivindicación, pedido (LAm) *nf, nm* demand *n* **reivindicación salarial** wage(s) claim/demand
reivindicar *vb* demand *vb*
relación *nf* list *n*, ratio *n* **con relación a** re,

with regard to... **relaciones con la clientela** customer relations **relaciones comerciales** business relations **relaciones humanas** human relations **relaciones industriales** industrial relations **relaciones laborales** labour relations **relaciones públicas** customer relations, public relations **con relación a nuestra carta de** we refer to our letter of... **relación de procedencia** statement of origin **relación real de intercambio** terms of trade **relación de trabajo** working relationship
relajar *vb* (restrictions) relax *vb*
rellenar *vb* (form) fill in *vb*, complete *vb*
rematar *vb* (price) knock down *vb*, bring down *vb*
remate *nm* (LAm) auction *n*
remesa *nf* consignment *n*, delivery *n*, remittance *n*
remitente *nmf* consigner/or *n*, sender *n*, shipper *n*
remitir *vb* send *vb* **remitir adjunto** enclose **remitir por correo** post
remodelación *nf* restructuring *n*, reorganization *n* **remodelación urbana** urban renewal
remuneración *nf* remuneration *n*, salary *n*
remunerado *adj* paid *adj* **bien remunerado** well-paid
remunerar *vb* remunerate *vb*
rendimiento *nm* output *n* **hay que mejorar nuestro rendimiento** we must improve our performance **rendimiento sobre acciones** yield on shares **rendimiento del capital** return on capital **rendimiento del capital social, plan de recapacitación** (LAm) return on equity **rendimiento económico, performance económico** (LAm) economic performance **rendimiento por hora** per hour output **rendimiento de la inversión** return on capital, return on investment **rendimiento del patrimonio neto, plan de recapacitación** (LAm) return on equity **rendimientos del capital** unearned income **rendimientos decrecientes** diminishing returns **rendimiento de las ventas** return on sales
rendir *vb* yield *vb*
renegociar *vb* renegotiate *vb* **renegociar una deuda** reschedule a debt
renovable *adj* renewable *adj*
renovación *nf* refurbishment *n*, renewal *n*, updating *n*
renovar *vb* refurbish *vb*, (policy, contract) renew *vb*

renta *nf* income *n*, rent *n* **renta anual** yearly income **renta fija** fixed income **renta nacional** national income **renta privada** private income **rentas públicas** revenue

rentabilidad *nf* profitability *n*

rentable *adj* moneymaking *adj*

rentar *vb* (LAm) hire *vb*

renuncia *nf* resignation *n*, waiver *n*

renunciar *vb* abandon *vb*, resign *vb*, waive *vb*

reparar *vb* make amends *vb*, repair *vb*

repartir *vb* allocate *vb* (goods) deliver *vb*

reparto *nm* delivery *n*, distribution *n* **reparto de ganancias** gain sharing **reparto rápido a domicilio** express delivery

repasar *vb* revise *vb*

repatriación *nf* repatriation *n*

repertorio *nm* directory *n*, index *n*

replantear *vb* restructure *vb*

reponer *vb* replace *vb*

reportaje, reporte (LAm) *nm* report *n* **reportaje de las noticias** news coverage **reportaje de prensa** newspaper report

reporte *nm* (LAm) report *n*

representación *nf* representation *n*, delegation *n* **representación falsa** false representation

representante, corredor, -ora (LAm) *nmf, nm,f* agent *n*, representative *n*, salesperson *n* **representante regional** area representative **representante sindical** shop steward, union representative

repudiar *vb* waive *vb*

repunte *nm* (economic) recovery *n* upswing *n*

requerimiento *nm* requirement *n* **requerimiento judicial** injunction

requerir *vb* demand *vb*, require *vb* **que requiere mucha mano de obra** labour-intensive

requisito *nm* requirement *n*, specification *n* **requisitos de la industria** needs of industry

resarcimiento *nm* compensation *n*, repayment *n* **resarcimiento no compensatorio** nominal damages

rescatar *vb* salvage *vb*, recover *vb*

rescate *nm* redemption *n*, rescue *n*

reserva, reservación (LAm) *nf* booking *n*, reservation *n*, supply *n* **con la más absoluta reserva** in strictest confidence **en reserva** in hand **reserva de divisas** currency reserve **reserva de libras esterlinas** sterling balance **reservas mínimas**

fractional reserves **reservas de oro** gold reserves

reservación *nf* reservation *n*

reservar *vb* reserve *vb* **reservar por adelantado** book in advance **reservar una habitación de hotel** book a hotel room **reservar un vuelo** book a flight

residual *adj* residual *adj*

residuos *nmpl* waste *n*

resistir *vb* withstand *vb*

resolución *nf* (decision) resolution *n*

resolver *vb* (dispute) settle *vb* **resolver hacer algo** resolve to do sth

respaldar *vb* back *vb*, support *vb* **respaldar una empresa** back a venture

respaldo *nm* backing *n*

respectar *vb* be concerned (with) *vb*

respecto *nm* matter *n* **respecto a** regarding, in respect of...

respetar *vb* respect *vb* **respetar las normas** comply with the rules **respetar las reglas** observe the rules

responder *vb* answer *vb*

responsabilidad *nf* accountability *n*, commitment *n*, liability *n* **responsabilidad conjunta/colectiva** joint responsibility **responsabilidad ilimitada** unlimited liability **responsabilidad limitada** limited liability

responsabilizar *vb* make responsible *vb* **responsabilizar a alguien** hold sb liable, hold sb responsible **responsabilizarse de algo** take charge of sth, take responsibility for sth

responsable *adj* accountable *adj*, liable *adj*, reliable *adj*, responsible *adj* **responsable de daños y perjuicios** liable for damages **responsable de la seguridad** safety officer

respuesta *nf* answer *n*, feedback *n* **en respuesta a** in response to...

restante *adj* (sum) remaining *adj*

restauración *nf* refurbishment *n*

restricción *nf* restriction *n* **restricciones comerciales** trade restrictions **restricciones de crédito** credit squeeze **restricciones a divisas** exchange restrictions **restricciones a la importación** import restrictions

restrictivo *adj* restrictive *adj*

restringir *vb* restrict *vb* (spending) squeeze *vb*

resultado *nm* balance *n*, consequence *n*, outcome *n* **resultado neto** net(t) result

resultar *vb* (end) turn out *vb* **resultar válido** (withstand scrutiny) hold up

resumen *nm* abstract *n*, summary *n*

resumido *adj* abbreviated *adj*
resumir *vb* abbreviate *vb*, summarise *vb*
retención *nf* retention *n* **retención de título** retention of title
retener *vb* retain *vb*, withhold *vb* **retener algo como garantía** hold sth as security **retener un documento** withhold a document
retirada, retiro (LAm) *nf, nm* withdrawal *n*
retirar *vb* withdraw *vb* **retirar una oferta** withdraw an offer **retirarse** retire
retiro *nm* retirement *n*, withdrawal (LAm) *n*
retransmisión *nf* broadcast *n*
retrasar, demorar (LAm) *vb* delay *vb*, hold back *vb*, hold up *vb*
reunión *nf* conference *n*, meeting *n* **reunión de la comisión** committee meeting **reunión del comité** committee meeting **reunión del consejo de administración** board meeting **reunión de la junta directiva** board meeting **reunión de negocios** business meeting **reunión de ventas** sales conference, sales talk
reutilizable *adj* (materials) reclaimable *adj*
revalorización *nf* (in value) appreciation *n*
revalorizar, revaluar (LAm) *vb* (currency) revalue *vb* **revalorizarse** gain in value
revaluación *nf* (of currency) revaluation *n*
revaluar *vb* (LAm) revalue *vb*
reventa *nf* resale *n*
revertir *vb* revert *vb* **revertir a** revert to *vb*
revisación *nf* (LAm) examination *n*
revisar *vb* inspect *vb*, revise *vb*, examine (LAm) *vb*
revisión, revisación (LAm) *nf* examination *n* (customs) inspection *n* **revisión de aduana** customs check
revisor, -ora *nm,f* supervisor *n*
revista *nf* journal *n*, magazine *n*
revocar *vb* (offer) revoke *vb*
riesgo *nm* hazard *n*, risk *n* **de alto riesgo, riesgoso** (LAm) high-risk **de bajo riesgo** gilt-edged **sin riesgo** safe **riesgo del cambio** exchange risk **riesgo natural** natural hazard **riesgo ocupacional** occupational hazard **riesgo de la profesión** occupational hazard **riesgos financieros** financial exposure
riqueza *nf* wealth *n*
ritmo *nm* timing *n* **ritmo de expansión, tasa de expansión** (LAm) rate of expansion **ritmo de facturación** turnover rate **ritmo de inversiones, tasa de inversión** (LAm) rate of investment **ritmo de reducción de la plantilla** wastage rate

ROM *abbr, nf* ROM (read only memory) *abbr*
rompehuelgas, carnero, -ra (LAm) *nm, nm,f* scab* *n*, strikebreaker *n*
romper *vb* split *vb* **romper un contrato** break an agreement
rotación *nf* rotation *n*, turnover *n*
rotundo *adj* total *adj*
rubro *nm* (LAm) bill *n*
rueda *nf* wheel *n* **rueda de prensa** press conference
s.r.c. (se ruega contestación), r.s.v.p. (LAm) *abbr* RSVP (répondez s'il vous plaît) *abbr*
saber *vb* know *vb* **se sabe muy bien** it is common knowledge **que yo sepa** to my knowledge
sabido *adj* known *adj* **bien sabido** well-known **es bien sabido** it is common knowledge
sacar *vb* (product) bring out *vb*, introduce *vb* **sacar algo a licitación** put sth out for tender
sala *nf* hall *n*, room *n* **sala de exposiciones** exhibition hall, showroom **sala de juntas** board room **sala para pasajeros en tránsito** (transport) transit lounge **sala de tránsito** (transport) transfer lounge, transit lounge
salario *nm* pay *n*, salary *n*, wage *n* **salario de entrada** starting wage **salario justo** fair wage **salario medio** average wage **salario mínimo** minimum wage **salario mínimo indexado** index-linked minimum wage **salario neto** net(t) wage **salario real** real wage
saldar *vb* liquidate *vb* (account) settle *vb* **saldar una cuenta** settle an account **saldar una deuda** pay off a debt
saldo *nm* balance *n* **con saldo acreedor** in credit **saldo bancario** bank balance **saldo de cuenta bancaria** bank balance **saldo disponible** balance in hand **saldo final** final balance **saldo deudor/negativo** debit balance, unpaid balance
salida *nf* departure *n*, exit *n* **salida a bolsa** flotation **salida de mercado** market outlet
salir *vb* (end) turn out *vb* **salir a la venta** go on sale **salir del trabajo** (finish work) knock off*
salón *nm* lounge *n* **salón de exposición** showroom
salud *nf* health *n* **salud industrial** industrial health
salvar *vb* salvage *vb*, save *vb*

sanción *nf* sanction *n* **sanción económica** economic sanction **sanciones económicas** trade sanctions
sanear *vb* (company) turn round *vb*, turn around (US)
sanidad *nf* health *n*
satisfacción *nf* satisfaction *n* **satisfacción del consumidor** consumer satisfaction **satisfacción laboral** job satisfaction **satisfacción por el trabajo** job satisfaction
sección *nf* department *n*, (of company) division *n*
secretaría *nf* (LAm) ministry *n*, Government Department *n*
secretario, -ria *nm,f* minister *n*, secretary *n* **secretario de la compañía** company secretary **secretario ejecutivo** executive secretary
secreto *nm* secret *n* **secreto comercial** trade secret
sector *nm* sector *n* **sector primario** primary sector **sector privado** private enterprise/sector **sector público** government/public sector **sector secundario** secondary industry/sector **sector de los servicios** tertiary industry **sector terciario** tertiary industry/sector
secundario *adj* minor *adj*
sede *nf* headquarters *npl*, HO (head office) *n*, registered office *n* **le referimos a nuestra sede** we refer you to our head office **sede central** head office **sede social** main office
seguir *vb* follow *vb*, continue *vb* **seguir instrucciones** follow instructions
según *prep* in accordance with **según lo establecido en el contrato** under the terms of the contract **según el ministro** according to the minister **según las normas** according to the regulations **según nuestros registros** according to our records **según lo planeado** according to plan **según sus requisitos** in accordance with your requirements
seguridad *nf* security *n* **Seguridad Social** National Health Service (GB), National Insurance (GB), Social Security (GB)
seguro 1. *adj* safe *adj*, secure *adj* 2. *nm* insurance *n* **seguros** insurance **seguro de automóviles** car insurance **seguro de casco de buque** hull insurance **seguro colectivo** group insurance **seguro de combinación aplazada y decreciente** endowment insurance **seguro contra incendios** fire insurance **seguro contra terceros** third-party insurance **seguro de**

crédito a la exportación export credit insurance **seguro de desempleo** unemployment insurance **seguro empresarial contra terceros** employer's liability insurance **seguro de enfermedad** health insurance **seguro de equipaje** luggage insurance **seguro de fidelidad** fidelity insurance **seguro de indemnización** indemnity insurance **seguro marítimo** hull/marine insurance **seguro médico** medical insurance **seguro de responsabilidad civil** third-party insurance **seguro a todo riesgo** all-risks/comprehensive insurance **seguro de viaje** travel insurance **seguro de vida** life assurance/insurance
selección *nf* choice *n*, selection *n* **selección aleatoria** random selection
sellar *vb* seal *vb*
sello *nm* seal *n*
semana *nf* week *n* **semana laboral** working week, workweek (US) **semana de trabajo** working week, workweek (US)
semestral *adj* biannual *adj*
semestre *nm* half-year *n*, semester *n*
semicualificado *adj* semi-skilled *adj*
seña *nf* (LAm) deposit *n*
señal *nf* brand *n*, index *n*, indication *n* **señal de alerta** warning sign **señal de comunicando, tono de ocupado; señal de ocupado** (LAm) engaged signal, busy signal (US)
señalar *vb* indicate *vb*, point *vb*
sensato *adj* well-advised *adj*, sensible *adj*
sentido *nm* direction *n*, way *n* **de doble sentido; de doble mano; de doble vía** (LAm) two-way
sentir *vb* experience *vb*, feel *vb*
ser *vb* be *vb* **ser declarado en quiebra** go to the wall **ser dueño de** own **ser gravemente afectado por** be hard hit by **ser noticia** hit the headlines **ser rechazado** (cheque) bounce* **ser responsable** be in charge **ser testigo de** witness
serio *adj* bona fide *adj*, businesslike *adj*, responsible *adj*, weighty *adj*
servicio *nm* commission *n*, facility *n*, service *n* **servicio de asistencia en carretera** breakdown service **servicio a domicilio** home service **servicio de enlace** shuttle **servicio incluido** service included **servicio post-venta** after-sales service **servicio público** public service **servicios** amenities **servicios postales** postal services **servicio urgente** express service **servicio de veinticuatro horas** twenty--four-hour service

sesión *nf* session *n* **sesión informativa** briefing **sesión de negociaciones** negotiating session **sesión a puerta cerrada** closed session/meeting

signatario, -ria *nm,f* signatory *n*

silicio *nm* silicon *n* **pastilla de silicio** microchip

simulador,- ora *nm,f* malingerer *n*

sindicalizar *vb* (LAm) unionize *vb*

sindicato, gremio (LAm) *nm* syndicate, trade union, union **sindicato industrial** industrial union **sindicato laboral** trade union, labor union (US)

síndico, -ica *nm,f* (bankruptcy) receiver *n*, administrator (US)

sinergia *nf* synergy *n*

síntesis *nf* synthesis *n*

sintético *adj* man-made *adj*, synthetic *adj*

sintonizar *vb* tune in *vb* **sintonizar con** be on the same wavelength as

sistema *nm* organization *n*, system *n* **sistema de archivo** filing system **sistema de cuotas** quota system **sistema de dos niveles** two-tier system **sistema experto** expert system **Sistema Monetario Europeo (SME)** European Monetary System (EMS) **sistemas de información** information systems **el sistema de tres turnos** the three-shift system **sistema tributario a tasa cero** zero-rate taxation

sistematización *nf* systematization *n*

sistematizar *vb* rationalize *vb*

situación, ubicación (LAm) *nf* location *n*, position *n*, status *n* **situación económica** financial status **situación financiera** financial situation

sobornar, coimear; morder (LAm) *vb* bribe *vb*

soborno, coima; mordida (LAm) *nm, nm; nf* backhander* *n*, bribe *n*, bribery *n*, payola (US) (bribe) sweetener* *n*

sobrante *adj* residual *adj*

sobre 1. *nm* envelope *n* **2.** *prep* on *prep*, about *prep*

sobrecargar *vb* overload *vb*

sobregirar *vb* **sobregirarse** overdraw *vb*

sobregiro *nm* bank overdraft *n*

sobrepasar *vb* exceed *vb*

sobrepoblación *nf* (LAm) overpopulation *n*

sobreproducción *nf* overproduction *n*

sobrepujar *vb* outbid *vb*

sobrestimar *vb* overvalue *vb*

sobrevalorar *vb* overvalue *vb*

sobrevendido *adj* oversold *adj*, oversubscribed *adj*

sociedad *nf* company *n*, society *n* **sociedad de ahorro y préstamo para la vivienda** building society **sociedad anónima** corporation, joint-stock company **sociedad anónima cuyas acciones se cotizan en bolsa** public limited company **sociedad anónima privada** private limited company **sociedad de ayuda mutua** Friendly Society **sociedad colectiva** partnership **sociedad comercial** trading company **sociedad de consumo** affluent/consumer society **sociedad cotizada en bolsa** public company **sociedad de crédito hipotecario** building society **sociedad cuyas acciones se cotizan en Bolsa** quoted company **sociedad filial** affiliated company **sociedad financiera** credit/finance company **sociedad inmobiliaria** property company **sociedad de inversión** investment trust **sociedad legalmente constituida** registered company **sociedad de primer orden** blue-chip company **sociedad próspera** affluent society **sociedad de responsabilidad limitada** limited company **sociedad tenedora** holding company **sociedad 'holding'** holding company

socio, -cia *nm,f* associate *n*, business associate *n*, member *n*, partner *n*, trading partner *n* **socio en comandita** sleeping partner **socio comanditario** sleeping partner, silent partner **socio general** general partner

solicitante *nmf* claimant *n*, applicant *n*

solicitar, aplicar por (LAm) *vb* apply for *vb* **solicitar un descubierto** request an overdraft **solicitar un mandamiento judicial** take out an injunction

solicitud, pedido (LAm) *nf, nm* request *n*, takeup *n* **solicitud de pago, pedido de pago** (LAm) request for payment

solvencia *nf* ability to pay *n*, creditworthiness *n*, solvency *n*

solventar *vb* pay *vb*, settle *vb* **solventar una reclamación** settle/adjust a claim

solvente *adj* creditworthy *adj*, solvent *adj*

someter *vb* subject *vb*, submit *vb* **someter algo a prueba** put sth to the test **someter a prueba de mercado** test-market

sondeo *nm* survey *n* **sondeo económico** economic survey **sondeo de opinión consumista** consumer survey

sopesar *vb* weigh the pros and cons *vb*

soportar *vb* withstand *vb*

soporte *nm* support *n*, computerware *n*

soporte físico del ordenador computer hardware
sospechoso adj (dealings) shady* adj
standing nm standing n de alto standing high-class, top-level
status nm status n statu quo status quo
suavizar vb water down vb, soften vb
suba nf (LAm) rise n
subalterno, -rna nm,f subordinate n
subasta, remate (LAm) nf, nm auction n
subastador, -ora, rematador, -ora (LAm) nm,f auctioneer n
subastar, rematar (LAm) vb auction vb subastar algo sell sth at auction
subcontratar vb farm out vb, subcontract vb
subcontratista nmf subcontractor n
subdirector, -ora nm,f assistant manager n, deputy director n
subempleado adj underemployed adj
subida, suba (LAm) nf rise n subida de precio price increase
subir vb (rise in value) appreciate vb (prices) bump up vb, increase vb, raise vb, rise vb subir a bordo go aboard subir tarifas raise tariffs
subproducto nm by-product n
subsidiar vb (LAm) subsidize vb
subsidio nm benefit n, subsidy n subsidio de enfermedad sickness benefit subsidio estatal government subsidy subsidio familiar, asignación familiar (LAm) family allowance subsidio del gobierno, subsidio del estado (LAm) state subsidy subsidio de paro, subsidio de cesantía (LAm) unemployment benefit, unemployment pay subsidios agrícolas farming subsidies subsidios sociales welfare benefits
subvención nf subsidy n subvenciones para exportaciones export subsidies subvención regional regional grant
subvencionar, subsidiar (LAm) vb subsidize vb
sucesión nf inheritance n
sucursal nf branch n, branch office n, subsidiary n, subsidiary company n sucursal de una cadena de grandes almacenes multiple store
sueldo nm pay n, salary n, wage n sueldo neto net(t) wage, wage packet, salary package (US) sueldo semanal weekly wages
suerte nf luck n suerte imprevista windfall n
sufrir vb suffer vb sufrir un bajón slump vb

sujetar vb (prices) peg vb
sujeto adj liable adj, subject adj sujeto a impuestos liable for tax
suma nf amount n suma bruta gross amount suma global net(t) amount, the grand total suma simbólica nominal amount
suministrador, -ora nm,f supplier n suministrador, -ora clave main supplier
suministrar vb (supply) provide vb suministrar algo bajo palabra supply sth on trust
suministro nm supply n
superable adj negotiable adj
superar vb exceed vb superarse improve vb
superávit nm surplus n superávit de la balanza de pagos balance of payments surplus superávit comercial trade surplus superávit de exportación export surplus superávit de fondos funds surplus superávit percibido earned surplus superávit presupuestario budget surplus
superfluo adj redundant adj, superfluous adj
superior adj senior adj, higher adj, superior adj
supermercado nm supermarket n
superpetrolero nm supertanker n
superpoblación, sobrepoblación (LAm) nf overpopulation n
superpotencia nf superpower n superpotencia económica economic superpower
superventas nm best seller n
supervisión nf oversight n
supervisor, -ora nm,f supervisor n
suplementario adj extra adj, supplementary adj
suplemento nm additional charge n suplemento salarial weighting
suplente nmf deputy n (person) replacement n
supresión nf abatement n, abolition n supresión de aranceles elimination of tariffs
suprimir vb abate vb, abolish vb, axe* vb, ax (US)
suscribir vb subscribe vb suscribir un tratado make a treaty
suscriptor, -ora nm,f insurance underwriter n, underwriter n
suspender vb adjourn vb suspender una cita cancel an appointment
suspensión nf adjournment n
sustituto, -uta nm,f (person) replacement n

tablero *nm* (notice) board *n*

tablón *nm* (notice) board *n* **tablón de anuncios** bulletin board

tabular *vb* (data) tabulate *vb*

tácito *adj* tacit *adj*

táctica *nf* tactic *n* **táctica de demora** delaying tactics **táctica de ventas** selling tactics

talla, talle (LAm) *nf, nm* size *n*

taller *nm* shopfloor *n*, workshop *n*

talón *nm* (LAm) counterfoil *n*

talonario *nm* cheque book *n*, receipt book *n* **talonario de cheques** cheque book, checkbook (US)

tamaño *nm* size *n*

tanto *nm* (given) amount *n* **tanto por ciento de los beneficios** percentage of profit

tapar *vb* (LAm) block *vb*

taquilla, boletería (LAm) *nf* box office *n*, ticket office *n*

tara *nf* defect *n*

tardanza, demora (LAm) *nf* delay *n* **sin tardanza, sin demora** (LAm) without delay

tardar *vb* delay *vb*, take one's time *vb*

tarifa *nf* scale *n*, tariff *n* **tarifa horaria** hourly rate **tarifas, tasas** (LAm) (tax) rates

tarjeta *nf* card *n* **tarjeta bancaria** bank card **tarjeta de cajero automático** cashpoint card **tarjeta de crédito** bank card, charge card, credit card **tarjeta de garantía de cheques** cheque card **tarjeta inteligente** smart card **tarjeta profesional** business card **tarjeta de visita** business card

tasa *nf* toll *n*, tax *n*, rate *n*, valuation *n* **tasa de abandono** wastage rate **tasa de acumulación** rate of accrual **tasa base** base rate, base lending rate, basic rate **tasa de beneficios decreciente** falling rate of profit **tasa de cambio flexible** flexible exchange rate **tasa de crecimiento** growth rate **tasa de crecimiento anual** annual growth rate **tasa de inflación** rate of inflation **tasa de interés** bank rate, interest rate **tasa de interés fija** flat rate **tasa de licencia** licence fee **tasa Lombard** Lombard Rate **tasa natural de incremento** natural rate of increase **tasa normal** basic rate **tasa de paro, tasa de cesantía** (LAm) rate of unemployment **tasa de rendimiento** rate of return **tasa de rendimiento justa** fair rate of return

tasa de rentabilidad rate of return **tasa variable** variable rate

tasación, avalúo (LAm) *nf, nm* appraisal *n*, valuation *n*

tasar *vb* ration *vb*, value *vb*

teclado *nm* keyboard *n*

teclear *vb* key in *vb*

técnica *nf* skill *n* **técnica de ventas** sales technique

técnico, -ica *nm,f* technician *n*

tecnología *nf* technology *n* **de alta tecnología** hi-tech **tecnología avanzada** advanced technology **tecnología de datos** information technology

telebanca *nf* telebanking *n*

telecomunicaciones *nfpl* telecommunications *n*

telecopiadora *nf* telecopier *n*

telefax *nm* facsimile (fax) *n*, telefax *n*

telefonista *nmf* operator *n*, switchboard operator *n*

teléfono *nm* telephone *n*, telephone number *n* **teléfono interno** house telephone **telefono visual** visual telephone

teleproceso *nm* teleprocessing *n*

telespectador, -ora *nm,f* viewer *n*

teletipo *nm* telecopier *n*

televentas *nfpl* telesales *npl*

televisar *vb* televise *vb*

télex *nm* telex *n*

temporada *nf* season *n* **temporada alta** high season **temporada baja** low season **temporada media** mid season

temporal, temporario; provisorio (LAm) *adj* temporary *adj*

temporario *adj* (LAm) temporary *adj*

tendencia *nf* tendency *n*, trend *n* **tendencia económica** economic trend **tendencia del mercado** market trend **tendencia de precios** price trend **tendencias del consumidor** consumer trends **tendencias de consumo** consumer trends **tendencias económicas** economic trends **tendencias del mercado** market forces, market tendencies

tender *vb* tend *vb*, have the tendency *vb* **tender a** tend toward *vb*

tenedor, -ora *nm,f* holder *n* **tenedor de acciones** shareholder, stockholder **tenedor de libros** book-keeper **tenedor de obligaciones** bondholder

teneduría *nf* (book/account) keeping *n*

tenencia *nf* occupation *n*, tenure *n*

tener *vb* have *vb*, own *vb*, possess *vb* **tener buena reputación** enjoy a good reputation **tener coherencia** (argument) hang together **tener algo en cuenta** take sth into account **tener en existencia** (stock) carry **tener mano de obra excesiva** overman **tener un presupuesto muy limitado** be on a tight budget **tener propiedades** have holdings **tener algo en reserva** hold sth in reserve **tener un saldo positivo** be in the black **tener tendencia a** tend toward **tener trabajo** be in work **¿tendría la amabilidad de...?** would you be so kind as to...?

teoría *nf* theory *n* **en teoría** in theory **teoría cuantitativa del dinero** quantity theory of money

tercero **1.** *adj* third *adj* **2.** *nm* third person *n*, third party *n*

terminal 1. *adj* terminal *adj* **2.** *n* **terminal aérea** air terminal *nf* **terminal del ordenador, terminal de la computadora** (LAm) *nm* computer terminal

terminar *vb* break up *vb*, complete *vb*, wind up *vb* **terminar una reunión** close a meeting

término *nm* term *n*, time limit *n* **bajo los términos del contrato** under the terms of the contract **a término** at term **términos y condiciones** terms and conditions **términos estrictamente netos** terms strictly net(t) **términos ventajosos** favourable terms

terrateniente *nmf* landowner *n*

terreno *nm* plot *n*, ground *n* **terreno edificable** building site

territorio *nm* territory *n* **territorio de ultramar** overseas territory

tesoro *nm* treasure *n*, Treasury *n* **el Tesoro público** the Treasury

testamento *nm* will *n*

testigo *nm* witness *n*

testimonio *nm* evidence *n*, attestation *n*, witness *n*

texto *nm* text *n*, wording *n*

tiempo *nm* time *n* **a tiempo completo** full-time **a tiempo parcial** part-time **tiempo real** real time

tienda *nf* shop *n*, store *n* **tienda bajo licencia** franchise outlet **tienda de una cadena** chain store **tienda al por menor** retail outlet

tierra *nf* land *n* **por tierra** by road

timador, -ora *nm,f* swindler* *n*

tipificar *vb* standardize *vb*

tipo *nm* type *n*, brand *n*, kind *n*, rate *n* **buen tipo de interés, alta tasa de interés** (LAm) fine rate of interest **tipo bancario,**

tasa de interés (LAm) bank rate **tipo base** base lending rate, base rate **tipo de cambio** exchange rate **tipo de cambio flexible** flexible exchange rate **tipo de cambio flotante** floating exchange rate **tipo de compra** buying rate **tipo de descuento** discount rate **tipo impositivo** tax rate **tipo de interés** bank rate, interest rate **tipo de interés mínimo establecido por el banco central** minimum lending rate **tipo de paridad, tasa de cambio** (LAm) rate of exchange **tipo preferencial de interés bancario** prime lending rate **tipo variable** variable rate

tiquete *nm* (LAm) ticket *n*

titular *nmf* bearer *n*, holder *n*, occupant *n* **titular del cargo** office holder **titular de una licencia** licence holder, licensee **titular de una póliza de seguros** policy holder

título *nm* (law) deed *n*, bond *n*, heading *n*, qualification *n*, (to goods) title *n* **título académico** academic qualification **título de acción** share certificate, stock certificate (US) **título docente** educational qualification **título del Estado** government bond/security **título nominativo** registered bond **título de obligaciones** bond certificate **título al portador** bearer bond **título provisional** scrip **títulos adecuados** necessary qualifications **títulos de la deuda pública** gilts **títulos del Estado** gilt-edged securities

tocar *vb* affect *vb*, touch *vb* **tocar fondo** bottom out

toma *nf* collecting *n*, taking *n*

tomar *vb* borrow *vb* **tomar apuntes, sacar apuntes** (LAm) take notes **tomar la delantera** take the lead **tomar la determinación** make a resolution **tomar la jubilación anticipada** take early retirement **tomar el mando** take the lead **tomar muestras** sample **tomar nota de algo** make a note of sth **tomar notas** take notes **tomarse un descanso** take a break **tomarse permiso, estar de licencia** (LAm) take leave **tomarse tiempo** take one's time

tonadilla *nf* jingle *n* **tonadilla de un anuncio** advertising jingle

tonelada *nf* ton *n* **tonelada métrica** metric ton

tonelaje *nm* tonnage *n* **tonelaje bruto** gross tonnage **tonelaje neto** net(t) tonnage

tono *nm* tone *n* **tono de marcar, tono de**

discado (LAm) (phone) dialling tone, dial tone (US)
tope *nm* (on prices) ceiling *n*
total **1.** *adj* absolute *adj*, total *adj* **2.** *nm* total *n* **total global** the grand total
totalidad *nf* total *n*
totalmente *adv* wholly *adv*
trabajador, -ora **1.** *adj* hard-working *adj* **muy trabajador** hard-working **2.** *nm,f* labourer *n* **trabajador autónomo** freelance, freelancer **trabajador no cualificado, obrero no calificado; peón** (LAm) unskilled worker **trabajadores por horas** hourly workers **trabajador eventual** casual worker, jobber **trabajador extranjero** migrant worker **trabajador extranjero temporal** guest worker **trabajador itinerante** migrant worker **trabajador manual, peón** (LAm) manual worker **trabajador en paro** (LAm) striker
trabajar *vb* work *vb* **que trabaja por cuenta propia** self-employed **trabajar fuera de horas normales** work unsocial hours **trabajar a jornada reducida** be on short time **trabajar a máquina** machine **trabajar a pleno rendimiento** work to full capacity
trabajo *nm* employment *n*, labour, labor (US) *n*, workplace *n* **sin trabajo, cesante** (LAm) jobless, unemployed **trabajo asignado** workload **trabajo de campo** field investigation/research **trabajo a contrata** contract work **trabajo defectuoso** faulty workmanship **trabajo a destajo** piecework **trabajo eventual** casual work **con trabajo excesivo** overworked **trabajo hecho deprisa** rush job **trabajo manual** factory work **trabajo de oficina** clerical work, office work **trabajo pagado por horas** hourly-paid work **trabajo por teléfono** teleworking **trabajo por turnos** job rotation, shift work
trabajoadicto, -cta *nm,f* workaholic *n*
tráfico *nm* traffic *n* **tráfico aéreo** air traffic **tráfico de armas** arms trade **tráfico por carretera** road traffic **tráfico por ferrocarril** rail traffic **tráfico marítimo** sea traffic **tráfico de mercancías, tráfico de mercaderías** (LAm) freight traffic
traje *nm* suit *n* **traje de oficina, vestido; terno** (LAm) business suit
tramitar *vb* process *vb* **tramitar el despacho de aduanas de algo** clear sth through customs **tramitar el pago de un cheque** clear a cheque
trámite *nm* business transaction *n* **trá-**

mites aduaneros customs formalities **trámites burocráticos** paperwork, red tape **trámites legales** legal procedures
transacción *nf* (business) transaction *n* **transacción de futuros** forward transaction
transbordar *vb* transship *vb*
transcribir *vb* transcribe *vb*
transferencia *nf* transfer *n* **transferencia bancaria** bank transfer **transferencia de capital** capital transfer **transferencia de divisas** currency transfer **transferencia electrónica de fondos** EFT (electronic funds transfer) **transferencia de fondos** credit transfer **transferencia de moneda** currency transfer **transferencia de tecnología** technology transfer
transferible *adj* transferable *adj*
transferir *vb* carry forward *vb*, hand over *vb* **transferir tecnología** transfer technology
transigir, transar (LAm) *vb* reach a compromise *vb*
tránsito *nm* transit *n*, traffic *n* **en tránsito** in transit
transmisión *nf* assignment *n*, broadcast *n*
transmitir *vb* broadcast *vb*, televise *vb*, transmit *vb* **transmitir en cadena** network *vb*
transnacional *adj* transnational *adj*
transporte *nm* forwarding *n*, freight *n*, transportation *n* **transporte aéreo** air freight/transport **transporte por carretera** haulage, road haulage/transport, freight (US) **transporte por ferrocarril** rail transport **transporte de géneros, transporte de mercaderías** (LAm) goods transport **transporte público** public transport
transportista *nmf* carrier *n*, haulier *n*
trasladar *vb* relocate *vb*, (transport) transfer *vb*, move *vb*
traslado *nm* relocation *n* **traslado temporal** secondment
traspasar *vb* (ownership) transfer *vb*
tratado *nm* treaty *n* **tratado comercial** commercial treaty **El Tratado de Roma** the Treaty of Rome
tratamiento *nm* treatment *n*
tratar *vb* address *vb* **tratar con cuidado** handle with care **tratar al personal** (staff) handle **tratar de resolver** (agreement, policy) thrash out
trato *nm* treatment *n*, deal *n* **¡trato hecho!** it's a bargain/deal **trato con información**

privilegiada insider dealing, insider trading (US)
tren *nm* train *n* en tren by rail tren de mercancías goods train, freight train (US) tren de pasajeros passenger train
tribunal *nm* tribunal *n* ante el tribunal in court tribunal agrario land tribunal Tribunal de Apelación Court of Appeal, Court of Appeals (US) Tribunal Europeo de Justicia European Court of Justice (ECJ) tribunal industrial industrial tribunal Tribunal Internacional de Justicia World Court tribunal penal criminal court
tributo *nm* tax *n*, testimonial *n*
trimestral *adj* quarterly *adj*
trimestre *nm* (of year) quarter *n*
triplicado *adv* triplicate *adv* por triplicado in triplicate
triquiñuelas *nf* sharp practice *n*
trituradora *nf* shredder *n*
trocar *vb* barter *vb*
trueque *nm* barter *n*
turismo *nm* tourism *n*, the tourist trade *n*
turista *nmf* tourist *n*
turno *nm* shift *n*
ubicación *nf* location *n*
UEO (Unión de la Europa Occidental) (La) *abbr,nf* WEU (Western European Union) *abbr*
último *adj* last *adj* última notificación final notice última oferta final offer
umbral *nm* threshold *n*
unánime *adj* unanimous *adj*
unidad *nf* unit *n* unidad central, computadora central (LAm) mainframe computer Unidad de Cuenta Europea (UCE) European Unit of Account (EUA) unidad de despliegue visual visual display unit (VDU) unidad de disco disk drive unidad familiar household unidad media average unit unidad principal, computadora central (LAm) (DP) mainframe unidad de proceso central (UPC) (DP) central processing unit (CPU) unidad de producción unit of production
unido *adj* united *adj*
unificación *nf* unification *n*
unilateral *adj* (contract) unilateral *adj*
unión *nf* union *n* unión aduanera customs union unión económica economic union Unión Económica y Monetaria Economic and Monetary Union Unión Europea European Union Unión Monetaria Europea (UME) European Monetary Union (EMU)

urbanismo *nm* town planning *n*
urbanización, colonia (LAm) *nf* housing complex *n*, housing estate *n*, housing tenement (US) *n*
urgencia *nf* urgency *n*
urgente *adj* urgent *adj*
urgentemente *adv* urgently *adv*
usar *vb* use *vb*, utilize *vb* usar algo make use of sth de usar y tirar non-returnable, disposable
uso *nm* (of machine) operation *n* para uso industrial heavy-duty uso intensivo intensive usage
usuario, -ria *nm,f* user *n* usuario final end consumer, end user usuario frecuente heavy user
usura *nf* usury *n*
usurero, -era *nm,f* shark* *n*
utensilios *nmpl* utensils *npl*, tools *npl* utensilios domésticos housewares (US)
útiles *nmpl* equipment *n*
utilidad *nf* utility *n* utilidades (LAm) profit, earnings, benefit utilidad final final utility utilidad marginal marginal utility
utilización *nf* utilization *n* con alta utilización de mano de obra labour-intensive
utilizar *vb* employ *vb*, utilize *vb*, use *vb*
vacación *nf* de vacaciones, tomando la licencia (LAm) on holiday, on leave, on vacation (US) vacaciones organizadas package tour vacaciones pagadas paid holiday
vacante 1. *adj* vacant *adj* 2. *nf* vacancy *n*
vaciamiento *nm* asset stripping *n*
vacío 1. *adj* empty *adj* 2. *nm* gap *n*, void *n* vacío inflacionario inflationary gap vacío poblacional population gap
vago *adj* idle *adj*
vago, -aga, fiacún, -una; flojonazo, -aza (LAm) *nm,f* shirker* *n*
vale *nm* coupon *n*, voucher *n*
valer *vb* be worth *vb*
validez *nf* validity *n*
valioso *adj* valuable *adj*
valor *nm* security *n*, share *n*, value *n* sin valor comercial no commercial value valores no admitidos a cotización unlisted securities valores bursátiles listed securities valores emitidos sin aumento de capital watered stock valores del Estado gilt-edged securities valores inmobiliarios stocks and shares valores seguros blue-chip securities valor extraordinario extraordinary value valor justo de mercado fair market value valor en libros book value valor de liquidación

liquidation value **valor de mercado** market value **valor nominal** face value, nominal price, nominal value **valor de primer orden** gilt-edged security **valor real** real value **valor de renta variable** equity share **valoración** *nf* appraisal *n*, assessment *n*, estimate *n*, valuation *n* **valoración de riesgos** risk assessment

valorar *vb* estimate *vb*

varianza *nf* variance *n*

vehículo *nm* vehicle *n* **vehículo comercial** commercial vehicle **vehículo de gran tonelaje** heavy goods vehicle

velocidad *nf* speed *n* **de velocidad doble** two-speed

vencer *vb* expire *vb*, fall due *vb* (business, economy) mature *vb*

vencido *adj* overdue *adj*, out of date (LAm) *adj*

vencimiento *nm* expiration *n*, expiry *n*

vendedor, -ora *nm,f* salesperson *n*, seller *n*, shop assistant *n*, vendor *n*, trader *n*, joint vendor *n* **vendedor de periódicos y revistas** newsdealer (US) **vendedor de seguros** insurance salesperson

vender *vb* market *vb*, sell *vb* **este artículo se vende bien** this article sells well **sin vender** unsold **vender barato** sell off **vender más barato** undercut, undersell **vender en la calle** peddle **vender algo a crédito** sell sth on credit **vender en exceso** oversell **vender algo a granel** sell sth in bulk **vender un inmueble a un mejor postor rompiendo un compromiso** gazump **vender algo al por mayor** sell sth wholesale **vender algo al por menor** sell sth retail **vender un negocio con todas sus existencias** sell up

vendido *adj* sold *adj* **vendido en exceso** oversold

venta *nf* sale *n* **esto nos va a afectar las ventas, esto tendrá implicancias para nuestras ventas** (LAm) this will have implications for our sales **en venta** for sale **venta agresiva** hard sell **venta blanda/suave** soft sell **venta por concurso** sale by tender **venta al contado** cash sale, cash transaction **venta por correo** mail order **venta domiciliaria** door-to-door selling **venta en efectivo** cash sale **venta ficticia** fictitious sale **venta inmobiliaria** house sale **venta piramidal** pyramid selling **ventas brutas** gross sales **ventas al exterior** export sales **ventas en el mercado interior** home sales

ventas netas net(t) sales **ventas totales** total sales

ventaja *nf* advantage *n* **ventaja comparativa** comparative advantage **ventaja sobre la competencia** competitive edge **ventaja competitiva** competitive advantage

ventajoso *adj* advantageous *adj*

ver *vb* see *vb* **verse obligado a hacer algo** be obliged to do sth

verdadero *adj* true *adj*, actual *adj*

verde *nm* (LAm) dollar *n*, buck*(US) *n*

verificar, checar; chequear (LAm) *vb* check *vb*

vetar *vb* veto *vb*

veto *nm* veto *n*

vez *nf* time *n* **dos veces a la semana** twice a week

viabilidad *nf* feasibility *n*, viability *n*

viable *adj* feasible *adj*, workable *adj*

viajante *nmf* traveller *n* **viajante comercial** commercial traveller, representative, traveler (US) **viajante de comercio, corredor, -ora** (LAm) commercial traveller, commercial traveler (US)

viajar *vb* travel *vb* **viajar por avión** air travel **viajar al exterior** foreign travel **viajar en grupo** group travel

viaje *nm* journey *n*, trip *n* **viaje de ida y vuelta, viaje redondo** (LAm) round trip **viaje de negocios** business trip **viajes al extranjero** foreign travel

viajero, -era *nm,f* passenger *n*, traveller *n*, traveler (US)

vida *nf* life *n* **vida activa** working life **vida laboral** working life

vigente *adj* valid *adj*

vigilancia *nf* vigilance *n* **bajo vigilancia** under observation

vinculante *adj* binding *adj*, legally binding *adj*

violación *nf* violation *n*

VIP *abbr, nmf* VIP (very important person) *n*

visado, visa (LAm) *nm*, *nf* visa *n* **visado de entrada** entry visa

visión *nf* vision *n* **visión para los negocios** business acumen

visita *nf* visit *n*, visitor *n*

visitar *vb* visit *vb*

visual *adj* visual *adj*

vocero, -era *nm,f* (LAm) spokesperson *n*

voltear *vb* (LAm) turn over *vb*

volumen *nm* bulk *n*, volume *n* **volumen de capital facturado** capital turnover **volumen comercial** trading volume **vo-**

lumen de negocios trading volume **volumen de ventas** sales figures, turnover **volumen de ventas acabado** finished turnover

voluntad *nf* will *n*

voluntario *adj* voluntary *adj*

volver *vb* return *vb* **volver a** revert to **volver a contratar** reappoint **volver a llamar, devolver el llamado** (LAm) (on phone) call back **volver a nombrar** reappoint

votación *nf* vote *n* **votación para decidir si se hace huelga, votación para decidir si se va al paro** (LAm) strike ballot

votar *vb* vote *vb*

voto *nm* vote *n* **voto de censura** vote of no confidence **voto de gracias** vote of thanks

vuelo *nm* (in plane) flight *n* **vuelo chárter** charter flight

vuelta, vuelto; vueltas (LAm) *nf, nm; nfpl* (from purchase) change *n* **dar vueltas** (LAm) turn over

xerografiar *vb* xerox *vb*

yacimiento *nm* deposit *n*, layer *n* **yacimiento petrolífero** oilfield

yen *nm* (currency) yen *n*

zona *nf* zone *n* **zona de comercio** trading area **zona de desarrollo** enterprise zone **zona de exclusión** exclusion zone **zona franca** franco zone, free trade area **zona industrial** industrial region, trading estate **zona de la libra esterlina** sterling area **zona de libre empresa** enterprise zone **zona monetaria** currency zone **zona salarial** wage zone

zonificación *nf* zoning *n* **zonificación fiscal** fiscal zoning

zonificar *vb* zone *vb*

English–Spanish

abandon *vb* abandonar *vb*, renunciar *vb*, dejar *vb*
abandoned *adj* **abandoned goods** *npl* mercancías abandonadas *nfpl*
abate *vb* disminuir *vb*, reducir *vb*, suprimir *vb*
abatement *n* disminución *nf*, reducción *nf*, supresión *nf*
abbreviate *vb* abreviar *vb*, resumir *vb*
abbreviated *adj* abreviado *adj*, resumido *adj*
abbreviation *n* abreviatura *nf*, abreviación *nf*
abeyance *n* **to fall into abeyance** *vb* caer en desuso *vb*
abide by *vb* atenerse (a) *vb*
ability *n* capacidad *nf*, aptitud *nf*, habilidad *nf* **ability to pay** solvencia *nf*, recursos *nmpl*, medios *nmpl*
able *adj* capaz *adj*
aboard *adv* a bordo *prep/adv* **to go aboard** subir a bordo *vb*, embarcarse *vb*
abolish *vb* abolir *vb*, suprimir *vb*
abolition *n* abolición *nf*, supresión *nf*, derogación *nf*
above-mentioned *adj* sobredicho *adj*, antedicho *adj*, arriba mencionado *adj*
aboveboard *adj* legítimo *adj*
abroad *adv* **to go abroad** ir al extranjero *vb*, irse al extranjero *vb*
absence *n* **in the absence of information** a falta de información *prep*, a falta de datos *prep*
absent *adj* ausente *adj*
absentee *adj* ausente *adj* **absentee landlord** propietario, -ria absentista *nm, f*
absenteeism *n* absentismo *nm*
absolute *adj* absoluto *adj*, total *adj*
absorb *vb* absorber *vb* **to absorb surplus stock** absorber existencias sobrantes
abstract *n* resumen *nm*
abundance *n* abundancia *nf*
abuse 1. *n* abuso *nm* **abuse of power/confidence** abuso de poder *nm*, abuso de

confianza *nm* **2.** *vb* abusar (de) *vb*, maltratar *vb*
accelerate *vb* acelerar *vb*
acceleration *n* aceleración *nf*
accept *vb* aceptar *vb* **accept delivery** *vb* aceptar la entrega de *vb*
acceptance *n* aceptación *nf* **consumer acceptance** aceptación por parte del consumidor *nf* **acceptance house** casa financiera *nf*, banco comercial de negocios *nm* **market acceptance** aceptación de mercado *nf*
access 1. *n* acceso *nm* **2.** *vb* entrar en *vb*, entrar a *vb*
accessibility *n* fácil acceso *nm*, accesibilidad *nf*
accident *n* accidente *nm* **industrial accident** accidente laboral *nm*, accidente de trabajo *nm*
accidental *adj* **accidental damage** daños por accidente *nmpl*
accommodation *n* alojamiento *nm*, espacio *nm* **accommodation allowance** *n* dieta para gastos de alojamiento *nf* **accommodation bill** pagaré de favor *nm* **to come to an accommodation** llegar a un acuerdo *vb*
accomplish *vb* cumplir *vb*, realizar *vb*, conseguir *vb*
accomplishment *n* logro *nm*, consecución *nf*
accordance *n* **in accordance with** de acuerdo con *prep*, conforme a *prep*, según *prep*
according to *prep* **according to plan** según lo planeado *prep* **according to the minister** según el ministro *prep*
account *n* cuenta *nf* **bank account** cuenta bancaria *nf* **Account Day** (stock exchange) día de liquidación *nm* **expense account** cuenta de gastos de representación *nf* **account-keeping** teneduría de cuentas *nf* **payment on account** pago a cuenta *nm* **profit and loss account** cuenta de pérdidas y

ganancias *nf* **savings account** cuenta de caja de ahorros *nf* **accounts receivable** cuentas a cobrar *nf* **statement of account** extracto de cuenta *nm*, estado de cuenta *nm* **to open an account** abrir una cuenta *vb* **to overdraw on an account** girar en descubierto una cuenta *vb*, rebasar una cuenta *vb* **to settle an account** saldar una cuenta *vb*, liquidar una cuenta *vb* **to take sth into account** tener algo en cuenta *vb* **trading account** cuenta de explotación *nf*, cuenta de ejercicio *nf*

account for *vb* dar cuentas de *vb*, justificar *vb*

accountability *n* responsabilidad *nf*

accountable *adj* responsable *adj*

accountancy *n* contabilidad *nf*

accountant *n* contable *nmf*, contador, -ora (LAm) *nm,f* **chartered accountant** contable colegiado, -ada *nm,f*, censor, -ora jurado, -ada de cuentas *nm,f*

accounting *n* **accounting conventions** métodos de contabilidad *nmpl* **financial accounting** contabilidad financiera *nf*, contabilidad de finanzas *nf* **management accounting** contabilidad gerencial *nf* **accounting period** período de contabilidad *nm*

accredit *vb* autorizar *vb*, reconocer *vb*

accrual *n* acumulación *nf* **rate of accrual** tasa de acumulación *nf*

accrued *adj* **accrued interest** interés acumulado *nm*

accumulate *vb* acumular *vb*

accumulated *adj* acumulado *adj*

accuracy *n* precisión *nf*, exactitud *nf*, fidelidad *nf*

accurate *adj* preciso *adj*, exacto *adj*

accuse *vb* acusar *vb*

achieve *vb* conseguir *vb*, lograr *vb*, obtener *vb*

achievement *n* logro *nm*, consecución *nf*, éxito *nm*

acknowledge *vb* reconocer *vb* **to acknowledge receipt of sth** acusar recibo de algo *vb*

acknowledgement *n* **acknowledgement of debt** reconocimiento de deuda *nm*

acquaintance *n* conocimiento *nm* **business acquaintance** conocido, -ida de negocios *nm, f* **to make the acquaintance of sb** conocer a alguien *vb*

acquire *vb* adquirir *vb*, obtener *vb*, hacerse con *vb*

acquisition *n* adquisición *nf*, compra *nf*

acquisitive *adj* codicioso *adj*

action *n* acto *nm*, acción *nf* **industrial action** acción laboral *nf*, acción industrial *nf*, huelga *nf*, paro (LAm) *nm* **legal action** pleito *nm*, demanda *nf* **out of action** estropeado *adj*, averiado *adj*, inutilizable *adj*, descompuesto (LAm) *adj*

actual *adj* real *adj*, verdadero *adj*

actuality *n* realidad *nf*

actuary *n* actuario, -ria (de seguros) *nm,f*

acumen *n* **business acumen** visión para los negocios *nf*

additional *adj* **additional charge** suplemento *nm*, recargo *nm*

address 1. *n* **home address** dirección privada *nf*, domicilio particular *nm* **registered address** dirección registrada *nf*, domicilio social *nm* **to change address** cambiar de domicilio *vb* 2. *vb* dirigir *vb*, dirigirse a *vb*, tratar *vb*

addressee *n* destinatario, -ria *nm,f*

adjourn *vb* suspender *vb*, aplazar *vb*, levantarse *vb*

adjournment *n* suspensión *nf*

adjust *vb* ajustar *vb*, adaptar *vb* **to adjust a claim** reajustar una reclamación *vb*, solventar una reclamación *vb* **to adjust the figures** ajustar las cifras *vb*

adjustment *n* ajuste *nm*

administer *vb* administrar *vb*, dirigir *vb*

administration *n* administración *nf*, dirección *nf*

administrative *adj* **administrative costs** gastos de administración *nmpl*, costes de administración *nmpl*, costos de administración (LAm) *nmpl*

administrator *n* administrador, -ora *nm,f*

advance 1. *adj* **advance notice** aviso previo *nm*, preaviso *nm* **payable in advance** pagadero por adelantado *adj* **advance payment** pago anticipado *nm* 2. *n* (on salary) avance *nm*, adelanto *nm*, progreso *nm* **cash advance** adelanto *nm*, préstamo *nm*, crédito *nm* 3. *vb* (salary) avanzar *vb*, adelantar *vb*, anticipar *vb*

advanced *adj* **advanced country** país desarrollado *nm* **advanced technology** tecnología avanzada *nf*

advantage *n* ventaja *nf* **comparative advantage** ventaja comparativa *nf* **competitive advantage** ventaja competitiva *nf*

advantageous *adj* ventajoso *adj*

adverse *adj* desfavorable *adj*, adverso *adj* **adverse balance of trade** balanza comercial negativa *nf*

advertise *vb* anunciar *vb*, hacerle propaganda a *vb*, hacerle réclame a (LAm) *vb*

advertisement *n* anuncio *nm*, mensaje publicitario *nm*, aviso (LAm) *nm*, réclame (LAm) *nm*

advertising *n* **advertising agency** agencia de publicidad *nf* **advertising budget** presupuesto de publicidad *nm* **advertising campaign** campaña de publicidad *nf* **advertising medium** medio publicitario *nm* **advertising revenue** ingresos de publicidad *nmpl*

advice *n* consejos *nmpl*, asesoramiento *nm*, notificación *nf*

advise *vb* **to advise sb about sth** aconsejarle a alguien sobre algo *vb*, asesorarle a alguien sobre algo *vb*

adviser/advisor *n* consejero, -era *nm,f*, asesor, -ora *nm,f*

advisory *adj* consultivo *adj*

advocate *vb* recomendar *vb*, abogar por *vb*

aerospace *adj* **aerospace industry** industria aeroespacial *nf*

affidavit *n* declaración jurada *nf*

affiliated *adj* afiliado *adj* **affiliated company** sociedad filial *nf*

affiliation *n* afiliación *nf*

affluent *adj* **affluent society** sociedad opulenta *nf*, sociedad de consumo *nf*, sociedad de la abundancia *nf*

afford *vb* **I can't afford (to buy a new printer)** no me puedo permitir el lujo (de comprar una nueva impresora) *vb* **we cannot afford (to take) the risk** no podemos correr el riesgo *vb*

after-sales service *n* servicio post-venta *nm*

agency *n* **advertising agency** agencia de publicidad *nf* **employment agency** agencia de empleo *nf*, oficina de empleo *nf* **travel agency** agencia de viajes *nf*

agenda *n* orden del día *nm*, agenda *nf*

agent *n* agente *nmf*, representante *nmf*

AGM (Annual General Meeting) *abbr* junta anual *nf*

agrarian *adj* agrario *adj*

agree *vb* estar de acuerdo *vb*, convenir *vb*

agreed *adj* acordado *adj*, convenido *adj*

agreement *n* acuerdo *nm*, convenio *nm*, consentimiento *nm* **by mutual agreement** de común acuerdo *prep* **verbal agreement** acuerdo verbal *nm*, acuerdo no escrito *nm* **wage agreement** convenio salarial *nm*

agribusiness *n* agroindustria *nf*

agriculture *n* agricultura *nf*

agronomist *n* agrónomo, -oma *nm,f*

aid *n* ayuda *nf*, apoyo *nm*, asistencia *nf* **financial aid** ayuda financiera *nf*

air *n* **by air** por avión *prep*, por vía aérea *prep* **air freight** carga aérea *nf*, transporte aéreo *nm* **air traffic controller** controlador, -ora aéreo, -rea *nm,f*

air-conditioned *adj* climatizado *adj*, con aire acondicionado *prep*

airline *n* línea aérea *nf*

airmail *n* correo aéreo *nm*

airport *n* aeropuerto *nm*

allocate *vb* asignar *vb*, repartir *vb*

allowance *n* complemento *nm*, dieta *nf*, prestación *nf* **family allowance** prestación estatal a la familia *nf*, subsidio familiar *nm*, asignación familiar (LAm) *nf*

amalgamate *vb* integrar *vb*, fusionarse *vb*

amalgamation *n* fusión *nf*

amend *vb* enmendar *vb*, corregir *vb* **to make amends** desagraviar *vb*, reparar *vb*, rectificar *vb*

amendment *n* enmienda *nf*, mejora *nf*

amenities *npl* servicios *nmpl*, instalaciones *nfpl*

amortization *n* amortización *nf*

amortize *vb* amortizar *vb*

amount *n* cantidad *nf*, suma *nf*, importe *nm*

amount to *vb* ascender a *vb*

analysis *n* **cost-benefit analysis** análisis coste-beneficio *nm* **systems analysis** análisis de sistemas *nm*

analyze *vb* analizar *vb*

annual *adj* **annual general meeting (AGM)** junta anual *nf* **annual report** informe anual *nm*

annuity *n* anualidad *nf*, pensión *nf*

annulment *n* anulación *nf*

Ansaphone (R) *n* contestador telefónico *nm*

answer 1. *n* contestación *nf*, respuesta *nf* 2. *vb* contestar *vb*, coger *vb*, responder *vb*, atender (LAm) *vb*

answering *n* **answering machine** contestador automático *nm*

anti-inflationary *adj* **anti-inflationary measures** medidas antiinflacionarias *nfpl*

anticipate *vb* anticipar *vb*

antitrust *adj* **antitrust laws** legislación antimonopolista *nf*

appeal 1. *n* interés *nm*, llamamiento *nm*, apelación *nf*, llamado (LAm) *nm*, pedido (LAm) *nm* 2. *vb* interesar *vb*, apelar *vb*

application *n* **application form** hoja de solicitud *nf*, formulario *nm*, impreso de aplicación (LAm) *nm* **letter of application**

carta de solicitud *nf*, carta de aplicación (LAm) *nf*
apply for *vb* solicitar *vb*, pedir *vb*, aplicar por (LAm) *vb*
appoint *vb* **to appoint sb to a position** nombrar a alguien para un puesto *vb*, nombrar a alguien para un cargo *vb*
appointment *n* (to meet) cita *nf*, compromiso *nm*, hora (LAm) *nf*, cita (LAm) *nf* (to a position) nombramiento *nm*, contratación *nf* **to make an appointment** concertar una cita *vb*, pedir una cita (LAm) *vb*
appraisal *n* evaluación *nf*, valoración *nf*, tasación *nf*
appreciate *vb* (rise in value) subir *vb*
appreciation *n* (in value) revalorización *nf*
apprentice *n* aprendiz, -iza *nm,f*
apprenticeship *n* aprendizaje *nm*
appropriate *adj* debido *adj*, adecuado *adj*, apropiado *adj*
appropriation *n* asignación *nf*, apropiación *nf*
approval *n* aprobación *nf*, autorización *nf* **on approval** a prueba *prep*
approve *vb* aprobar *vb*, autorizar *vb*, acreditar *vb*
approximate *adj* aproximado *adj*
approximately *adv* aproximadamente *adv*
arbitrage *n* arbitraje *nm*
arbitrary *adj* arbitrario *adj*
arbitrate *vb* arbitrar *vb*
arbitration *n* arbitraje *nm*
arbitrator *n* árbitro, -tra *nm,f*
area *n* área *nf*, zona *nf*, polígono *nm* **area manager** director, -ora regional *nm,f*, gerente regional *nmf*
argument *n* discusión *nf*, polémica *nf*, argumentos *nmpl*
arithmetic *n* aritmética *nf*
arithmetical *adj* **arithmetical mean** promedio aritmético *nm*
arms *npl* **arms trade** tráfico de armas *nm*, comercio armamentístico *nm*
arrangement *n* (agreement) plan *nm*, arreglo *nm*, disposición *nf*
arrears *npl* atrasos *nmpl* **in arrears** atrasado *adj* **to fall/get into arrears** atrasarse en los pagos *vb*
articulated *adj* **articulated lorry** camión articulado *nm*, camión con remolque *nm*
asap (as soon as possible) *abbr* lo antes posible, cuanto antes
asking *adj* **asking price** precio de oferta *nm*

assembly *n* **assembly line** cadena de montaje *nf*, cadena de ensamblaje *nf*
assess *vb* evaluar *vb*, calcular *vb*
assessment *n* evaluación *nf*, valoración *nf*, cálculo *nm*
asset *n* activo *nm* **capital assets** activo fijo *nm* **asset stripping** liquidación de activo *nf*, vaciamiento *nmf*
assign *vb* asignar *vb*, destinar *vb*, nombrar *vb*
assignee *n* cesionario, -ria *nm,f*
assignment *n* misión *nf*, transmisión *nf*, cesión *nf*
assistant *n* ayudante *nmf* **assistant manager** subdirector, -ora *nm,f*, ayudante de dirección *nmf*
associate **1.** *adj* **associate director** director, -ora adjunto, -nta *nm,f* **2.** *n* socio, -cia *nm,f*, asociado, -ada *nm,f*, colega *nmf*
attend *vb* acudir *vb*, asistir a *vb*, atender *vb*
attendance *n* asistencia *nf*
attestation *n* testimonio *nm*, autorización *nf*
attorney *n* **power of attorney** poder notarial *nm*
auction **1.** *n* subasta *nf*, remate (LAm) *nm* **2.** *vb* subastar *vb*, rematar (LAm) *vb*
auctioneer *n* subastador, -ora *nm,f*, rematador, -ora (LAm) *nm,f*
audit *n* auditoría *nf*
auditor *n* auditor, -ora *nm,f*, censor, -ora *nm,f*, interventor, -ora de cuentas *nm,f*
authority *n* (official) autoridad *nf*
authorize *vb* autorizar *vb*
authorized *adj* **authorized dealer** agente oficial *nmf*, distribuidor, -ora autorizado, -ada *nm,f*
automatic *adj* **automatic cash dispenser** cajero automático *nm*
automation *n* automatización *nf*
automobile *adj* **automobile industry** industria del automóvil *nf*
autonomous *adj* autónomo *adj*
auxiliary *adj* auxiliar *adj*
average **1.** *adj* medio *adj* **2.** promedio *nm*, media *nf* **average unit** unidad media *nf*, unidad promedio *nf*
avoid *vb* evitar *vb*, evadir *vb*, eludir *vb*
avoidance *n* **tax avoidance** evasión de impuestos *nf*, evasión fiscal *nf*
axe, ax (US) *vb* recortar *vb*, despedir *vb*, suprimir *vb* **to axe expenditure** recortar gastos *vb*
back *vb* respaldar *vb*, apoyar *vb* **to back a venture** respaldar una empresa *vb*

back pay *n* atrasos de sueldo *nmpl*
backdate *vb* antedatar *vb* **to backdate a cheque** poner una fecha anterior a un cheque *vb*
backer *n* garante *nmf*, capitalista *nmf*, partidario, -ria *nm,f*, patrocinador, -ora *nm,f*
backhander* *n* soborno *nm*, mordida (LAm) *nf*, coima (LAm) *nf*
backing *n* apoyo *nm*, respaldo *nm*, ayuda *nf*
backlog *n* acumulación de trabajo atrasado *nf*
bad *adj* **bad cheque** cheque sin fondos *nm*, cheque descubierto *nm* **bad debt** deuda incobrable *nf*
bail *n* fianza *nf*
bailiff *n* alguacil *nmf*, administrador, -ora *nm,f*
balance 1. *n* (financial) saldo *nm*, resultado *nm*, balanza *nf* **bank balance** saldo de cuenta bancaria *nm* **final balance** saldo final *nm*, balance final *nm* **balance in hand** saldo disponible *nm* **balance of payments** balanza de pagos *nf* **balance of payments deficit** déficit de la balanza de pagos *nm* **balance of payments surplus** superávit de la balanza de pagos *nm* **balance of trade** balanza comercial *nf* **balance sheet** balance general *nm*, balance de situación *nm* **trade balance** balanza comercial *nf* 2. *vb* equilibrar *vb* **to balance the books** hacer cuadrar las cuentas *vb* **to balance the budget** ajustar el presupuesto *vb*, equilibrar el presupuesto *vb*
bank 1. *adj* **bank account** cuenta bancaria *nf* **bank balance** estado de cuenta *nm*, saldo bancario *nm* **bank card** tarjeta de crédito *nf*, tarjeta bancaria *nf*, tarjeta de garantía *nf* **bank charges** gastos bancarios *nmpl* **bank clerk** empleado, -ada de banco *nm,f*, bancario, -aria (LAm) *nm,f* **bank details** domiciliación *nf* **bank draft** cheque bancario *nm*, giro bancario *nm* **bank holiday** día festivo *nm*, día feriado (LAm) *nm* **bank loan** préstamo bancario *nm* **bank manager** director, -ora de banco *nm,f* **bank overdraft** descubierto *nm*, sobregiro *nm* **bank payment** domiciliación *nf* **bank rate** tipo bancario *nm*, tipo de interés *nm*, tasa de interés (LAm) *nf* **bank statement** estado de cuentas *nm*, extracto de cuentas *nm* 2. *n*

banco *nm* 3. *vb* **to bank a cheque** ingresar un cheque *vb*
banker *n* banquero, -era *nm,f* **banker's order** domiciliación bancaria *nf*, orden permanente de pago *nf*
banking *n* banca *nf* **banking circles** el mundo de la banca *nm* **banking hours** horario bancario *nm* **banking system** *n* banca *nf*
banknote *n* billete de banco *nm*, pagaré *nm*
bankrupt *adj* insolvente *adj*, en bancarrota *prep* **to be bankrupt** estar insolvente *vb*
bankruptcy *n* quiebra *nf*, bancarrota *nf*, insolvencia *nf*
bar code *n* código de barras *nm*
bargain 1. *adj* **bargain offer** oferta de rebaja *nf* **bargain price** precio de ocasión *nm* 2. *n* trato *nm*, ganga *nf*, oferta *nf*, pichincha (LAm) *nf* **it's a bargain** ¡trato hecho! *nm* 3. *vb* regatear *vb*, negociar *vb*
barrier *n* **trade barrier** barrera comercial *nf*
barrister, lawyer (US) *n* abogado, -ada (que actúa únicamente en el juicio oral) *nm,f*
barter 1. *adj* **barter agreement** acuerdo de trueque *nm* **barter transaction** operación de trueque *nf* 2. *n* trueque *nm* 3. *vb* permutar *vb*, trocar *vb*
base *adj* **base lending rate** tipo base *nm*, tasa base (LAm) *nf*
basic *adj* **basic commodity** producto básico *nm* **basic income** ingresos básicos *nmpl* **basic rate** tasa normal *nf*, tasa base *nf* **basic training** preparación básica *nf*
basis *n* **basis of assessment** base de evaluación *nf*
basket *n* **basket of currencies** cesta de monedas *nf*, canasta de divisas (LAm) *nf*
batch *n* (of goods) lote *nm*, serie *nf* **batch processing** (DP) procesamiento por lotes *nm*
bear 1. *adj* **bear market** mercado bajista *nm* 2. *n* (stock exchange) bajista *nmf* 3. *vb* **to bear interest** devengar intereses *vb*
bearer *n* portador, -ora *nm,f*, titular *nmf*, poseedor, -ora *nm,f* **bearer bond** título al portador *nm* **bearer cheque** cheque al portador *nm* **bearer share** acción al portador *nf*
bench *n* **bench mark** punto de referencia *nm*, prueba patrón *nf* **bench mark price** precio de referencia *nm*

benefactor *n* bienhechor, -ora *nm,f*
benefit 1. *n* (social security) beneficio *nm*, provecho *nm*, subsidio *nm* **2.** *vb* aprovecharse *vb* beneficiar *vb*
bequeath *vb* legar *vb*
bequest *n* legado *nm*, donación *nf*
best *adj* **best-before date** fecha de caducidad *nf* **best seller** bestseller *nm*, superventas *nm*
biannual *adj* semestral *adj*
bid 1. *n* oferta *nf*, licitación *nf*, intento *nm* **2.** *vb* (auction) licitar *vb*, hacer una oferta *vb*, ofrecer *vb*, licitar (LAm) *vb*
biennial *adj* bianual *adj*
bilateral *adj* **bilateral trade** comercio bilateral *nm*
bill 1. *n* (invoice) factura *nf*, cuenta *nf*, adición (LAm) *nf*, rubro (LAm) *nm* **bill of exchange** letra de cambio *nf* **bill of lading** conocimiento de embarque *nm* **bill of sale** factura de venta *nf* **bills discounted** letras descontadas *nfpl* **to pay a bill** pagar una cuenta *vb*, liquidar una factura *vb* **2.** *vb* (invoice) presentar una factura *vb*
bimonthly *adj* bimensual *adj*
binding *adj* obligatorio *adj*, vinculante *adj* **legally binding** con fuerza jurídica, vinculante *prep*
biweekly *adj* quincenal *adj*
black *adj* **black economy** economía sumergida *nf*, economía informal (LAm), economía paralela (LAm) **black market** mercado negro *nm*, estraperlo *nm* **to be in the black** tener un saldo positivo *vb*
blackmail chantaje *nm*
blank *adj* **blank cheque** cheque en blanco *nm*
block 1. *n* bloque *nm*, parte *nf*, manzana *nf*, cuadra (LAm) *nf* **2.** *vb* bloquear *vb*, impedir *vb*, obstaculizar *vb*, tapar (LAm) *vb*
blockade 1. *n* bloqueo *nm* **2.** *vb* bloquear *vb*
blocked *adj* **blocked account** cuenta bloqueada *nf*
blue *adj* **blue-chip company** empresa de primera clase *nf*, sociedad de primer orden *nf* **blue-collar worker** obrero, -era *nm,f* **blue-chip securities** valores seguros *nm pl*
board *n* junta *nf* **Board of Trade** Departamento de Comercio y Exportación *nm*, Cámara de Comercio *nf* **board meeting** reunión del consejo de administración *nf*, reunión de la junta directiva *nf* **board of**

directors (GB) consejo de administración *nm*, junta directiva *nf*, directorio *nm*
board room sala de juntas *nf*
body *n* cuerpo *nm*, organismo *nm*, masa *nf*
bona fide *adj* de buena fe *prep*, serio *adj*
bond *n* bono *nm*, título *nm*, obligación *nf* **bond certificate** título de obligaciones *nm* **government bond** bono del Estado *nm*, obligación del Estado *nf*, título del Estado *nm* **in bond** en depósito aduanero *prep*
bonded *adj* **bonded warehouse** depósito aduanero *nm*, almacén de depósito *nm*
bondholder *n* tenedor, -ora de obligaciones *nm,f*, bonista *nmf*
bonus *n* prima *nf*, bonificación *nf*, plus *nm*
book 1. *n* libro *nm* **cheque book** talonario de cheques *nm*, chequera (LAm) *nf* **book profit** beneficios contables *nm*, beneficios en libros *nm*, utilidades contables (LAm) *nf* **the books** las cuentas *nf* **book value** valor en libros *nm* **2.** *vb* **to book a hotel room** reservar una habitación de hotel *vb* **to book in advance** reservar por adelantado *vb*
book-keeper *n* contable *nmf*, tenedor, -ora de libros *nm,f*
book-keeping *n* contabilidad *nf*
booking *n* (reservation) reserva *nf*, reservación (LAm) *nf*
bookseller *n* librero, -era *nm,f*
bookshop, bookstore (US) *n* librería *nf*
boom 1. *n* boom *nm*, bonanza *nf* **economic boom** boom económico *nm* **boom in demand** alza de la demanda *nf*, aumento rápido de la demanda *nm* **2.** *vb* prosperar *vb*, aumentar *vb*
booming *adj* próspero *adj*, en fuerte expansión *prep*, en auge *prep*
boost 1. *n* estímulo *nm*, impulso *nm*, aumento *nm* **2.** *vb* **to boost demand** potenciar la demanda *vb*, fomentar la demanda *vb* **to boost morale** reforzar la moral *vb* **to boost production** estimular la producción *vb* **to boost sales** incrementar las ventas *vb*
boot *vb* **to boot a computer** cargar un ordenador *vb*, cargar una computadora (LAm) *vb*
booth *n* (voting) cabina *nf*, puesto *nm*, casilla (LAm) *nf*, caseta (LAm) *nf*
borrow *vb* pedir prestado *vb*, sacar *vb*, tomar *vb*
borrowing *n* préstamo *nm*, deuda *nf*, préstamos *nmpl*

boss *n* jefe, -efa *nm,f*, patrón, -ona *nm,f*, amo, -a *nm,f*
bottleneck *n* atasco *nm*, embotellamiento *nm* **bottleneck inflation** inflación de demanda por cambio de estructura *nf*
bottom 1. *adj* **bottom price** precio más bajo *nm* **2.** *n* **at the bottom** en el fondo *prep* **3.** *vb* **to bottom out** tocar fondo *vb*
bought *adj* **bought ledger** libro mayor de compras *nm*
bounce* *vb* (cheque) ser rechazado *vb*, no tener fondos *vb*
bound *n* **out of bounds** fuera de los límites *prep*, prohibido *adj*
box 1. *n* caja *nf*, apartado *nm*, casilla *nf* **box number** apartado de correos *nm*, número de referencia *nm* **box office** taquilla *nf*, boletería (LAm) *nf* **PO box** apartado de correos *nm*, apartado postal (LAm) *nm*, casilla postal (LAm) *nf* **2.** *vb* **to box sth up** embalar algo *vb*
boycott 1. *n* boicot *nm* **2.** *vb* boicotear *vb*
bracket *n* **tax bracket** banda impositiva *nf*
branch *n* sucursal *nf*, rama *nf*, ramo *nm* **branch company** empresa filial *nf* **branch manager** director, -ora de sucursal *nm,f* **branch office** sucursal *nf*
brand *n* marca *nf*, tipo *nm*, señal *nf* **brand image** imagen de marca *nf* **brand leader** producto principal de la marca *nm*
breach *n* **breach of contract** incumplimiento de contrato *nm*
break 1. *n* **to take a break** descansar *vb*, tomarse un descanso *vb* **2.** *vb* romper *vb* **to break an agreement** romper un contrato *vb*
break even *vb* cubrir gastos *vb*
break up *vb* deshacerse *vb*, desintegrar *vb*, terminar *vb*
break-even *adj* **break-even point** punto crítico *nm*
breakdown *n* (of figures) desglose de estadísticas *nm*, análisis de cifras *nm* **breakdown service** servicio de asistencia en carretera *nm*
breakthrough *n* avance *nm* **to make a breakthrough** hacer un avance importante *vb*
breakup *n* desintegración *nf*, disolución *nf*, división *nf*
brevity *n* brevedad *nf*
bribe 1. *n* soborno *nm*, cohecho *nm*, coima (LAm), mordida (LAm) **2.** *vb* sobornar *vb*, comprar *vb*, coimear (LAm) *vb*, morder (LAm) *vb*

bribery *n* soborno *nm*, cohecho *nm*, coima (LAm) *nf*
bridging *adj* **bridging loan, bridge loan** (US) préstamo puente *nm*, crédito puente *nm*
brief 1. *n* instrucciones *nfpl*, órdenes *nfpl* **2.** *vb* dar instrucciones *vb* pl, informar *vb* pl
briefing *n* informe *nm*, sesión informativa *nf*
bring down *vb* (prices) reducir *vb*, rebajar *vb*
bring forward *vb* presentar *vb*, adelantar *vb*
bring out *vb* (product) sacar *vb*, lanzar *vb*
brinkmanship *n* política arriesgada *nf*
Britain *n* Gran Bretaña *nf*, La Gran Bretaña (LAm) *nf*
British *adj* británico *adj* **British Council** Consejo Británico *nm* **British Isles** Islas Británicas *nfpl*
broad *adj* **broad market** mercado amplio *nm*
broadcast 1. *n* emisión *nf*, transmisión *nf*, retransmisión *nf* **2.** *vb* emitir *vb*, transmitir *vb*, divulgar *vb*
broadsheet *n* periódico de formato grande *nm*
brochure *n* folleto publicitario *nm*
broker *n* agente comercial *nmf*, comisionista *nmf*, corredor, -ora *nm,f*
brokerage *n* corretaje *nm*, comisión *nf* **brokerage firm** agencia de corredores *nf*, agentes de bolsa *nm*
buck* (US) *n* dólar *nm*, verde (LAm) *nf* **pass the buck*** pasar la pelota
budget *n* presupuesto *nm* **to draw up a budget** preparar el presupuesto *vb*, elaborar el presupuesto *vb*
budget for *vb* presupuestar *vb*, asignar *vb*
budgetary *adj* **budgetary deficit** déficit presupuestario *nm*, déficit presupuestal (LAm) *nm* **budgetary policy** política presupuestaria *nf*, política presupuestal (LAm) *nf*
bug 1. *n* virus *nm*, peste (LAm) *nf* (listening device) micrófono oculto *nm*, (computer) error *nm* **2.** *vb* **to bug a call** pinchar el teléfono *vb*, intervenir un llamado (LAm) *vb*
build *vb* **to build a reputation** hacerse conocer *vb*, hacerse buena reputación *vb*
builder *n* contratista *nmf*, albañil *nmf*, empresa constructora *nf*
building *adj* **building contractor** contratista de obras *nmf* **building firm** empresa

constructora *nf* **building industry/trade**
industria de la construcción *nf* **building
permit** licencia de obras *nf* **building site**
obra *nf*, terreno edificable *nm* **building
society** sociedad de crédito hipotecario *nf*
built-in *adj* fijo *adj*, incorporado *adj*
built-up *adj* **built-up area** zona muy
urbanizada *nf*
bulk *n* volumen *nm* **the bulk of** la mayor
parte de *nf* **to buy in bulk** comprar a
granel *vb*, comprar en grandes
cantidades *vb*
bull 1. *n* (stock exchange) alcista *nmf* **bull
market** mercado alcista *nm* **2.**
vb (stock exchange) especular al alza *vb*
bulletin *n* boletín *nm*, anuncio *nm*,
comunicado *nm* **bulletin board** tablón/
tablero de anuncios *nm*
bullion *n* oro y plata en lingotes *nm* & *nf*
bump up *vb* (prices) aumentar *vb*, subir *vb*
bundle *n* paquete *nm*, legajo *nm*, (financial) dineral *nm*, platal (LAm) *nm*, lanón
(LAm) *nm*
bundle up *vb* liar *vb*
buoyant *adj* **buoyant market** mercado
alcista *nm*
bureau *n* **bureau de change** oficina de
cambio *nf*, casa de cambio *nf*, cambio *nm*
Federal Bureau (US) Agencia Federal *nf*,
Departamento de Estado *nm*
bureaucracy *n* burocracia *nf*
bureaucrat *n* burócrata *nmf*
bureaucratic *adj* burocrático *adj*
bursar *n* administrador, -ora *nm,f*
bus *n* **bus station** estación de autobuses
nf, estación de micros (LAm) *nf*, estación
de colectivos (LAm) *nf*
business *n* negocios *nmpl*, comercio *nm*,
empresa *nf* **to go out of business** quebrar
vb **business address** dirección comercial
nf **business associate** socio, -cia *nm,f* **big
business** las grandes empresas *nfpl*
business consultant asesor, -ora de
empresas *nm,f* **business expenses** gastos de explotación *nmpl* **family business**
empresa familiar *nf* **business hours** horas
de oficina *nfpl* **business premises** local
comercial *nm* **business studies** ciencias
empresariales *nfpl* **business suit** traje de
oficina *nm*, vestido (LAm) *nm*, terno
(LAm) *nm* **to set up in business** montar
un negocio *vb*, poner un negocio (LAm)
vb **business transaction** operación
comercial *nf*, transacción *nf*, trámite *nm*
business trip viaje de negocios *nm*

businesslike *adj* formal *adj*, serio *adj*,
práctico *adj*
busy *adj* ocupado *adj* **busy signal (US)**
señal de comunicando *nf*, tono de ocupado (LAm) *nm*, señal de ocupado (LAm)
nf
buy 1. *n* **a good buy** una buena compra *nf*
2. *vb* **to buy sth at a high price** comprar
algo caro *vb* **to buy sth on credit** comprar
algo a crédito *vb* **to buy sth second hand**
comprar algo de segunda mano *vb* **to
buy sth wholesale** comprar algo al por
mayor *vb*
buy out *vb* comprarle su parte a *vb*
buy-out *n* compra *nf*, adquisición *nf*
buyer *n* comprador, -ora *nm,f*, cliente, -nta
nm,f, encargado, -ada de compras *nm,f*
buyer's market mercado de oferta *nm*,
mercado favorable a los compradores *nm*
buying *n* **buying and selling** compraventa
nf **buying power** poder adquisitivo *nm*
buying price precio de compra *nm*,
cambio comprador *nm* **buying rate** tipo
de compra *nm*, tasa de compra (LAm) *nf*
by-product *n* subproducto *nm*, derivado
nm
bypass *vb* circunvalar *vb*, pasar por
encima *vb*
byte *n* byte *nm*, octeto *nm*
c.i.f. (cost, insurance and freight) *abbr* cif
(coste, seguro y flete) *abbr,nm*
**CAD (computer-aided or assisted
design)** *abbr* CAD (diseño asistido por
ordenador) *abbr,nm*
calculate *vb* calcular *vb*
calculation *n* cálculo *nm*
calculator *n* calculadora *nf*
call 1. *n* llamada *nf* **call money** dinero a la
vista *nm* **person-to-person call** conferencia personal *nf* **reverse-charge call,
collect call (US)** llamada a cobro revertido
nf, llamado por cobrar (LAm) *nm* **2.** *vb*
llamar *vb* **to call a meeting** convocar una
reunión *vb* **to call it a deal** cerrar un trato
vb, llegar a un acuerdo *vb*
call back *vb* (on phone) volver a llamar *vb*,
devolver la llamada *vb*, devolver el llamado (LAm) *vb*
call for *vb* pasar a buscar *vb*, exigir *vb*,
pedir *vb*
call in *vb* (demand the repayment of a
loan) exigir el pago inmediato de un
préstamo *vb*
campaign *n* campaña *nf* **advertising
campaign** campaña publicitaria *nf* **publicity campaign** campaña publicitaria *nf*

sales campaign campaña de ventas *nf* **to run a campaign** hacer una campaña *vb*, preparar una campaña *vb*
cancel *vb* **cancel a contract** anular un contrato *vb* **cancel an appointment** cancelar una cita *vb*
cancellation *n* cancelación *nf*, anulación *nf* **cancellation charge** cobro por cancelación *nm*
candidate *n* (for job) candidato, -ata *nm,f*, aspirante *nmf*
cap *vb* **to cap the interest rate** limitar el tipo de interés *vb*, limitar la tasa de interés (LAm) *vb*
CAP (Common Agricultural Policy) *abbr* PAC (Política Agrícola Común) *abbr,nf*
capable *adj* capaz *adj*
capacity *n* **earning capacity** capacidad de rendimiento *nf*, grado de rendimiento *nm*, escala de rendimiento *nf* **industrial capacity** capacidad industrial *nf* **in my capacity as chairman** en mi calidad de presidente *prep* **manufacturing capacity** capacidad de producción *nf* **storage capacity** capacidad de almacenamiento *nf* **to expand capacity** ampliar la capacidad *vb* **to work to full capacity** trabajar a pleno rendimiento *vb*
capital *n* (financial) capital *nm*, (city) capital *nf* **capital assets** activo fijo *nm*, bienes de capital *nmpl*, capital disponible *nm* **capital budget** presupuesto de gastos de capital *nm* **capital cost** coste de capital *nm*, costo de capital (LAm) *nm* **capital expenditure** gastos en capital *nmpl*, inversión de capital *nf* **capital exports** exportaciones de capital *nfpl* **fixed capital** capital fijo *nm* **capital funds** fondos para invertir *nmpl*, capital operativo *nm*, capital circulante *nm* **capital gains** ganancias de capital *nfpl*, plusvalía *nf* **capital gains tax** impuesto sobre la plusvalía *nm* **capital goods** bienes de capital *nmpl*, bienes de equipo *nmpl* **initial capital** capital inicial *nm* **invested capital** capital invertido *nm* **capital loss** minusvalía *nf* **capital market** mercado de capitales *nm* **to raise capital** movilzar fondos *vb* **capital turnover** movimientos de capitales *nmpl* **venture capital** capital riesgo *nm*, capital de riesgo *nm* **working capital** capital operativo *nm*, capital circulante *nm*
capitalism *n* capitalismo *nm*
capitalist *n* capitalista *nmf*
capitalize *vb* capitalizar *vb*

card *n* carné *nm*, tarjeta *nf* **bank card** tarjeta de cajero automático *nf* **business card** tarjeta profesional *nf*, tarjeta de visita *nf* **chargecard** tarjeta de cuenta *nf*, tarjeta de pago *nf* **cheque card** tarjeta de garantía de cheques *nf* **credit card** tarjeta de crédito *nf* **identity card** carné de identidad *nm* **smart card** tarjeta inteligente *nf*
career *n* profesión *nf*, carrera *nf*, desarrollo profesional *nm* **careers advice** orientación profesional *nf*, orientación vocacional (LAm) *nf*
cargo *n* carga *nf*, cargamento *nm* **bulk cargo** carga *nf*, carga a granel *nf* **cargo ship** barco de carga *nm*, carguero *nm*
carriage *n* porte *nm* **carriage charge** gasto de transporte *nm* **carriage costs** gasto de transporte *nm*, costes de transporte *nmpl*, costos de transporte (LAm) *nmpl* **carriage forward** porte debido *nm*, portes a pagar *nmpl* **carriage included** porte incluido *nm* **carriage paid** porte pagado *nm*, franco a domicilio *adv*, franco de porte *adv*
carrier *n* transportista *nmf*, empresa de transportes *nf*, línea aérea *nf* **bulk carrier** carguero de graneles *nm* **express carrier** empresa de transportes urgentes *nf*
carry *vb* (stock) tener en existencia *vb*
carry forward *vb* pasar a cuenta nueva *vb*, transferir *vb*
carry out *vb* llevar a cabo *vb*, realizar *vb*, cumplir *vb*
carry over *vb* (to next month) trasladar *vb*, pasar a cuenta nueva *vb*
carrying *adj* **carrying cost** coste de transporte *nm*, costo de transporte (LAm) *nm*
cartel *n* cartel *nm*, cártel *nm*
case *n* caso *nm*
cash 1. *n* dinero *nm*, dinero en efectivo *nm*, efectivo *nm*, plata (LAm) *nf* **cash and carry** autoservicio *nm*, mayorista de pago al contado *nmf* **cash before delivery** pago anticipado *nm*, pago al hacer el pedido *nm* **cash crop** cultivo comerciall *nm* **cash desk** caja *nf* **cash discount** descuento por pago al contado *nm* **cash flow** cash flow *nm*, flujo de caja *nm* **for cash** al contado *prep* **cash machine/dispenser** cajero automático *nm* **cash offer** oferta de pago en efectivo *nf* **cash on delivery (COD)** cobro a la entrega *nm*, entrega contra reembolso *nf* **cash on receipt of goods** cobro al recibo de

mercancías *nm* **cash payment** pago en efectivo *nm*, pago al contado *nm* **cash sale** venta al contado *nf*, venta en efectivo *nf* **to pay in cash** pagar al contado *vb*, pagar en efectivo *vb* **cash transaction** venta al contado *nf*, venta en efectivo *nf* **cash with order** pago al hacer el pedido *nm* **2.** *vb* **to cash a cheque** cobrar un cheque *vb*

cash up *vb* hacer la caja *vb*

cashier *n* cajero, -era *nm,f*

category *n* categoría *nf*, clase *nf*

cater for *vb* atender a *vb*, abastecer *vb*

caution *n* **caution money** fianza *nf*, garantía *nf*

ceiling *n* (on prices) límite *nm*, tope *nm* **to put a ceiling on sth** imponer un límite a algo *vb*

central *adj* **central bank** banco central *nm* **central planned economy** planificación económica estatal *nf* **central planning** planificación estatal *nf* **central processing unit (CPU)** (DP) unidad de proceso central (UPC) *nf*

centralization *n* centralización *nf*

centralize *vb* centralizar *vb*

centre *n* **business centre** centro comercial *nm*, centro financiero *nm* **Jobcentre** oficina de empleo *nf*, agencia de colocaciones *nf*, bolsa de empleo *nf*

certificate **1.** *n* certificado *nm* **clearance certificate** certificado de haber efectuado el despacho de aduana *nm* **marriage certificate** certificado de matrimonio *nm* **certificate of employment** certificado de empleo *nm* **certificate of origin** certificado de origen *nm* **certificate of ownership** certificado de propiedad *nm* **share certificate, stock certificate** (US) título de acción *nm* **2.** *vb* certificar *vb*

certified *adj* certificado *adj* **certified cheque** cheque certificado *nm*, cheque conformado *nm*

certify *vb* certificar *vb*

chain *n* cadena *nf* **chain of shops** cadena de tiendas *nf* **retail chain** cadena de minoristas *nf* **chain store** tienda de una cadena *nf*

chair *vb* **to chair a meeting** presidir una reunión *vb*

chamber *n* cámara *nf* **Chamber of Commerce** Cámara de Comercio *nf*

chancellor *n* **Chancellor of the Exchequer (GB)** ministro, -tra de Economía y Hacienda *nm,f*

change *n* (from purchase) cambio *nm*, vuelta *nf*, vuelto (LAm) *nm*, vueltas (LAm) *nfpl* **bureau de change** cambio *nm*, oficina de cambio *nf* **loose/small change** (coins) monedas *nfpl*, calderilla *nf*, sencillo (LAm) *nm*, feria (LAm) *nf*, menudo (LAm) *nm*

charge **1.** *n* **charge account** cuenta de crédito *nf*, cuenta abierta *nf* **bank charges** gastos bancarios *nmpl* **delivery charges** gastos de envío *nmpl*, gastos de transporte *nmpl* **handling charges** gastos de tramitación *nmpl*, costes de manipulación *nmpl*, costos de manipulación (LAm) *nmpl* **legal charges** costes judiciales *nmpl* **2.** *vb* **to charge (a price)** cobrar *vb*, cargar *vb*, encomendar *vb* **to charge commission** cobrar comisión *vb* **to charge for sth** cobrar por algo *vb*, cargar algo *vb* **to charge sth to an account** cargar algo a una cuenta *vb* **to be in charge** estar encargado *vb* **to take charge of sth** hacerse cargo de *vb*, responsabilizarse de algo *vb* **to charge sb with sth** encargar a alguien con algo *vb*

chargeable *adj* cobrable *adj*

charitable *adj* **charitable trust** fundación benéfica *nf*, entidad caritativa *nf*

charity *n* caridad *nf*, obras de beneficencia *nfpl*

chart *n* gráfico *nm* **bar chart** gráfico de barras *nm* **flow chart** organigrama *nm*, diagrama de flujos *nm*, diagrama de secuencias *nm* **pie chart** gráfico sectorial *nm*

charter *n* **charter flight** vuelo chárter *nm*

chartered *adj* **chartered accountant** contable colegiado, -ada *nm,f*, contador, -ora público, -ica (LAm) *nm,f* **chartered bank** banco fundado antiguamente por cédula real *nm* **chartered surveyor** agrimensor, -ora colegiado, -ada *nm,f*

chattels *npl* bienes *nmpl*

check **1.** *n* **customs check** control de aduana *nm*, revisión de aduana *nf* **to make a check on sth** verificar algo *vb*, inspeccionar algo *vb*, chequear *vb*, checar (LAm) *vb* **2.** *vb* comprobar *vb*, verificar *vb*

check in 1. *n* (at airport) facturación *nf*, chequeo (LAm) *nm* **2.** *vb* (at airport) presentarse *vb*, facturar el equipaje *vb*, chequear (LAm) *vb* (register in an hotel) registrarse *vb*, inscribirse *vb*

check out *vb* (pay the hotel bill) pagar la cuenta y marcharse *vb*

checkbook (US) *n* talonario de cheques *nm*, chequera (LAm) *nf*

chemical *adj* **chemical industry** industria química *nf* **chemical products** productos químicos *nmpl*

cheque, check (US) *n* cheque *nm* **return a cheque to drawer** devolver un cheque *vb* **blank cheque** cheque en blanco *nm* **cheque book** talonario de cheques *nm,* chequera (LAm) *nf* **crossed cheque** cheque cruzado *nm* **dud cheque** cheque sin fondos *nm,* cheque no cubierto *nm* **a cheque for the amount of £100** cheque por valor de cien libras *nm* **to bounce a cheque** rechazar un cheque *vb* **to cash a cheque** cobrar un cheque *vb* **to make out a cheque** extender un cheque *vb* **to pay by cheque** pagar con cheque *vb* **to sign a cheque** firmar un cheque *vb* **to stop a cheque** detener el pago de un cheque *vb* **traveller's cheque, traveler's cheque** (US) cheque de viaje *nm,* cheque de viajero *nm*

chief *adj* **chief accountant** jefe, -efa de contabilidad *nm,f* **chief cashier** cajero, -era jefe *nm,f* **chief executive** director, -ora general *nm,f,* jefe, -efa ejecutivo, -iva *nm,f,* presidente, -nta *nm,f* **chief financial officer** jefe, -efa de finanzas *nm,f*

choice *n* selección *nf*

circular *n* (letter) circular *nf*

circulate *vb* (document) hacer circular *vb,* divulgar *vb*

circulation *n* **in circulation** en circulación *prep*

circumstance *n* circunstancias *nfpl* **circumstances beyond our control** circunstancias ajenas a nuestra voluntad *nfpl* **due to unforeseen circumstances** debido a circunstancias imprevistas *prep* **under no circumstances** bajo ningún concepto *prep*

civil *adj* **civil engineering** ingeniería civil *nf,* ingeniería de caminos *nf* **civil servant** funcionario, -ria *nm,f* **civil service** administración pública *nf*

claim 1. *n* demanda *nf,* reivindicación *nf,* reclamación *nf* **claim form** impreso de reclamación *nm* **claims department** departamento de reclamaciones *nm* **claims procedure** tramitación de reclamaciónes *nf* **to put in a claim** presentar una reclamación *vb,* presentar una solicitud *vb* **to settle a claim** liquidar una reclamación *vb* **wage claim** reivindicación salarial *nf,* demanda de aumento salarial *nf* 2. *vb* **to claim for damages** presentar una demanda de

indemnización *vb,* presentar una reclamación *vb*

claimant *n* solicitante *nmf,* demandante *nmf*

class *n* **business class** (plane) clase preferente *nf* **first class** (plane) primera clase *nf*

classification *n* clasificación *nf*

classified *adj* **classified advertisement** anuncio por palabras *nm,* aviso clasificado (LAm) *nm* **classified information** información clasificada como secreta *nf*

clause *n* (in contract) cláusula *nf* **escape clause** cláusula de excepción *nf,* cláusula de salvaguardia *nf* **option clause** cláusula de opción *nf*

clear 1. *adj* **clear loss** pérdida neta *nf* **to make oneself clear** explicarse claramente *vb* 2. *vb* (a cheque) tramitar el pago de *vb,* compensar *vb* **to clear sth through customs** tramitar el despacho de aduanas de algo *vb*

clearance *n* **clearance offer** oferta por liquidación *nf,* oferta por realización (LAm) *nf* **clearance sale** liquidación *nf,* realización (LAm) *nf*

clearing *adj* **clearing bank** banco comercial *nm,* banco de compensación *nm* **clearing house** cámara de compensación *nf* **clearing payment** pago de compensación *nm*

clerical *adj* de oficina *prep* **clerical error** error de copia *nm* **clerical work** trabajo de oficina *nm*

clerk *n* oficinista *nmf,* empleado, -ada *nm,f,* recepcionista *nmf,* bancario, -ria (LAm) *nm,f*

client *n* cliente, -nta *nm,f*

clientele *n* clientela *nf*

clinch *vb* **clinch a deal** cerrar un trato *vb*

clock in *vb* fichar a la entrada al trabajo *vb,* checar tarjeta al entrar al trabajo (LAm) *vb*

clock out *vb* fichar a la salida del trabajo *vb,* checar tarjeta al salir del trabajo (LAm) *vb*

close *vb* **to close a business** cerrar una empresa *vb* **to close a deal** cerrar un trato *vb* **to close a meeting** terminar una reunión *vb* **to close an account** cerrar una cuenta *vb*

closed *adj* cerrado *adj* **closed session/ meeting** sesión a puerta cerrada *nf* **closed shop** empresa que emplea exclusivamente a trabajadores sindicados *nf*

closing *adj* **closing bid** oferta final *nf*

closing price precio al cierre *nm* **closing time** hora de cierre *nf*

closure *n* **closure of a company** cierre de una empresa *nm*

co-efficient *n* coeficiente *nm*

COD (cash on delivery), (collect on delivery) (US) *abbr* cobro a la entrega *nm*

code *n* **bar code** código de barras *nm* **professional code of practice** código de práctica *nm* **post code, zip code (US)** código postal *nm* **telephone code** prefijo *nm* **tax code** código fiscal *nm*

collaborate *vb* colaborar *vb*

collaborative *adj* **collaborative venture** empresa conjunta *nf*, negocio en participación *nm*, agrupación temporal de empresas *nf*

collapse *n* (of company) quiebra *nf*, (of economy) desplome *nm*, caída *nf* **on stock market** hundimiento de la bolsa *nm*, caída bursátil *nf*

collateral 1. *adj* **collateral security** garantía colateral *nf* 2. *n* garantía *nf*, fianza *nf*

colleague *n* colega *nmf*

collect *vb* recoger *vb*, recaudar *vb*, coleccionar *vb* **to collect a debt** cobrar una deuda *vb*

collecting *adj* **collecting agency** banco de cobros *nm*

collection *n* toma *nf*, recogida *nf*, recaudación *nf* **debt collection** cobro de morosos *nm*

collective 1. *adj* **collective agreement** convenio colectivo *nm* **collective bargaining** negociación colectiva *nf* 2. *n* colectivo *nm*, cooperativa *nf* **workers' collective** propiedad colectiva *nf*

colloquium *n* coloquio *nm*

combination *n* combinación *nf*

command *n* mando *nm*

comment *n* comentario *nm*, observación *nf*

commerce *n* comercio *nm*

commercial *adj* comercial *adj*, mercantil *adj* **commercial bank** banco comercial *nm*, banco mercantil *nm* **commercial traveller, commercial traveler (US)** viajante de comercio *nmf*, corredor, -ora (LAm) *nm,f* **commercial vehicle** vehículo comercial *nm*

commission *n* comisión *nf*, encargo *nm*, servicio *nm*, comisión (LAm) *nf* **commission agent** comisionista *nmf* **commission broker** agente de bolsa *nmf*, comisionista *nmf* **commission fee** cuota

de comisión *nf* **to charge commission** cobrar comisión *vb*

commit *vb* cometer *vb*, comprometer *vb*, asignar *vb*

commitment *n* compromiso *nm*, obligación *nf*, responsabilidad *nf*

committee *n* comité *nm*, comisión *nf* **advisory committee** comisión asesora *nf* **committee meeting** reunión del comité *nf*, reunión de la comisión *nf*

common *adj* común *adj* **Common Agricultural Policy (CAP)** Política Agrícola Común *nf* **Common Market** Mercado Común *nm* **common law** derecho consuetudinario *nm*

communication *n* comunicación *nf*, comunicado *nm* **communication network** red de comunicaciones *nf*

community *n* comunidad *nf*

companion *n* compañero, -era *nm,f*

company *n* compañía *nf*, empresa *nf*, sociedad *nf* **holding company** sociedad "holding" *nf* **incorporated company (US)** compañía constituida legalmente *nf* **joint-stock company** sociedad anónima *nf* **company law** ley de sociedades anónimas *nf* **limited company** sociedad de responsabilidad limitada *nf* **parent company** sociedad matriz *nf* **company policy** política de la empresa *nf* **private limited company** sociedad anónima privada *nf* **public limited company** sociedad anónima cuyas acciones se cotizan en bolsa *nf* **registered company** sociedad legalmente constituida *nf* **company secretary** secretario, -ria de la compañía *nm,f* **sister company** compañía asociada *nf* **subsidiary company** filial *nf*, sucursal *nf*

comparative *adj* comparativo *adj*

comparison *n* comparación *nf*, equiparación *nf*

compatible *adj* compatible *adj*

compensate for *vb* compensar por *vb*, indemnizar por *vb*

compensation *n* indemnización *nf*, compensación *nf*, resarcimiento *nm* **to claim compensation** pedir indemnización *vb* **to pay compensation** indemnizar *vb*, conceder indemnización *vb*

compete *vb* competir *vb*, hacer la competencia *vb*, participar *vb* **to compete with a rival** competir con un(a) rival *vb*

competing *adj* **competing company** empresa rival *nf*

competition n competencia nf, competición nf, concurso nm **cut-throat competition** competencia encarnizada nf **market competition** competencia de mercado nf **unfair competition** competencia desleal nf

competitive adj competitivo adj

competitiveness n competitividad nf

competitor n competidor, -ora nm,f

complain vb quejar vb **to complain about sth** quejarse de algo vb, protestar por algo vb

complaint n queja nf, protesta nf, reclamación nf, reclamo (LAm) nm **to make a complaint** presentar una queja vb, reclamar vb, protestar vb **complaints department** departamento de reclamaciones nm

complete vb terminar vb, acabar vb, rellenar vb

complex 1. adj complejo adj, complicado adj **2.** n **housing complex** complejo habitacional nm, complejo de viviendas nm, urbanización nf, colonia (LAm) nf

complimentary adj elogioso adj

comply vb acatar vb, obedecer vb **to comply with legislation** cumplir con las leyes vb **to comply with the rules** cumplir el reglamento vb, respetar las normas vb

compound adj **compound interest** interés compuesto nm

comprehensive adj amplio adj **comprehensive insurance policy** seguro a todo riesgo nm

compromise n acuerdo mutuo nm, transacción (LAm) nf **to reach a compromise** llegar a un acuerdo mutuo vb, llegar a un arreglo vb, transigir vb, transar (LAm) vb

computer n ordenador nm, computadora (LAm) nf **computer-aided design (CAD)** diseño asistido por ordenador (CAD) nm **computer-aided learning (CAL)** aprendizaje asistido por ordenador (CAL) nm **computer-aided manufacture (CAM)** fabricación asistida por ordenador (CAM) nf **computer centre, center** (US) centro informático nm **computer file** archivo nm **computer language** lenguaje de ordenador nm **laptop computer** ordenador portátil nm **computer literate** con conocimientos de informática prep **mainframe computer** ordenador central nm, unidad central nf **computer operator** operador, -ora de teclado nm,f **personal computer (PC)** ordenador personal (PC)

nm **portable computer** ordenador portátil nm **computer program** programa de ordenador nm, programa informático nm **computer programmer** programador, -ora de ordenadores nm,f, programador, -ora (LAm) nm,f **computer terminal** terminal del ordenador nm **computer ware** n soporte nm

concern 1. n **going concern** negocio en marcha nm, negocio en plena marcha nm **2.** vb (be of importance to) interesar vb, importar vb, incumbir vb, respectar vb

concur vb coincidir vb, concurrir vb

condition n **living conditions** condiciones de vida nfpl **conditions of purchase** condiciones de compra nfpl **conditions of sale** condiciones de venta nfpl **working conditions** condiciones de trabajo nfpl

conduct n conducta nf, comportamiento nm

conference n congreso nm, conferencia nf, reunión nf **conference proceedings** actas de conferencia nfpl **to arrange a conference** organizar una conferencia vb **conference venue** lugar de la conferencia nm

confidence n **in strictest confidence** con la más absoluta reserva prep

confidential adj confidencial adj

confirm vb confirmar vb **to confirm receipt of sth** acusar recibo de algo vb

confirmation n confirmación nf, ratificación nf

conglomerate n conglomerado nm

congress n congreso nm

connect vb **could you connect me to...** (telephone) ¿me pone con...? vb, comuníqueme con... (LAm) vb

connection n conexión nf **business connections** contactos comerciales nmpl, conexiones comerciales (LAm) nfpl

consent 1. n consentimiento nm **2.** vb consentir vb

consequence n consecuencia nf, resultado nm

consideration n (for contract) consideración nf

consignee n consignatario, -ria nm,f, destinatario, -ria nm,f

consigner/or n consignador, -ora nm,f, remitente nmf

consignment n consignación nf, envío nm, remesa nf

consolidate vb consolidar vb, reforzar vb

consolidated *adj* **consolidated figures** estadísticas consolidadas *nf*
consortium *n* consorcio *nm*
construction *n* **construction industry** industria de la construcción *nf,* construcción *nf*
consul *n* cónsul *nmf*
consulate *n* consulado *nm*
consult *vb* consultar *vb,* asesorar *vb* **to consult with sb** consultar a alguien *vb*
consultancy *n* asesoría *nf* **consultancy fees, consulting fees** (US) honorarios por asesoría *nmpl* **consultancy firm, consulting firm** (US) asesoría *nf,* consultoría *nf* **consultancy work, consulting work** (US) asesoría *nf,* labor de asesoría *nf*
consultant *n* asesor, -ora *nm,f,* consultor, -ora *nm,f,* especialista *nmf*
consumer *n* consumidor, -ora *nm,f* **consumer credit** crédito al consumidor *nm* **consumer demand** demanda de consumo *nf* **consumer habits** conducta del consumidor *nf* **consumer research** investigación sobre el consumo *nf* **consumer satisfaction** satisfacción del consumidor *nf* **consumer survey** estudio de mercado *nm,* sondeo de opinión consumista *nm* **consumer trends** tendencias del consumidor *nfpl,* tendencias de consumo *nfpl*
consumerism *n* consumismo *nm*
contact 1. *n* contacto *nm* **business contacts** contactos comerciales *nmpl,* conocidos de negocios *nmpl,* enchufes *nmpl,* conexiones comerciales (LAm) *nfpl,* palancas (LAm) *nfpl* **to get in contact with sb** ponerse en contacto con alguien *vb* **2.** *vb* contactar (con) *vb*
container *n* contenedor *nm* **container depot** depósito de contenedores *nm* **container ship** portacontenedores *nm* **container terminal** terminal de portacontenedores *nf*
contract *n* contrato *nm* **breach of contract** incumplimiento de contrato *nm* **draft contract** proyecto de contrato *nm* **contract labour** mano de obra empleada a base de contrato *nf* **law of contract** derecho contractual *nm* **the terms of the contract** los términos del contrato *nmpl* **the signatories to the contract** los firmantes del contrato *nmpl* **to cancel a contract** anular un contrato *vb* **to draw up a contract** redactar un contrato *vb* **to sign a contract** firmar un contrato *vb* **to tender for a contract** licitar para un

contrato *vb* **under the terms of the contract** según lo establecido en el contrato *prep,* bajo los términos del contrato *prep* **contract work** trabajo a contrata *nm*
contracting *adj* **the contracting parties** las partes contratantes *nf pl*
contractor *n* contratista *nmf* **building contractor** contratista de la construcción *nmf* **haulage contractor** contratista de transporte por carretera *nm*
contractual *adj* **contractual obligations** obligaciones contractuales *nfpl*
contravene *vb* contravenir *vb,* infringir *vb*
contravention *n* infracción *nf*
contribute *vb* contribuir *vb,* aportar *vb,* hacer aportes (LAm) *vb*
contribution *n* contribución *nf,* aportación *nf* **social security contributions** cotizaciones a la Seguridad Social *nfpl,* aportes a la seguridad social (LAm) *nmpl*
control *n* **financial control** control de finanzas *nm,* control financiero *nm* **production control** control de producción *nm* **quality control** control de calidad *nm* **stock control** control de existencias *nm*
convene *vb* **to convene a meeting** convocar una reunión *vb*
convenience *n* **at your earliest convenience** a su mayor brevedad posible *prep*
convenient *adj* oportuno *adj,* práctico *adj*
convertible *adj* **convertible currency** moneda convertible *nf*
copier *n* (photocopier) fotocopiadora *nf*
copy 1. *n* copia *nf,* número *nm* **2.** *vb* (photocopy) copiar *vb,* fotocopiar *vb*
copyright *n* derechos de autor *nmpl,* derechos de reproducción *nmpl,* "copyright" *nm* **copyright law** ley sobre la propiedad intelectual *nf*
corporate *adj* empresarial *adj,* de empresa *prep* **corporate image** imagen pública de la empresa *nf* **corporate investment** inversión de empresa *nf*
corporation *n* sociedad anónima *nf,* empresa *nf,* corporación *nf* **corporation tax** impuesto de sociedades *nm*
correspondence *n* correspondencia *nf*
corruption *n* corrupción *nf*
cosignatory *n* cosignatario, -ria *nm,f*
cost 1. *n* coste *nm,* gasto *nm,* costo (LAm) *nm* **cost breakdown** análisis de costes *nm* **cost centre** centro de coste *nm* **cost-cutting** reducción de gastos/costes *nf* **cost of living** coste de vida *nm* **operating cost** coste de explotación *nm,* costo de operación (LAm) *nm* **cost price** precio de

coste *nm* **running cost** coste de explotación *nm*, costo de operación (LAm) *nm* **2.** *vb* **to cost a job** calcular el coste de un trabajo *vb*
counterfeit 1. *n* falsificación *nf* **2.** *vb* falsificar *vb*
counterfoil *n* matriz *nf*, talón (LAm) *nm*
countersign *vb* refrendar *vb*
country *n* **developing country** país en vías de desarrollo *nm* **third-world country** país del Tercer Mundo *nm*
coupon *n* cupón *nm*, vale *nm*, boleto *nm*
courier 1. *n* mensajero, -era *nm,f*, correo *nmf*, guía de turismo *nmf* **by courier service** por servicio de correo *prep* **2.** *vb* entregar por servicio de mensajero *vb*
court *n* corte *nf* **Court of Appeal, Court of Appeals** (US) Tribunal de Apelación *nm* **criminal court** tribunal penal *nm* **in court** ante el tribunal *prep*
covenant *n* pacto *nm*, convenio *nm*
covenantee *n* parte contratada *nf*
covenantor *n* parte contratante *nf*
cover *n* cobertura *nf* **insurance cover** cobertura del seguro *nf* **cover note** póliza provisional *nf*, nota de cobertura *nf*
credit 1. *adj* **credit agency** agencia de informes comerciales *nf* **credit card** tarjeta de crédito *nf* **credit company** sociedad financiera *nf* **credit control** control de crédito *nm* **credit enquiry** petición de informe sobre el crédito *nf* **credit note** nota de abono *nf*, nota de crédito *nf* **credit rating** clasificación crediticia *nf* **credit terms** condiciones de crédito *nfpl* **2.** *n* crédito *nm* **to buy sth on credit** comprar algo a crédito *vb*, comprar algo a plazos *vb* **in credit** con saldo acreedor *prep* **letter of credit** carta de crédito *nf* **long credit** crédito a largo plazo *nm* **3.** *vb* **to credit sth to an account** abonar algo en una cuenta *vb*, ingresar algo en una cuenta *vb*
creditor *n* acreedor, -ora *nm,f*
creditworthiness *n* solvencia *nf*, capacidad de pago *nf*
creditworthy *adj* solvente *adj*
crossed *adj* **crossed cheque** cheque cruzado *nm*
currency *n* moneda *nf*, divisa *nf* **convertible currency** moneda convertible *nf* **foreign currency** moneda extranjera *nf*, divisas *nfpl* **hard currency** moneda convertible *nf*, moneda fuerte *nf* **legal currency** moneda de curso legal *nf* **paper**

currency papel moneda *nm* **soft currency** divisa débil *nf*, moneda no convertible *nf* **currency transfer** transferencia de divisas *nf*, transferencia de moneda *nf*
current *adj* **current account** cuenta corriente *nf*
curriculum vitae (CV), résumé (US) *n* currículum (vitae) (CV) *nm*
customer *n* cliente, -nta *nm,f* **customer loyalty** fidelidad a un establecimiento *nf* **regular customer** cliente, -nta de la casa *nm,f* **customer relations** relaciones con la clientela *nfpl*, relaciones públicas *nfpl*
customs *npl* aduana *nf* **customs charges** derechos de aduana *nmpl* **customs clearance** formalidades aduaneras *nfpl* **customs declaration** declaración de aduana *nf* **customs office** despacho de aduana *nm* **customs officer** aduanero, -era *nm,f*, funcionario, -ria de aduana *nm,f* **customs regulations** disposiciones aduaneras *nfpl* **to clear sth through customs** despachar algo por aduana *vb* **customs union** unión aduanera *nf* **customs warehouse** depósito aduanero *nm*
cut 1. *n* recorte *nm* **tax cut** reducción en los impuestos *nf* **2.** *vb* (reduce) recortar *vb*, rebajar *vb*
damage 1. *n* daño *nm*, daños *nmpl* **to cause extensive damage** ocasionar daños graves *vb* **to claim damages** (legal) reclamar por daños y perjuicios *vb* **damage to goods in transit** daños sufridos por mercancías durante el transporte *nmpl* **damage to property** daños materiales *nmpl* **2.** *vb* dañar *vb*, estropear *vb*, perjudicar *vb*
data *n* datos *nmpl*, información *nf* **data bank** banco de datos *nm* **database** base de datos *nf* **data capture** captación de datos *nf* **data processing** proceso de datos *nm*, procesamiento de datos *nm*
date *n* fecha *nf* **delivery date** fecha de entrega *nf* **out-of-date** anticuado *adj*, caducado *adj*, obsoleto *adj*, vencido (LAm) *adj*, perimido (LAm) *adj* **up-to-date** moderno *adj*, actualizado *adj*, al día *prep*
deal *n* trato *nm*, negocio *nm* **it's a deal!** ¡trato hecho! *nm*
dealer *n* comerciante *nmf*, agente mediador, -ora *nm,f* **foreign exchange dealer** agente de cambio *nmf*, operador, -ora de cambios *nm,f*, cambista *nmf*
dealing, trading (US) *n* comercio *nm*,

operaciones en bolsa *nfpl* **foreign exchange dealings** cambio *nm*, operaciones de cambio *nfpl* **insider dealing** operaciones de iniciado *nfpl*, trato con información privilegiada *nm*
debenture *n* obligación *nf*, bono *nm*, pagaré *nm* **debenture bond** obligación no hipotecaria *nf* **debenture capital**, **debenture stock** (US) obligaciones garantizadas por los activos de la compañía *nfpl* **debenture loan** préstamo garantizado por obligaciones *nm*
debit **1.** *n* débito *nm*, pasivo *nm*, cargo *nm* **debit balance** saldo negativo *nm*, saldo deudor *nm* **2.** *vb* (account) adeudar *vb*, cargar *vb*
debiting *n* **direct debiting** domiciliación bancaria *nf*
debt *n* deuda *nf*, endeudamiento *nm* **corporate debt** endeudamiento de una sociedad *nm* **to get into debt** endeudarse *vb* **to pay off a debt** saldar una deuda *vb* **to reschedule a debt** renegociar una deuda *vb* **debt service** pago de intereses de una deuda *nm*
debtor *n* deudor, -ora *nm,f*
decline *n* (economic) baja *nf*
decrease **1.** *n* disminución *nf* **2.** *vb* disminuir *vb*, bajar *vb*, reducir *vb*
deduct *vb* deducir *vb*, desgravar *vb*
deductible *adj* deducible *adj*, desgravable *adj*
deduction *n* deducción *nf*, desgravación *nf*, descuento *nm*
deed *n* (law) escritura *nf*, título *nm* **deed of sale** escritura de venta *nf* **deed of transfer** escritura de transferencia *nf*
default **1.** *n* falta *nf*, omisión *nf* **2.** *vb* incumplir *vb*
defect *n* defecto *nm*, tara *nf*
defective *adj* defectuoso *adj*
defer *vb* (postpone) posponer *vb*, aplazar *vb*
deferment *n* aplazamiento *nm*
deferred *adj* (tax) diferido *adj*, aplazado *adj*
deficiency *n* deficiencia *nf*, escasez *nf*
deficient *adj* deficiente *adj*, insuficiente *adj*
deficit *n* **deficit financing** financiación de déficit *nf*
deflation *n* deflación *nf*
deflationary *adj* deflacionista *adj*
defraud *vb* estafar *vb*
del credere *adj* **del credere agent** agente que recibe una comisión elevada porque garantiza el pago *nmf*
delay **1.** *n* retraso *nm*, tardanza *nf*,

demora (LAm) *nf* **without delay** sin tardanza *prep*, sin demora (LAm) *prep* **2.** *vb* retrasar *vb*, tardar *vb*, demorar (LAm) *vb*
delegate **1.** *n* delegado, -ada *nm,f* **2.** *vb* delegar *vb*
delegation *n* delegación *nf*, delegación de poderes *nf*, representación *nf*
deliver *vb* (goods) entregar *vb*, repartir *vb*, cumplir *vb*
delivery *n* entrega *nf*, reparto *nm*, remesa *nf* **cash on delivery** entrega contra reembolso *nf*, cobro a la entrega *nm* **delivery date** fecha de entrega *nf* **free delivery** entrega gratuita *nf* **general delivery** (US) entrega general *nf* **recorded delivery** correo certificado con acuse de recibo *nm* **delivery time** plazo de entrega *nm*
demand **1.** *n* demanda *nf*, reivindicación *nf*, petición *nf*, pedido (LAm) *nm* **supply and demand** oferta y demanda *nf & nf* **2.** *vb* exigir *vb*, reivindicar *vb*, reclamar *vb*
demography *n* demografía *nf*
demote *vb* (employee) rebajar *vb*
denationalize *vb* privatizar *vb*
department *n* departamento *nm*, sección *nf* **government department** ministerio *nm*, secretaría (LAm) *nf* **personnel department** departamento de personal *nm* **department store** grandes almacenes *nmpl*, tienda de departamentos (LAm) *nf*
depletion *n* reducción *nf*, disminución *nf*, agotamiento *nm*
deposit **1.** *adj* **deposit account** cuenta de ahorros *nf* **2.** *n* depósito *nm*, imposición *nf*, entrada *nf*, pie (LAm) *nm*, seña (LAm) *nf* **3.** *vb* depositar *vb*, ingresar *vb*
depository *n* depositario, -ria *nm,f*, guardamuebles *nm*
depreciate *vb* depreciarse *vb*, perder valor *vb*, amortizar *vb*
depreciation *n* depreciación *nf*, amortización *nf*, pérdida de valor *nf*
depression *n* (economic) recesión *nf*, crisis *nf*
deputy **1.** *adj* adjunto *adj* **deputy director** subdirector, -ora *nm,f*, director, -ora adjunto, -nta *nm,f* **2.** *n* suplente *nmf*
design **1.** *n* diseño *nm*, motivo *nm* **a machine of good/bad design** una máquina bien/mal diseñada *nf* **2.** *vb* diseñar *vb*, proyectar *vb*, planear *vb*
designer *n* (commercial) diseñador, -ora *nm,f*
devaluation *n* devaluación *nf*

developer *n* promotor, -ora *nm,f*, promotor, -ora de contrucciones *nm,f*
digital *adj* digital *adj*
diminishing *adj* **diminishing returns** rendimientos decrecientes *nmpl*
director *n* director, -ora *nm,f*, directivo, -iva *nm,f*, consejero, -era *nm,f* **board of directors** consejo de administración *nm*, junta directiva *nf* **managing director** director, -ora gerente *nm,f*, director, -ora ejecutivo, -iva *nm,f*
disburse *vb* desembolsar *vb*
discount *n* descuento *nm*, bonificación *nf* **at a discount** con descuento *prep*, descontado *adj* **discount rate** tipo de descuento *nm*
discounted *adj* **discounted cash flow (DCF)** "cash flow" actualizado *nm*, flujo de caja descontado *nm*
disk *n* diskette *nm*, disquete *nm* **disk drive** unidad de disco *nf* **floppy disk** disco flexible *nm*, "floppy" *nm* **hard disk** disco duro *nm* **magnetic disk** disco magnético *nm*
dismiss *vb* (employee) despedir *vb*, botar (LAm) *vb*
dispatch **1.** *n* **date of dispatch** fecha de expedición *nf* **2.** *vb* (goods) despachar *vb*, enviar *vb*
dispatcher *n* expedidor, -ora *nm,f*
display **1.** *n* (of goods) exhibición *nf*, exposición *nf* **2.** *vb* exhibir *vb*, exponer *vb*, demostrar *vb*
disposable *adj* (not for reuse) desechable *adj* **disposable income** ingresos disponibles *nmpl*
dispute *n* disputa *nf*, conflicto *nm*, diferendo (LAm) *nm* **industrial dispute** conflicto laboral *nm*
distribution *n* distribución *nf*, reparto *nm*
distributor *n* distribuidor, -ora *nm,f*
diversification *n* diversificación *nf*
diversify *vb* diversificarse *vb*
dividend *n* dividendo *nm*, beneficio *nm*
division *n* (of company) división *nf*, sección *nf* **division of labour** división del trabajo *nf*
dock **1.** *n* (for berthing) muelle *nm* **2.** *vb* (ship) entrar en dársena *vb*, atracar *vb*, fondear *vb*
dockyard *n* astillero *nm*
document documento *nm*, papel *nm* **document retrieval** recuperación de documentos *nf*
domestic *adj* **domestic policy** política nacional *nf*

door *n* **door-to-door selling** venta domiciliaria *nf*
double *adj* **double-entry** (bookkeeping) de partida doble *prep*
Dow-Jones average (US) *n* índice Dow Jones *nm*
down *adv* **down payment** entrada *nf*, pago inicial *nm*, pie (LAm) *nm*
downturn *n* (economic) descenso *nm*, bajón *nm*
downward *adj* & *adv* hacia abajo *prep*, a la baja *prep*, descendente *adj*
draft **1.** *n* (financial) giro *nm*, efecto bancario *nm*, borrador *nm* **2.** *vb* redactar *vb*
draw *vb* (cheque) girar *vb*
dry *adj* **dry goods** artículos de mercería *nmpl*
dumping *n* dumping *nm*
durable *adj* **durable goods** bienes duraderos *nm*
duty *n* (customs) derecho *nm*, deber *nm* **duty-free** (goods) libre de impuestos, libre de derechos de aduana *adj*, *adv*
dynamic *adj* dinámico *adj*
dynamics *npl* dinámica *nf*
early *adj* **early retirement** jubilación anticipada *nf*
earn *vb* ganar *vb*, percibir *vb*, devengar *vb*
earned *adj* ganado *adj*, percibido *adj* **earned income** ingresos en concepto de sueldo *nmpl* **earned surplus** superávit percibido *nm*
earnest *adj* serio *adj* **earnest money** fianza *nf*
earning *adj* **earning capacity** capacidad de ganar dinero *nf*, grado de rendimiento *nm* **earning power** capacidad de ganar dinero *nf*, grado de rendimiento *nm*, escala de rendimiento *nf*
earnings *npl* ingresos *nmpl*, ganancias *nfpl*, beneficios *nmpl*, utilidades (LAm) *nfpl* **earnings drift** deriva de ingresos *nf* **loss of earnings** pérdida de ingresos *nf* **earnings-related pension** pensión proporcional al sueldo *nf* **earnings yield** rédito *nm*
easy *adj* fácil *adj* **easy-money policy** política monetaria expansiva *nf*
EC (European Community) *abbr* CE (Comunidad Europea) *abbr,nf*
econometrics *n* econometría *nf*
economic *adj* **economic adviser** asesor, -ora económico, -ica *nm,f* **economic analysis** análisis económico *nm* **economic crisis** crisis económica *nf* **eco-**

nomic cycle ciclo económico *nm* **economic decline** declive económico *nm* **economic development** desarrollo económico *nm* **Economic and Monetary Union** Unión Económica y Monetaria *nf* **economic expansion** expansión económica *nf* **economic forecast** previsión económica *nf* **economic geography** geografía económica *nf* **economic growth** crecimiento económico *nm* **economic infrastructure** infraestructura económica *nf* **economic integration** integración económica *nf* **economic objective** objetivo económico *nm* **economic performance** rendimiento económico *nm*, performance económico (LAm) *nm* **economic planning** planificación económica *nf* **economic policy** política económica *nf* **economic sanction** sanción económica *nf* **economic slowdown** desaceleración económica *nf* **economic strategy** estrategia económica *nf* **economic superpower** superpotencia económica *nf* **economic survey** estudio económico *nm*, sondeo económico *nm* **economic trend** tendencias económicas *nfpl* **economic union** unión económica *nf*
economical *adj* económico *adj*
economics *n* economía *nf*
economist *n* economista *nmf*
economy *n* (system) economía *nf* **advanced economy** economía avanzada *nf* **developing economy** economía en vías de desarrollo *nf* **free market economy** economía de mercado libre *nf* **global economy** economía global *nf* **economies of scale** economías de escala *nfpl* **national economy** economía nacional *nf* **planned economy** economía planificada *nf* **underdeveloped economy** economía subdesarrollada *nf*
ECSC (European Coal and Steel Community) *abbr* Comunidad Europea del Carbón y del Acero *nf*
ECU (European Currency Unit) *abbr* ecu (European Currency Unit) *nm*
edge *n* **competitive edge** margen competitivo *nm*, ventaja sobre la competencia *nf*
effect *n* efecto *nm* **financial effects** efectos financieros *nmpl*
efficiency *n* eficiencia *nf*
efficient *adj* eficiente *adj*, eficaz *adj*
EFT (electronic funds transfer) *abbr* transferencia electrónica de fondos *nf*
EFTA (European Free Trade Association)

abbr EFTA (la) *abbr,nf,* Asociación Europea de Libre Comercio *nf*
elasticity *n* elasticidad *nf* **income elasticity** elasticidad de ingresos *nf* **elasticity of demand** elasticidad de demanda *nf* **elasticity of production** elasticidad de producción *nf*
election *n* elección *nf* **general election** elecciones generales *nfpl*, comicios *nmpl* **local election** elecciones municipales *nfpl*
electronic *adj* electrónico *adj* **electronic banking** banca electrónica *nf* **electronic data processing** proceso electrónico de datos (EDP) *nm* **electronic mail** correo electrónico *nm*
elimination *n* eliminación *nf* **elimination of tariffs** supresión de aranceles *nf*
email *n* correo electrónico *nm*
embargo *n* embargo *nm* **to impose an embargo** imponer un embargo *vb* **to lift an embargo** levantar un embargo *vb* **trade embargo** embargo comercial *nm*
embassy *n* embajada *nf*
embezzle *vb* malversar *vb*
embezzlement *n* malversación *nf,* desfalco *nm*
embezzler *n* malversador, -ora *nm,f*
emergency *n* emergencia *nf* **emergency fund** fondo de emergencia *nm*
emigration *n* emigración *nf*
employ *vb* contratar *vb*, emplear *vb*, utilizar *vb*
employee *n* empleado, -ada *nm,f* **employee recruitment** contratación de empleados *nf*, contratación de personal *nf* **employee training** formación de empleados *nf*
employer *n* patrón, -ona *nm,f*, empresario, -ria *nm,f* **employer's federation** organización patronal *nf* **employers' liability insurance** seguro empresarial contra terceros *nm*
employment *n* empleo *nm*, ocupación *nf*, trabajo *nm* **employment agency** agencia de trabajo *nf*, agencia de colocaciones *nf*, oficina de empleo *nf* **employment contract** contrato de trabajo *nm* **full employment** pleno empleo *nm* **employment law** derecho laboral *nm*
encashment *n* cobro (en metálico) *nm*
enclose *vb* adjuntar *vb*, remitir adjunto *vb*
enclosure *n* anexo *nm*
end *n* fin *nm*, final *nm*, extremo *nm* **end consumer** usuario, -ria final *nm,f*, consumidor, -ora final *nm,f* **end user** usuario, -ria final *nm,f*

endorse vb (cheque) endosar vb
endorsement n aprobación nf
endowment n donación nf, legado nm,
dotación nf **endowment insurance** seguro de combinación aplazada y
decreciente nm **endowment policy** póliza dotal nf
enforce vb (policy) aplicar vb, ejecutar vb
enforcement n aplicación nf, ejecución nf
engagement n (meeting) compromiso
nm, cita nf
engineering n ingeniería nf **civil engineering** ingeniería civil nf **electrical engineering** ingeniería eléctrica nf
mechanical engineering ingeniería
mecánica nf **precision engineering** ingeniería de precisión nf
enhance vb (value) incrementar vb
enlarge vb ampliar vb, aumentar vb
enquire vb preguntar vb
enquiry n pregunta nf, petición de
informes nf, investigación nf
enterprise n (project) empresa nf,
iniciativa nf **private enterprise** iniciativa
privada nf, sector privado nm, empresa
privada nf
entertain vb **to entertain a client** recibir a
un cliente vb, invitar a un cliente vb
entrepôt n depósito nm, centro de almacenaje y distribución nm
entrepreneur n empresario, -ria nm,f,
contratista nmf
entrepreneurial adj empresarial adj
entry n entrada nf, asiento nm **entry for
free goods** entrada para mercancías
exentas de derechos de aduana nf,
entrada para mercaderías exentas de
derechos de aduana (LAm) nf **entry into
force** entrada en vigor nf, entrada a vigor
(LAm) nf **port of entry** puerto de entrada
nm **entry visa** visado de entrada nm, visa
de entrada (LAm) nf
equalization n **equalization of burdens**
equiparación de cargas nf
equalize vb igualar vb, compensar vb
equilibrium n equilibrio nm
equip vb equipar vb, proveer vb
equipment n equipo nm, útiles nmpl,
equipamiento nm, enseres nmpl **equipment leasing** arrendamiento de medios
de producción nm
equity n patrimonio neto nm, derechos
sobre el activo nmpl **equity capital**
capital social nm **equity financing** financiación de valores nf, financiación de
acciones nf **equity interests** intereses en

títulos nmpl **equity share** valor de renta
variable nm **equity trading** comercio de
acciones nm **equity transaction** operación en el mercado de valores nf
ergonomics n ergonomía nf
escalate vb aumentar vb, intensificarse vb
escalation n (prices) escalada nf
escalator n escalera mecánica nf
escudo n escudo nm
establish vb establecer vb, montar vb,
instalar vb
establishment n establecimiento nm,
creación nf, casa nf
estate n **estate agency, real estate agency**
(US) agencia inmobiliaria nf **estate
agent, real estate agent** (US) agente
inmobiliario, -ria nm,f
estimate 1. n cálculo nm, valoración nf
estimate of costs presupuesto de costes
nm, presupuesto de gastos nm, presupuesto de costos (LAm) nm **2.** vb calcular
vb, valorar vb, estimar vb
eurobond n eurobono nm
eurocapital n eurocapital nm
eurocheque n eurocheque nm
eurocracy n eurocracia nf
eurocrat n eurócrata nmf
eurocredit n eurocrédito nm
eurocurrency n eurodivisa nf **eurocurrency market** mercado de la eurodivisa
nm
eurodollar n eurodólar nm
eurofunds npl eurofondos nm
euromarket n euromercado nm
euromerger n eurofusión nf
euromoney n euromoneda nf
European adj europeo adj **Council of
Europe** Consejo de Europa nm **European
Advisory Committee** Comisión Consultiva Europea nf **European Commission**
Comisión Europea nf **European Community (EC)** Comunidad Europea (CE) nf
European Court of Justice (ECJ) Tribunal
Europeo de Justicia nm **European Development Fund (EDF)** Fondo Europeo de
Desarrollo (FED) nm **European Investment Bank (EIB)** Banco Europeo de
Inversiones (BEI) nm **European Monetary Agreement (EMA)** Acuerdo Monetario Europeo (AME) nm **European
Monetary Cooperation Fund (EMCF)**
Fondo Europeo de Cooperación Monetaria (FECM) nm **European Monetary System (EMS)** Sistema Monetario Europeo
(SME) nm **European Monetary Union
(EMU)** Unión Monetaria Europea (UME) nf

nf **European Parliament** Parlamento Europeo *nm* **European Recovery Plan** Plan Europeo de Recuperación *nm* **European Regional Development Fund (ERDF)** Fondo Europeo de Desarrollo Regional (FEDR) *nm* **European Social Fund (ESF)** Fondo Social Europeo (FSE) *nm* **European Union** Unión Europea *nf* **European Unit of Account (EUA)** Unidad de Cuenta Europea (UCE) *nf*

eurosceptic *n* euroescéptico *adj*

evade *vb* evadir *vb*

evasion *n* **tax evasion** evasión fiscal *nf*, evasión de impuestos *nf*, fraude fiscal *nm*

eviction *n* desahucio *nm*, lanzamiento *nm*

ex *prep* **ex factory/works** en fábrica *prep*, franco en fábrica, en almacén *prep* **ex gratia payment** paga voluntaria *nf*, pago ex-gratia *nm* **ex interest** sin interés *prep*, sin intereses *prep* **ex quay** en el muelle *prep* **ex repayment** sin reembolso *prep* sin pago *prep* **ex ship** en buque *prep* **ex stock** de existencias disponibles *prep* **ex store/warehouse** en almacén *prep* **ex wharf** en el muelle *prep*

examination *n* examen *nm*, revisión *nf*, revisación (LAm) *nf*

examine *vb* examinar *vb*, estudiar *vb*, revisar (LAm) *vb*

exceed *vb* sobrepasar *vb*, superar *vb*

excess *adj* **excess capacity** capacidad excesiva *nf* **excess demand inflation** inflación provocada por la demanda excesiva *nf* **excess profit(s) tax** impuesto sobre beneficios extraordinarios *nm* **excess reserves** exceso de reservas *nm*

exchange *n* **exchange broker** operador, -ora de cambios *nm,f*, cambista *nmf* **exchange cheque** cheque en divisas *nm* **exchange clearing agreement** convenio de compensación de cambio *nm* **exchange control** control de divisas *nm* **foreign exchange** divisas *nf*, moneda extranjera *nf* **exchange market** mercado de divisas *nm* **exchange rate** tipo de cambio *nm*, tasa de cambio (LAm) *nf* **exchange rate mechanism (ERM)** mecanismo de tasas de cambio *nm*, mecanismo de paridades *nm* **exchange restrictions** restricciones a divisas *nfpl* **exchange risk** riesgo del cambio *nm* **Stock Exchange** bolsa *nf*, bolsa de valores *nf*

excise *n* **excise duty** impuesto sobre la venta *nm* **the Board of Customs and**

Excise administración de aduanas e impuestos sobre el consumo *nf*

exclude *vb* excluir *vb*

exclusion *n* **exclusion clause** cláusula de exclusión *nf* **exclusion zone** zona de exclusión *nf*

executive 1. *adj* **executive committee** comisión ejecutiva *nf* **executive compensation** recompensa de directivos *nf* **executive duties** funciones ejecutivas *nfpl* **executive hierarchy** jerarquía de dirección *nf* **executive personnel** personal directivo *nm* 2. *n* ejecutivo, -iva *nm,f*, director, -ora *nm,f*

exempt *adj* exento *adj*, libre *adj* **tax-exempt** exento de impuestos *adj*

exemption *n* exención *nf*, exoneración *nf*, desgravación *nf*

exhaust *vb* (reserves) agotar *vb*

exhibit *vb* exponer *vb*, exhibir *vb*

exhibition *n* exposición *nf*, muestra *nf*

exorbitant *adj* excesivo *adj*

expand *vb* expandir *vb*, ampliar *vb*, aumentar *vb*

expansion *n* expansión *nf*, ampliación *nf*, desarrollo *nm* **expansion of capital** aumento de capital *nm*, incremento de capitales *nm* **expansion of trade** expansión del comercio *nf*, ampliación comercial *nf*

expectation *n* expectativa *nf* **consumer expectations** expectativas del consumidor *nfpl*

expedite *vb* expeditar *vb*, acelerar *vb*

expenditure *n* gasto *nm*, gastos *nmpl*, desembolso *nm* **expenditure rate** coeficiente de gastos *nm* **state expenditure** gasto público *nm* **expenditure taxes** impuestos sobre gastos *nmpl*

expense *n* gasto *nm* **expense account** cuenta de gastos de representación *nf* **expense control** control de gastos *nm* **entertainment expenses** gastos de representación *nmpl* **travelling expenses, travel expenses** (US) gastos de viaje *nmpl*, gastos de desplazamiento *nmpl*

experience 1. *n* experiencia *nf* **experience curve** curva de la experiencia *nf* 2. *vb* experimentar *vb*, sentir *vb*

experienced *adj* con experiencia *prep*

expert 1. *adj* perito *adj* 2. *n* experto, -rta *nm,f*

expertise *n* competencia *nf*, conocimientos *nmpl*

expiration n expiración nf, terminación nf, vencimiento nm
expire vb caducar vb, vencer vb
expiry, expiration (US) n caducidad nf, expiración nf, vencimiento nm **expiry date, expiration** (US) fecha de caducidad nf, fecha de vencimiento nf
export 1. adj **export bill of lading** conocimiento de embarque de exportación nm **export credit** crédito a la exportación nm **export credit insurance** seguro de crédito a la exportación nm **export department** departamento de exportación nm **export-led growth** crecimiento regido por la exportación nm **export licence** permiso de exportación nm **export marketing** promoción de las exportaciones nf **export operations** operaciones de exportación nfpl **export strategy** estrategia de exportación nf **export subsidies** subvenciones dirigidas a fomentar las exportaciones nfpl **export surplus** superávit de exportación nm **export tax** impuesto a la exportación nm **export trade** comercio de exportación nm **2.** n exportación nf **export of capital** exportación de capitales nf **3.** vb exportar vb
exporter n exportador, -ora nm,f
express adj exprés adj, expreso adj **express agency** agencia exprés nf **express delivery** entrega urgente nf, reparto rápido a domicilio nm **express service** servicio urgente nm
expropriate vb expropiar vb
expropriation n expropiación nf
extend vb **to extend a contract** extender un contrato vb **to extend credit** otorgar crédito vb **to extend the range** ampliar la gama vb
extension n (of contract) extensión nf, ampliación nf, prórroga nf
extent n **extent of cover** nivel de cobertura nm
external adj externo adj, exterior adj **external audit** auditoría externa nf
extortion n extorsión nf
extra adj extra adj, adicional adj, suplementario adj **extra cost** coste adicional nm, gasto complementario nm, costo adicional (LAm) nm **extra profit** beneficios extraordinarios nmpl
extraordinary adj **extraordinary meeting** junta extraordinaria nf **extraordinary value** valor extraordinario nm
facility n facilidad nf, servicio nm,

instalación nf **facility planning** planificación de servicios nf
facsimile (fax) n facsímile nm, telefax nm, fax nm
factor 1. adj **factor income** ingresos de los factores nmpl **factor market** mercado de factores (de producción) nm **factor price** precio de los factores de producción nm **2.** n (buyer of debts) agente al por mayor nmf **limiting factor** factor limitativo nm **factor of production** factor de producción nm **3.** vb (debts) hacer factoring vb
factoring n (of debts) factoring nm, gestión de deudas de otras compañías con descuento nf
factory n **factory board** comisión de fábricas nf, consejo de la fábrica nm **factory costs** gastos de fábrica nmpl, costos de fábrica (LAm) nmpl **factory inspector** inspector, -ora de fábrica nm,f **factory ledger** libro mayor de la fábrica nm, registro de fábricas nm **factory overheads** gastos generales de fabricación nmpl **factory price** precio en fábrica nm, precio franco fábrica nm
fail vb (negotiations) fracasar vb, fallar vb
failure n fracaso nm, fallo nm, quiebra nf
fair adj justo adj, limpio adj **fair competition** competencia leal nf **fair market value** valor justo de mercado nm **fair rate of return** tasa de rendimentio justa nf **fair-trade agreement** convenio sobre los precios mínimos de venta al público nm **fair-trade policy** política de comercio de reciprocidad arancelaria nf **fair-trade practice** práctica de vender a precio mínimo al público nf **fair trading** prácticas comerciales leales nfpl **fair wage** salario justo nm
fall due vb vencer vb
falling adj **falling prices** precios con tendencia a la baja nmpl **falling rate of profit** tasa de beneficios decreciente nf
false adj **false representation** representación falsa nf
falsification n falsificación nf **falsification of accounts** falsificación de cuentas nf
family n **family allowance** prestación estatal a la familia nf, asignación familiar (LAm) nf **family branding** identificación por marca nf **family corporation** empresa familiar nf **family income** ingresos familiares nmpl **family industry** industria familiar nf

farm out *vb* subcontratar *vb*, delegar *vb*, encargar *vb*

farming *n* agricultura *nf*, cultivo *nm*, crianza *nf* **farming of taxes** cesión por el gobierno de la acción recaudatoria a un particular *nf* **farming subsidies** subsidios agrícolas *nmpl*

FAS (free alongside ship) *abbr* franco en muelle *adj, adv*

fast *adj* **fast-selling goods** artículos de venta rápida *nmpl*, mercancías de venta fácil *nfpl*, mercaderías de venta rápida (LAm) *nfpl* **fast track** pista de máxima velocidad *nf*

fault *n* defecto *nm*, culpa *nf*, avería *nf* **minor fault** defecto menor *nm*, fallo de poca importancia *nm* **serious fault** defecto grave *nm*, avería importante *nf* **to find fault with** criticar *vb*, parecerle mal a *vb*

faulty *adj* **faulty goods** artículos defectuosos *nmpl* **faulty workmanship** trabajo defectuoso *nm*

favour *n* favor *nm* **to do sb a favour** hacerle un favor a alguien *vb*

favourable *adj* **favourable balance of payments** balanza de pagos favorable *nf* **favourable balance of trade** balanza comercial favorable *nf* **favourable exchange** cambio favorable *nm* **favourable price** precio favorable *nm* **favourable terms** términos ventajosos *nmpl*

fax **1.** *n* fax *nm*, telefax *nm*, facsímil *nm* **2.** *vb* enviar por fax *vb*

feasibility *n* viabilidad *nf*, posibilidad *nf* **feasibility study** estudio de viabilidad *nm*

feasible *adj* viable *adj*, factible *adj*, posible *adj*

federal *adj* federal *adj*

federation *n* federación *nf*

fee *n* honorarios *nmpl*, comisión *nf* **to charge a fee** cobrar honorarios *vb* **to pay a fee** pagar una cuota *vb*

feedback *n* reacción *nf*, respuesta *nf*, información *nf* **to give feedback** comunicar la reacción *vb*

fiat *n* **fiat money** dinero de curso forzoso *nm*

fictitious *adj* ficticio *adj*, falso *adj* **fictitious assets** activos ficticios *nmpl* **fictitious purchase** compra ficticia *nf* **fictitious sale** venta ficticia *nf*

fidelity *n* fidelidad *nf* **fidelity bond** bono de fidelidad *nm*, obligación de fidelidad *nf* **fidelity insurance** seguro de fidelidad *nm*

fiduciary *adj* **fiduciary bond** fianza fiduciaria *nf*, obligación fiduciaria *nf* **fiduciary issue** emisión fiduciaria *nf*

field *n* **field investigation** investigación de campo *nf*, trabajo de campo *nm* **field manager** director, -ora de campo *nm,f* **field personnel** personal de campo *nm* **field research** investigación de campo *nf*, trabajo de campo *nm*, investigación directa *nf* **field test** prueba sobre el terreno *nf* **field work** estudios sobre el terreno *nm*

FIFO (first in first out) *abbr* primeras entradas, primeras salidas *nfpl* & *nfpl*

file **1.** *n* carpeta *nf*, archivo *nm* **2.** *vb* archivar *vb*, presentar *vb*, entregar *vb*

filing *n* **filing cabinet** archivador *nm*, archivero (LAm) *nm* **filing system** sistema de archivo *nm*

final *adj* **final accounts** cuentas definitivas *nfpl* **final demand** petición final *nf* **final entry** asiento final *nm* **final invoice** última factura *nf* **final offer** última oferta *nf* **final products** productos finales *nmpl*, productos acabados *nmpl* **final settlement** acuerdo final *nm*, ajuste definitivo *nm* **final utility** utilidad final *nf*

finance **1.** *adj* **finance bill** ley presupuestaria *nf* **finance company** sociedad financiera *nf*, compañía de crédito comercial *nf* **Finance Act** Ley Presupuestaria *nf* **2.** *n* finanzas *nfpl* **3.** *vb* financiar *vb*

financial *adj* financiero *adj*, económico *adj* **financial accounting** contabilidad financiera *nf* **financial assets** activos financieros *nmpl* **financial balance** balance financiero *nm* **financial company** entidad financiera *nf* **financial consultancy** asesoría financiera *nf* **financial consultant** asesor, -ora financiero, -era *nm,f* **financial control** control financiero *nm* **financial crisis** crisis económica *nf* **financial difficulty** dificultad financiera *nf* **financial exposure** riesgos financieros *nmpl* **financial incentives** incentivos financieros *nmpl* **financial institution** entidad financiera *nf* **financial investment** inversión financiera *nf* **financial loan** préstamo financiero *nm* **financial management** gestión financiera *nf*, dirección financiera *nf* **financial market** mercado financiero *nm* **financial measures** medidas financieras *nfpl* **financial operation** operación financiera *nf* **financial planning** planificación financiera *nf*

financial policy política financiera *nf*
financial report informe financiero *nm*
financial resources recursos financieros
nmpl **financial risk** riesgo financiero *nm*
financial situation situación financiera *nf*
financial stability estabilidad financiera
nf **financial statement** estado financiero
nm, balance general *nm* **financial stra-**
tegy estrategia financiera *nf* **financial**
structure estructura financiera *nf* **finan-**
cial year año fiscal *nm*, ejercicio
(económico) *nm*
financier *n* financiero, -era *nm,f*
financing *n* financiación *nf* **financing**
surplus excedente de financiación *nm*
fine *adj* **fine rate of interest** buen tipo de
interés *nm*, alta tasa de interés (LAm) *nf*
finished *adj* **finished goods** productos
acabados *nmpl* **finished stock** existencias acabadas *nfpl* **finished turnover**
volumen de ventas acabado *nm*
fire* *vb* despedir *vb*, echar *vb*
firm *adj* **firm offer** oferta en firme *nf* **firm**
price precio en firme *nm*
first *adj* **first bill of exchange** primera letra
de cambio *nf* **first class** primera clase *nf*
first-class paper papel de primera clase
nm, ponencia de primera categoría *nf*
first customer primer, -era cliente, -nta
nm,f **first-hand** de primera mano *prep*,
directamente *adv* **first mortgage** primera
hipoteca *nf* **first-rate** (investment) de
primer orden *prep*
fiscal *adj* **fiscal agent** agente fiscal *nmf*
fiscal balance balance fiscal *nm* **fiscal**
charges costes fiscales *nmpl*, costos
fiscales (LAm) *nmpl* **fiscal measures**
medidas fiscales *nfpl* **fiscal policy** política fiscal *nf* **fiscal receipt** ingreso fiscal
nm **fiscal year** año fiscal *nm*, ejercicio
fiscal *nm* **fiscal year end (fye)** fin de año
fiscal *nm* **fiscal zoning** zonación fiscal *nf*
fix *vb* **to fix the price** fijar el precio *vb*
fixed *adj* **fixed assets** activo fijo *nm*,
inmovilizado *nm* **fixed asset turnover**
facturación de activo fijo *nf* **fixed budget**
presupuesto fijo *nm* **fixed charges** precios fijos *nmpl* **fixed costs** costes fijos
nmpl, costos fijos (LAm) *nmpl* **fixed**
credit crédito fijo *nm* **fixed income**
ingresos fijos *nmpl*, renta fija *nf* **fixed**
interest interés fijo *nm* **fixed liabilities**
deudas a largo plazo *nfpl* **fixed price**
precio fijo *nm*
fixture *n* **fixtures and fittings** instalaciones fijas y accesorios *nfpl & nmpl*

flat *adj* **flat bond** bono sin intereses *nm*
flat market mercado inactivo *nm* **flat**
rate cuota fija *nf*, tasa de interés fija
(LAm) *nf* **flat-rate income tax** impuesto
sobre la renta a cuota fija *nm*, impuesto a
los réditos a cuota fija (LAm) *nm* **flat-rate**
tariff precio a cuota fija *nm*
flexibility *n* (of prices) flexibilidad *nf*
flexible *adj* **flexible budget** presupuesto
flexible *nm* **flexible exchange rate** tipo
de cambio flexible *nm*, tasa de cambio
flexible (LAm) *nf* **flexible price** precio
flexible *nm*
flexitime, flextime (US) *n* horario flexible
nm
flight *n* (in plane) vuelo *nm*, trayectoria *nf*,
fuga *nf* **flight capital** capitales de fuga
nmpl **to book a flight** reservar un vuelo
vb
float *vb* (currency) dejar flotar *vb*
floating *adj* **floating assets** activo
circulante *nm* **floating exchange rate**
tipo de cambio flotante *nm*, tasa de
cambio flotante (LAm) *nf* **floating rate**
interest interés de tipo flotante *nm*,
interés de tasa flotante (LAm) *nf*
floor *n* **floor broker** corredor, -ora de bolsa
nm,f, corredor, -ora de parquet *nm,f*
shopfloor taller *nm*, obreros *nmpl*
flotation *n* salida a bolsa *nf*, emisión *nf*
flow *n* **cash flow** flujo de caja *nm*, "cash
flow" *nm* **flow chart** organigrama *nm*,
diagrama de flujos *nm*, diagrama de
secuencia *nm* **flow line production** fabricación en cadena *nf*, nivel de
producción *nm* **flow of income** flujo de
ingresos *nm* **flow production** fabricación
en cadena *nf*
fluctuate *vb* fluctuar *vb*
fluctuation *n* fluctuación *nf* **fluctuation in**
sales fluctuaciones de ventas *nfpl*
fluid *adj* fluido *adj*, líquido *adj* **fluid**
market mercado fluido *nm*, mercado
inestable *nm*
FOB (free on board) *abbr* fab (franco a
bordo) *abbr*
for *prep* **for sale** en venta *prep*, se vende
vb
forced *adj* **forced currency** divisas
forzosas *nfpl*
forecast 1. *n* previsión *nf*, predicción *nf*
2. *vb* prever *vb*, pronosticar *vb*, predecir
vb
forecasting *n* previsión *nf*
foreclose *vb* entablar juicio hipotecario *vb*

foreclosure n ejecución nf, ejecución de un juicio hipotecario nf
foreign adj extranjero adj, exterior adj, extraño adj **foreign aid** asistencia económica al exterior nf **foreign aid programme** programa de asistencia al exterior nm **foreign bank** banco extranjero nm, banco exterior nm **foreign company** compañía extranjera nf, empresa exterior nf **foreign competition** competencia extranjera nf **foreign currency** divisas nfpl, moneda extranjera nf **foreign exchange** divisas nfpl, moneda extranjera nf, cambio de moneda extranjera nm **foreign exchange dealer** cambista nmf, operador, -ora de cambios nm,f **foreign exchange market** mercado de divisas nm **foreign currency holdings** cartera de valores extranjeros nf **foreign investment** inversión exterior nf **foreign loan** préstamo extranjero nm, crédito extranjero nm **foreign travel** viajes al extranjero nmpl, viajar al exterior nm
foreman n capataz nmf, encargado, -ada nm,f
forestall vb prevenir vb, impedir vb
forestalling adj **forestalling policy** politica de acaparamiento nf, politica de monopolización nf
forfeit 1. n decomiso nm, confiscación nf, multa nf (shares) confiscación de acciones nf **2.** vb perder el derecho a vb
forfeiture n pérdida nf, confiscación nf
forgery n falsificación nf
form n (document) hoja nf, formulario nm, impreso nm, forma (LAm) nf
formal adj formal adj, oficial adj **formal agreement** acuerdo oficial nm **formal contract** contrato en firme nm
formality n **customs formalities** formalidades aduaneras/legales nfpl, trámites aduaneros/legales nmpl **to observe formalities** cumplir formalidades vb
formation n (of company) fundación nf **capital formation** formación de capital nf
forward 1. adj **forward contract** contrato a plazo fijo nm **forward cover** cobertura a plazo nf **forward market** mercado de futuros nm **forward transaction** transacción de futuros nf **2.** vb enviar vb, mandar vb
forwarder n agente de transportes nmf, agente fletero (LAm) nm
forwarding n envío nm, expedición nf, transporte nm, flete de mercancías (LAm) nm **forwarding agency** agencia de

transporte nf, agencia de fletes (LAm) nf **forwarding agent** agente de transporte nmf, agente de transportes nmf, agente de despacho nmf, agente de flete de mercancías (LAm) nmf **forwarding charges** costes de transporte nmpl, costos de flete (LAm) nmpl **forwarding note** nota de envío nf, nota de expedición nf, nota de flete (LAm) nf
found vb fundar vb **to found a company** fundar una empresa vb, montar un negocio vb
founder n fundador, -ora nm,f
fraction n fracción nf, mínima parte nf
fractional adj fraccionario adj, mínimo adj **fractional money** dinero fraccionario nm **fractional shares** reservas mínimas nfpl
franc n **Belgian franc** franco belga nm **French franc** franco francés nm **Swiss franc** franco suizo nm
franchise 1. n franquicia nf, concesión nf, licencia nf **franchise outlet** franquicia nf, tienda bajo licencia nf **2.** vb conceder en franquicia vb
franchisee n concesionario, -ria nm,f, licenciatario, -ria nm,f
franchising n concesión de franquicias nf, franchising nm
franchisor n persona que concede la licencia nf, persona que otorga la concesión nf
franco adj **franco domicile** franco a domicilio adv **franco price** franco de precio adv **franco zone** zona franca nf
frank vb franquear vb
franked adj **franked income** ingresos franqueados nmpl
franking n **franking machine** máquina franqueadora nf
fraud n fraude nm, estafa nf
fraudulent adj fraudulento adj
free adj gratuito adj, libre adj, franco adj, gratis adv **free agent** dueño, -eña de hacer lo que quiera nm,f **free alongside ship (FAS)** franco en el muelle **free competition** libre competencia nf **free delivery** entrega incluida en el precio nf **duty free** libre de impuestos adj, libre de derechos de aduana adj **free economy** economía libre nf **free entry** entrada gratuita nf, entrada libre nf **free goods** productos gratuitos nmpl, mercaderías gratuitas (LAm) nfpl **free market** mercado libre nm **free market economy** economía de mercado nf **free movement of goods** movimiento libre de mercancías

nm, movimiento libre de mercaderías (LAm) *nm* **free of charge** gratuito *adj*, gratis *adv* **free of freight** franco de porte *adj*, *adv* franco de flete (LAm) *adj*, *adv* **free of tax** libre de impuestos *adj*, *adv* **free on board (FOB)** franco a bordo *adj*, *adv* **free on quay** franco en muelle *adj*, *adv* **free port** puerto franco *nm* **free trade** librecambio *nm* **free trade area** puerto franco *nm*, zona franca *nf*

freedom *n* **freedom of choice** libertad de elección *nf*

Freefone (R) (GB) *n* llamadas telefónicas gratuitas *nfpl*

freelance 1. *adj* freelance *nmf*, por cuenta propia *prep* **2.** *n* trabajador, -ora autónomo, -oma *nm,f*, persona que trabaja por libre *nf*

freelancer *n* persona que trabaja por su propia cuenta *nf*, trabajador, -ora autónomo, -oma *nm,f*, persona que trabaja por libre *nf*

Freepost (R) (GB) *n* franqueo pagado *nm*

freeze 1. *n* (on prices, wages) congelación *nf* **2.** *vb* (prices, wages) congelar *vb*

freight *n* carga *nf*, transporte *nm*, flete *nm*, mercaderías (LAm) *nfpl*, flete (LAm) *nm*

freight forwarder agente de transporte *nmf*, agente de transportes *nmf*, fletador (LAm) *nm* **freight traffic** tráfico de mercancías *nm*, tráfico de mercaderías (LAm) *nm*

freighter *n* buque de carga *nm*, avión de carga *nm*, fletador, -ora *nm,f*

frequency *n* frecuencia *nf*

friendly *adj* **Friendly Society** sociedad de ayuda mutua *nf*

fringe *adj* **fringe benefits** incentivos *nmpl*, beneficios extrasalariales *nmpl* **fringe market** mercado marginal *nm*

frontier *n* frontera *nf*

fronting *n* presentación *nf*, dirección *nf*

frozen *adj* **frozen assets** activo congelado *nm* **frozen credits** crédito congelado *nm*

FT Index (Financial Times Index) *n* índice de cotización bursátil del "Financial Times" *nm*

full *adj* **full cost** coste total *nm*, costo total (LAm) *nm* **full liability** plena responsabilidad *nf* **full payment** pago íntegro *nm*, pago total *nm*

full-time *adj & adv* a tiempo completo *prep*, a jornada completa *prep*

function 1. *n* (role) función *nf*, papel *nm*, acto *nm* **2.** *vb* marchar *vb*, funcionar *vb*

functional *adj* **functional analysis** análisis funcional *nm* **functional organization** organización funcional *nf*

fund 1. *n* fondo *nm* **funds flow** movimiento de capital *nm*, flujo de fondos *nm* **funds surplus** superávit de fondos *nm* **2.** *vb* financiar *vb*, destinar fondos *vb*

funded *adj* **funded debt** deuda consolidada *nf*

funding *n* financiación *nf*, asignación de fondos *nf* **funding bonds** bonos de financiación *nmpl*

furlough (US) 1. *n* permiso *nm*, licencia *nf* **2.** *vb* permitir *vb*, conceder una licencia *vb*, conceder un permiso *vb*

future *adj* futuro *nm* **future commodity** futuro *nm* **future delivery** entrega futura *nf* **future goods** géneros futuros *nmpl* **futures contract** contrato de futuros *nm* **futures exchange** cambio de futuros *nm* **futures market** mercado de futuros *nm* **futures marketing** comercialización de futuros *nf* **futures price** precio de futuros *nm* **futures trading** comercio de futuros *nm*

fye (fiscal year end) *abbr* fin de año fiscal *nm*

gain 1. *n* **capital gain** plusvalía *nf* **capital gains tax** impuesto sobre la plusvalía *nm* **gain sharing** reparto de ganancias *nm* **2.** *vb* conseguir *vb*, obtener *vb*, ganar *vb* **gain in value** aumentar de valor *vb*, revalorizarse *vb*

gainful *adj* **gainful employment** empleo remunerado *nm*

galloping *adj* **galloping inflation** inflación galopante *nf*

Gallup poll (R) *n* encuesta Gallup *nf*, sondeo Gallup *nm*

gap *n* **population gap** vacío poblacional *nm*, desequilibrio demográfico *nm* **trade gap** déficit comercial *nm*

gas *n* **natural gas** gas natural *nm*

GATT (General Agreement on Tariffs and Trade) *abbr* GATT (Acuerdo General sobre Aranceles Aduaneros y Comercio) *abbr,nm*

gazump *vb* vender un inmueble a un mejor postor, rompiendo un compromiso *vb*

GDP (Gross Domestic Product) *abbr* PIB (Producto Interior Bruto) *abbr,nm*

general *adj* **general accounting** contabilidad general *nf* **general agencies (US)** agencias generales *nfpl* **general agent**

agente general *nmf* **general average** media general *nf* **general election** elecciones generales *nfpl* **general management** dirección general *nf* **general manager** director, -ora general *nm,f* **general partner** socio, -cia general *nm,f* **general partnership** asociación general *nf* **general strike** huelga general *nf*, paro general (LAm) *nm*

generate *vb* **to generate income** generar ingresos *vb*

generation *n* **income generation** generación de ingresos *nf*

generosity *n* generosidad *nf*

gentleman *n* **gentleman's agreement** acuerdo entre caballeros *nm*

gilt-edged *adj* de la máxima confianza *prep*, de bajo riesgo *prep* **gilt-edged market** mercado de valores de primera clase *nm* **gilt-edged security** valor de primer orden *nm*

gilts *npl* bonos del Tesoro *nmpl*, títulos de la deuda pública *nmpl*

giveaway *n* regalo *nm*, obsequio *nm*

global *adj* global *adj*, mundial *adj* **global economy** economía global *nf* **global market** mercado global *nm*, mercado mundial *nm* **global marketing** márketing global *nm*

globalization *n* globalización *nf*

GMT (Greenwich Mean Time) *abbr* hora de Greenwich *nf*

gnome *n* **the Gnomes of Zurich** "los gnomos de Zurich" *nmpl*, los banqueros suizos *nm*

GNP (Gross National Product) *abbr* PNB (Producto Nacional Bruto) *abbr,nm*

go-slow *n* (strike) huelga de celo *nf*, huelga pasiva *nf*, trabajo a reglamento (LAm) *nm*

going *adj* corriente *adj*, de mercado *prep* **going concern** negocio en marcha *nm*

gold *n* oro *nm* **gold bullion** oro en lingotes *nm* **gold coin** moneda de oro *nf* **gold market** mercado de oro *nm* **gold reserves** reservas de oro *nfpl* **gold standard** patrón-oro *nm*

golden *adj* dorado *adj*, de oro *adj* **golden handcuffs** prima de permanencia *nf* **golden handshake** gratificación por fin de servicio *nf*, indemnización por despido *nf* **golden hello** prima de enganche *nf* **golden parachute** gratificación por fin de servicio *nf*, indemnización por despido *nf*

goods *npl* mercancías *nfpl*, productos *nmpl*, bienes *nmpl*, mercaderías (LAm)

nfpl **bulk goods** mercancías a granel *nfpl*, artículos de producción en serie *nmpl*, mercaderías a granel (LAm) *nfpl* **domestic goods** enseres domésticos *nmpl* **export goods** mercancías de exportación *nfpl*, mercaderías de exportación (LAm) *nfpl* **import goods** artículos de importación *nmpl*, mercaderías de importación (LAm) *nfpl* **goods on approval** mercancías a prueba *nfpl*, productos a prueba *nmpl*, mercaderías a prueba (LAm) *nfpl* **goods in process** mercancías en curso *nfpl*, mercaderías en curso (LAm) *nfpl* **goods in progress** productos en construcción *nmpl*, mercancías en curso *nfpl*, mercaderías en curso (LAm) *nfpl* **goods on consignment** artículos consignados *nmpl*, mercaderías en consignación (LAm) *nfpl* **goods transport** transporte de géneros *nm*, transporte de mercaderías (LAm) *nm*

goodwill *n* fondo de comercio *nm*, clientela *nf*, crédito *nm*, llave (LAm) *nf*

govern *vb* gobernar *vb*, determinar *vb*, dominar *vb*

government *n* gobierno *nm*, administración *nf*, estado *nm* **government body** organismo gubernamental *nm*, organización estatal *nf* **government bond** obligación del Estado *nf*, acción del Tesoro *nf* **government enterprise** empresa pública *nf*, empresa estatal *nf*, iniciativa del gobierno *nf* **government loan** préstamo estatal *nm* **government policy** política del gobierno *nf* **government sector** sector público *nm* **government security** título del Estado *nm* **government subsidy** subsidio estatal *nm*

graduate 1. *n* (of university) licenciado, -ada *nm,f*, egresado, -ada (LAm) *nm,f* 2. *vb* escalonar *vb*, graduar *vb*

grant 1. *n* (of a patent) concesión *nf* **regional grant** subvención regional *nf* 2. *vb* conceder *vb*, otorgar *vb*

graphics *npl* **computer graphics** gráficos (de ordenador) *nmpl*

gratuity *n* propina *nf*, gratificación *nf*

green *adj* **green card** carta verde *nf*, permiso de residencia y trabajo (LAm) *nm* **green currency** moneda verde *nf* **green pound** libra verde *nf*

Greenwich *n* **Greenwich Mean Time (GMT)** hora de Greenwich *nf*

grievance *n* queja *nf*, motivo de queja *nm*

gross *adj* bruto *adj* **gross amount** suma bruta *nf* **gross domestic product (GDP)**

producto interior bruto (PIB) *nm* **gross interest** interés bruto *nm* **gross investment** inversión bruta *nf* **gross loss** pérdida bruta *nf* **gross margin** margen bruto *nm* **gross national product (GNP)** producto nacional bruto (PNB) *nm* **gross negligence** culpa grave *nf* **gross output** producción bruta *nf* **gross sales** ventas brutas *nfpl* **gross weight** peso bruto *nm* **group** *n* **group insurance** seguro colectivo *nm* **group of countries** grupo de países *nm* **group travel** viajar en grupo *vb*

growth *n* crecimiento *nm*, desarrollo *nm*, expansión *nf* **annual growth rate** tasa de crecimiento anual *nf* **economic growth** crecimiento económico *nm*, desarrollo económico *nm* **export-led growth** crecimiento regido por las exportaciones *nm* **market growth** expansión del mercado *nf* **growth rate** tasa de crecimiento *nf* **sales growth** aumento de ventas *nm* **growth strategy** estrategia de desarrollo *nf*, estrategia de crecimiento *nf*

guarantee *n* garantía *nf*, prenda *nf* **quality guarantee** garantía de calidad *nf*

guarantor *n* garante *nmf*, garantía (LAm) *nmf*

guest *n* **guest worker** trabajador, -ora extranjero, -era temporal *nm,f*, obrero, -era *nm,f*

guild *n* gremio *nm*, corporación *nf*

guilder *n* florín *nm*

h *abbr* (hour) h. *abbr*

half *n* mitad *nf*, parte *nf* **half-an-hour** media hora *nf* **half-board** media pensión *nf* **half-pay** medio sueldo *nm* **half-price** mitad de precio *nf* **to reduce sth by half** rebajar algo a mitad de precio *vb* **half-year** semestre *nm*

hall *n* sala *nf* **exhibition hall** salón de exposiciones *nm*, sala de exposiciones *nf*

hallmark *n* contraste *nm*, marca de contraste *nf*

halt *vb* (inflation) parar *vb*, frenar *vb*

halve *vb* reducir a la mitad *vb*, partir por la mitad *vb*

hand *n* **in hand** entre manos *prep*, en reserva *prep* **to hand** a mano *prep*

hand over *vb* entregar *vb*, transferir *vb*, pasar *vb*

handbook *n* manual *nm*, guía *nf*

handle *vb* (deal) encargarse de *vb*, manejar *vb* (money) manejar dinero *vb*, (staff, people) tratar al personal *vb* **handle with care** tratar con cuidado *vb*

handling *n* **handling charges** gastos de

tramitación *nmpl*, costos de manipulación (LAm) *nmpl* **data handling** manejo de datos *nm*, proceso de datos *nm*

handmade *adj* hecho a mano *adj*

handshake *n* apretón de manos *nm*

handwritten *adj* escrito a mano *adj*

handy *adj* a mano *prep*, práctico *adj*

hang on *vb* (wait) esperar *vb* (on phone) esperar *vb*, no colgar *vb*

hang together *vb* (argument) tener coherencia *vb*

hang up *vb* (telephone) colgar *vb*, cortar (LAm) *vb*

harbour *n* puerto *nm* **harbour authorities** dirección portuaria *nf* **harbour dues** derechos portuarios *nmpl*, derechos de dársena *nmpl* **harbour facilities** instalaciones portuarias *nfpl* **harbour fees** derechos portuarios *nmpl*

hard *adj* **hard bargain** negocio difícil *nm* **hard cash** dinero en metálico *nm*, efectivo *nm* **hard currency** divisas fuertes *nfpl*, moneda convertible *nf* **hard disk** disco duro *nm* **hard-earned** bien merecido *adj* **hard-hit** muy afectado *adj* **hard-line** de línea dura *prep* **hard loan** crédito en condiciones desventajosas *nm*, préstamo exterior pagadero en moneda fuerte *nm* **hard news/information** información concreta *nf* **hard price** precio fijo *nm* **hard sell** venta agresiva *nf* **the hard facts** los hechos puros y duros *nmpl* **hard-working** trabajador *adj*, muy trabajador *adj*

hardware *n* **computer hardware** "hardware" *nm*, equipo *nm*, soporte físico del ordenador *nm*

haul *n* **long-haul** de largo recorrido *prep*, a largo plazo *prep* **short-haul** de corto recorrido *prep*, a corto plazo *prep*

haulage, freight (US) *n* **road haulage** transporte por carretera *nm* **haulage company** compañía de transportes *nf*, empresa de transporte por carretera *nf*

haulier *n* transportista *nmf*, contratista de transporte por carretera *nmf*

hazard *n* peligro *nm*, riesgo *nm*, obstáculo *nm* **natural hazard** riesgo natural *nm*, peligro inevitable *nm* **occupational hazard** riesgo ocupacional *nm*

hazardous *adj* peligroso *adj*

head 1. *adj* **head accountant** director, -ora de contabilidad *nm,f* **head office** oficina central *nf*, sede central *nf*, casa matriz *nf* 2. *n* **at the head of** a la cabeza de *prep* **head of department** jefe, -efa de departamento *nm,f* **head of government** jefe, -efa de gobierno *nm,f* **per head** per cápita *prep*, por persona *prep* **to be head of** encabezar *vb* **3.** *vb* (department) dirigir *vb*, estar a la cabeza de *vb*

head for *vb* ir camino de *vb*, dirigirse a *vb* **headed** *adj* **headed notepaper** papel con membrete *nm*

heading *n* encabezamiento *nm*, título *nm*, acápite (LAm) *nm*

headquarters *n* sede *nf*, oficina central *nf*, domicilio social *nm*

headway *n* **to make headway** hacer progresos *vb*

health *n* salud *nf*, sanidad *nf* **health benefits** compensaciones por enfermedad *nfpl* **health care industry** industria de asistencia médica *nf* **health hazard** peligro para la salud *nm* **industrial health** salud industrial *nf*, prosperidad industrial *nf* **health insurance** seguro de enfermedad *nm* **Ministry of Health** Ministerio de Salud *nm*

healthy *adj* (finances) próspero *adj*, sustancial *adj*

heavy *adj* **heavy-duty** para uso industrial **heavy goods vehicle** vehículo de gran tonelaje *nm* **heavy industry** industria pesada *nf* **heavy trading** mucho movimiento (en la bolsa) *nm* **heavy user** usuario, -ria frecuente *nm,f*

hedge *n* **hedge against inflation** barrera contra la inflación *nf* **hedge clause (US)** cláusula de protección *nf*

hidden *adj* **hidden assets** bienes ocultos *nmpl* **hidden defect** defecto oculto *nm*

hierarchy *n* (corporate) jerarquía *nf* **data hierarchy** jerarquía de datos *nf* **hierarchy of needs** jerarquía de necesidades *nf*

high *adj* **high-class** de alta clase *prep*, de alto standing *prep* **high finance** las altas finanzas *nfpl* **high-grade** de alto grado *prep*, de calidad superior *prep* **high-income** de altos ingresos *prep* **high-level** de alto nivel *prep* **high-powered** dinámico *adj*, muy potente *adj* **high-priced** de precio alto *adj* **high-ranking** de alto rango *prep* **high-risk** de alto riesgo *prep*, riesgoso (LAm) *adj* **high season** temporada alta *nf* **high-tech*** de alta tecnología, high tech* *prep*

higher *adj* **higher bid** oferta superior *nf*

hire 1. *adj* **hire charges** alquiler *nm*, arriendo (LAm) *nm* **hire contract** contrato de alquiler *nm*, contrato de arriendo

(LAm) *nm* **hire purchase** compra a plazos *nf* **2.** *n* alquiler *nm*, arriendo (LAm) *nm* **for hire** se alquila *vb*, se arrienda (LAm) *vb*, se renta (LAm) *vb* **3.** *vb* (person) contratar *vb*, alquilar *vb*, arrendar (LAm) *vb*, rentar (LAm) *vb*

history *n* **employment/work history** historial de empleo *nm*, historia profesional (LAm) *nf*

hit *vb* **hit-or-miss** una lotería *nf*, a la buena de Dios *prep*, a la sanfasón (LAm) *prep* **to hit the market** lanzarse al mercado *vb* **to be hard hit by** ser gravemente afectado por *vb* **to hit the headlines** ser noticia *vb*

HO (head office) *abbr* sede *nf*, oficina central *nf*, domicilio social *nm*

hoard *vb* acumular *vb*, esconder *vb*

hold 1. *adj* **hold area** área de la bodega *nf* **hold queue, hold line** (US) lista de espera *nf*, cola de comunicantes *nf* **2.** *n* **on hold** (on phone) esperando para hablar *vb*, sin colgar *prep* **3.** *vb* **to hold a meeting** celebrar una reunión *vb* **to hold sth as security** retener algo como garantía *vb* **to hold sb liable, responsible** hacer responsable a alguien *vb*, responsabilizar a alguien *vb*

hold back *vb* (not release) retrasar *vb*, contener *vb*, postergar (LAm) *vb*

hold on *vb* (on phone) esperar *vb*, no cortar (LAm) *vb*

hold over *vb* (to next period) aplazar *vb*, postergar (LAm) *vb*

hold up *vb* (delay) retrasar *vb*, detener *vb*, (criminal act) atracar *vb* (withstand scrutiny) resultar válido *vb*

holder *n* titular *nmf*, portador, -ora *nm,f*, tenedor, -ora *nm,f* **joint holder** cotitular *nmf* **licence holder** titular de un permiso *nmf*, titular de una licencia *nmf* **office holder** titular del cargo *nmf* **policy holder** titular de una póliza de seguros *nmf*

holding 1. *adj* **holding company** holding *nm*, sociedad de cartera *nf*, sociedad tenedora *nf* **2.** *n* participación *nf*, cartera de valores *nf*, propiedad *nf* **foreign exchange holdings** cartera de valores en divisas *nf* **majority/minority holding** participación mayoritaria/minoritaria *nf* **to have holdings** poseer valores en cartera *vb*, tener propiedades *vb*

holdup *n* demora *nf*, atraco *nm*

holiday, vacation (US) *n* fiesta *nf* **bank holiday (GB)** fiesta nacional *nf*, día festivo *nm*, día feriado (LAm) *nm*, fiesta patria (LAm) *nf* **on holiday** de vacaciones *prep*,

tomando la licencia (LAm) *vb* **holiday pay** paga de vacaciones *nf*, sueldo gozado durante la licencia (LAm) *nm* **tax holiday** exención fiscal concedida a una nueva empresa *nf*
home *n* domicilio *nm*, hogar *nm* **home address** dirección particular *nf*, domicilio particular *nm* **home buyer** comprador, -ora de vivienda *nm,f* **home country** país de origen *nm* **home delivery** entrega a domicilio *nf* **home industry** industria nacional *nf* **home loan** préstamo de ahorro-vivienda *nm* **home market** mercado nacional *nm*, mercado interior *nm* **home owner** propietario, -ria de una vivienda *nm,f* **home sales** ventas en el mercado interior *nfpl* **home service** servicio a domicilio *nm* **home shopping** compras hechas sin salir del hogar *nfpl*
honorary *adj* de honor *prep*
horizontal *adj* **horizontal analysis** análisis horizontal *nm* **horizontal integration** fusión horizontal *nf*
host *n* anfitrión, -ona *nm,f* **host country** país anfitrión *nm*
hot *adj* **hot line** línea directa *nf* **hot money** dinero caliente *nm*, dinero especulativo *nm* **hot seat** línea de fuego *nf* **to be in hot demand** haber mucha demanda *vb*
hotel *n* hotel *nm* **hotel accommodation** alojamiento hotelero *nm* **hotel chain** cadena hotelera *nf* **five-star hotel** hotel de cinco estrellas *nm* **hotel industry/ trade** industria hotelera *nf*, hostelería *nf* **hotel management** dirección hotelera *nf* **to run a hotel** dirigir un hotel *vb*
hour *n* hora *nf* **after hours** fuera del horario de trabajo *prep* **business hours** horas de oficina *nfpl*, horas de trabajo *nfpl*, horario de oficina *nm* **busy hours** (US) horas punta *nfpl*, horas pico (LAm) *nfpl* **fixed hours** horario fijo *nm* **office hours** horario de oficina *nm*, horas de oficina *nfpl* **per hour** por hora, a la hora *prep* **per hour output** rendimiento por hora *nm*
hourly *adj* por hora *prep* **hourly-paid work** trabajo pagado por horas *nm* **hourly rate** tarifa horaria *nf* **hourly workers** trabajadores, - oras por horas *nm,fpl*
house *n* **clearing house** cámara de compensación *nf* **house duty (US)** impuesto sobre la propiedad residencial *nm* **house journal/magazine** revista interno

de la casa *nf* **mail-order house** compañía de venta por correo *nf* **packing house (US)** empresa envasadora *nf* **house prices** el precio de la vivienda *nm* **publishing house** editorial *nf* **house sale** venta inmobiliaria *nf* **house telephone** teléfono interno *nm*
household *n* casa *nf*, hogar *nm*, unidad familiar *nf* **household expenditure** gastos del hogar *nmpl* **household goods** enseres domésticos *nmpl* **household survey** encuesta familiar *nf*
householder *n* dueño, -eña de casa *nm,f*
housewares (US) *npl* utensilios domésticos *nmpl*
housing *n* **housing estate, tenement** (US) urbanización *nf*, complejo habitacional *nm*, colonia (LAm) *nf* **housing industry** industria de construcción de viviendas *nf* **housing project** complejo de viviendas subvencionadas *nm* **housing scheme** proyecto relativo a la vivienda *nm*
hull *n* casco *nm* **hull insurance** seguro de casco de buque *nm*, seguro marítimo *nm*
human *adj* **human relations** relaciones humanas *nfpl* **human resources** recursos humanos *nmpl* **human resource management (HRM)** gestión de recursos humanos (GRH) *nf*
hundred *n* cien *nm* **one hundred per cent** cien por cien *nm*
hydroelectricity *n* hidroelectricidad *nf*
hype *n* bombo *nm*
hyperinflation *n* hiperinflación *nf*
hypermarket *n* hipermercado *nm*
hypothesis *n* hipótesis *nf*
idle *adj* inactivo *adj*, desocupado *adj*, vago *adj* **idle capacity** capacidad no utilizada *nf*
illegal *adj* ilegal *adj*
implication *n* implicación *nf* **this will have implications for our sales** esto nos va afectar las ventas, esto tendrá implicancias para nuestras ventas (LAm)
import 1. *adj* **import agent** agente de importación *nmf* **import barrier** barrera a la importación *nf* **import control** control de importaciones *nm* **import department** departamento de importación *nm* **import duty** derecho de importación *nm* **import licence** permiso de importación *nm* **import office** oficina de importación *nf* **import quota** cuota de importación *nf*, cupo de importación *nm* **import restrictions** restricciones a la importación *nfpl* **import surplus** excedente de

importaciones *nm* **2.** *n* importación *nf* **3.** *vb* importar *vb*
importation *n* importación *nf*
importer *n* importador, -ora *nm,f*
importing *adj* **importing country** país importador *nm*
impose *vb* **to impose a tax** gravar con un impuesto *vb* **to impose restrictions** poner restricciones *vb*
imposition *n* (of tax) imposición *nf*
impound *vb* confiscar *vb*, embargar *vb*
imprint *n* **to take an imprint** (credit card) hacer impresión *vb*
improve *vb* mejorar *vb*, aumentar *vb* perfeccionarse *vb*, superarse *vb* **we must improve our performance** hay que mejorar nuestro rendimiento
inadequate *adj* inadecuado *adj*, insuficiente *adj*, incompetente *adj*
incentive *n* incentivo *nm*, aliciente *nm*
incidental *adj* **incidental expenses** gastos menores *nmpl*
include *vb* **our price includes delivery** nuestro precio incluye la entrega *n* **taxes are included** van incluidos los impuestos *vb*
inclusive *adj* **inclusive of tax and delivery costs** incluidos impuestos y gastos de entrega *adj* **the prices quoted are inclusive** los precios citados incluyen *n*
income *n* ingresos *nmpl*, renta *nf* **gross income** ingresos brutos *nmpl* **net(t) income** ingresos netos *nmpl*, renta neta *nf* **private income** renta privada *nf* **income tax** impuesto sobre la renta *nm*, impuesto a los réditos (LAm) *nm*
inconvenience *n* inconveniente *nm*, molestias *nfpl*
inconvenient *adj* inconveniente *adj*, inoportuno *adj*
increase **1.** *n* aumento *nm*, auge *nm*, incremento *nm* **increase in the cost of living** aumento del coste de vida *nm*, aumento del costo de vida (LAm) *nm* **price increase** subida de precio *nf* **wage increase** aumento de sueldo *nm* **2.** *vb* (prices, taxes) subir *vb*, incrementar *vb*
incur *vb* (expenses) incurrir en *vb*
indebted *adj* endeudado *adj*
indemnify *vb* indemnizar *vb*, asegurar *vb*
indemnity *n* indemnidad *nf* **indemnity insurance** seguro de indemnización *nm*
index *n* índice *nm*, lista *nf*, señal *nf* **cost of living index** índice del coste de la vida *nm*, índice del costo de la vida (LAm) *nm* **growth index** índice de crecimiento *nm*

price index índice de precios *nm* **share index** índice de acciones *nm*
indicate *vb* indicar *vb*, señalar *vb*
indication *n* indicio *nm*, pauta *nf*, señal *nf*
indirect *adj* indirecto *adj* **indirect cost** coste indirecto *nm*, gasto indirecto *nm*, costo indirecto (LAm) *nm* **indirect expenses** gastos indirectos *nmpl* **indirect tax** impuesto indirecto *nm*
industrial *adj* industrial *adj* **industrial accident** accidente laboral *nm* **industrial arbitration** arbitraje laboral *nm* **industrial democracy** democracia industrial *nf* **industrial dispute** conflicto laboral *nm*, conflicto colectivo *nm* **industrial expansion** expansión industrial *nf* **industrial region** zona industrial *nf* **industrial relations** relaciones industriales *nfpl* **industrial tribunal** tribunal industrial *nm* **industrial union** sindicato industrial *nm*
industry *n* industria *nf*
inefficient *adj* ineficiente *adj*, incompetente *adj*
inferior *adj* (goods) inferior *adj*
inflation *n* inflación *nf* **rate of inflation** tasa de inflación *nf*
inflationary *adj* inflacionario *adj*, inflacionista (LAm) *adj* **inflationary gap** vacío inflacionario *nm* **inflationary spiral** espiral inflacionista *nm*
inform *vb* informar *vb*, notificar *vb*, comunicar *vb*
information *n* información *nf*, datos *nmpl* **information desk** información *nf*, oficina de información *nf* **information management** dirección de información *nf* **information office** oficina de información *nf* **information processing** proceso de datos *nm* **information retrieval** recuperación de datos *nf* **information storage** almacenaje de datos *nm* **information systems** sistemas de información *nmpl* **information technology (IT)** informática *nf*
infrastructure *n* infraestructura *nf*
inherit *vb* heredar *vb*
inheritance *n* herencia *nf*, legado *nm*, sucesión *nf* **inheritance laws** leyes sobre la herencia *nfpl*
inhouse *adj* **inhouse training** *n* formación en el puesto de trabajo *nf*
injunction *n* mandamiento judicial *nm*, requerimiento judicial *nm*, orden *nf* **to take out an injunction** solicitar un mandamiento judicial *vb*
inland *adj* interior *adj*, nacional *adj* **the Inland Revenue, The Internal Revenue**

Service (IRS) (US) Hacienda *nf*, fisco *nm*, Dirección General Impositiva (LAm) *nf*, Impuestos Internos (LAm) *nmpl*
insider *n* iniciado, -ada *nm,f* **insider dealing, insider trading** (US) trato con información privilegiada *nm*
insist on *vb* insistir en *vb*, exigir *vb*
insolvency *n* insolvencia *nf*
insolvent *adj* insolvente *adj*
inspect *vb* inspeccionar *vb*, examinar *vb*, revisar *vb*
inspection *n* (customs) control *nm*, revisión *nf*
inspector *n* inspector, -ora *nm,f*, interventor, -ora *nm,f* **customs inspector** aduanero, -era *nm,f*
instability *n* inestabilidad *nf*
instal(l) *vb* instalar *vb*
installation *n* instalación *nf*, investidura *nf*
instalment, installment (US) *n* plazo *nm*, cuota (LAm) *nf*
institute *n* instituto *nm*
institution *n* institución *nf*, entidad *nf*, establecimiento *nm* **credit institution** institución crediticia *nf*
instruction *n* instrucción *nf*, orden *nf*, formación *nf* **instruction book** libro de instrucciones *nm* **instruction sheet** hoja de instrucciones *nf* **to follow instructions** seguir instrucciones *vb*
insurable *adj* **insurable risk** riesgo asegurable *nm*
insurance *n* seguro *nm*, seguros *nmpl* **insurance agent** agente de seguros *nmf*, corredor, -ora de seguros *nm,f* **insurance broker** agente de seguros *nmf*, corredor, -ora de seguros *nm,f* **car insurance** seguro de automóviles *nm* **insurance certificate** certificado de seguros *nm*, póliza de seguros *nf* **insurance company** compañía de seguros *nf*, aseguradora *nf* **comprehensive insurance** seguro a todo riesgo *nm* **insurance contract** contrato de seguros *nm* **fire insurance** seguro contra incendios *nm* **insurance fund** fondo de seguros *nm* **National Insurance (GB)** Seguridad Social *nf* **insurance policy** póliza de seguros *nf* **insurance premium** prima de seguros *nf*, cuota de seguros (LAm) *nf* **insurance representative** agente de seguros *nmf*, asesor, -ora de seguros *nm,f* **insurance salesperson** vendedor, -ora de seguros *nm,f* **third party insurance** seguro contra terceros *nm* **to take out insurance** hacerse un seguro *vb* **insurance underwriter** suscriptor, -ora *nm,f* **unemployment insurance** seguro de desempleo *nm*
insure *vb* asegurar *vb*
intangible *adj* **intangible asset** activo intangible *nm*
intensive *adj* intensivo *adj* **capital-intensive** intensivo en capital *adj* **labour-intensive** con alta utilización de mano de obra, con alto coeficiente de mano de obra *prep*
interest *n* interés *nm*, intereses *nmpl*, participación *nf* **interest-bearing** con interés *prep*, que produce intereses *rel pron* **interest-free** sin interés *prep*, sin intereses *prep*, a bajo interés *prep* **interest period** período de vigencia del tipo de interés *nm*, período de vigencia de la tasa de interés (LAm) *nm* **interest rate** tipo de interés *nm*, tasa de interés (LAm) *nf* **to bear interest** devengar interés *vb*, dar interés *vb*, rendir interés *vb* **to charge interest** cobrar interés *vb*, cargar en concepto de interés *vb* **to pay interest** pagar interés *vb*, abonar interés *vb*
interface *n* interface *nm*, punto de contacto *nm*, interrelación *nf*
interim *adj* provisional *adj*, interino *adj*, intermedio *adj*, provisorio (LAm) *adj*
intermediary *adj* intermediario *adj*, intermedio *adj*
internal *adj* **internal audit** auditoría interna *nf* **internal auditor** censor, -ora de cuentas interior *nm,f* **the Internal Revenue Service (IRS) (US)** Hacienda *nf*, Hacienda Pública *nf*, el fisco *nm*, Dirección General Impositiva (LAm) *nf*, Impuestos Internos (LAm) *nmpl*
international *adj* internacional *adj* **international agreement** convenio internacional *nm* **international competition** competencia internacional *nf* **International Date Line** línea (de cambio) de fecha *nf* **international organization** organización internacional *nf* **international trade** comercio internacional *nm*
intervene *vb* intervenir *vb*, participar *vb*
intervention *n* intervención *nf*, intercesión *nf* **state intervention** intervención estatal *nf*, intervención del estado *nf*
interview 1. *n* entrevista *nf* **to attend for interview** asistir a una entrevista *vb* **to hold an interview** entrevistar *vb* **to invite sb to interview** llamar a alguien para la entrevista *vb* 2. *vb* entrevistar *vb*

introduce *vb* (product) introducir *vb*, lanzar *vb*, sacar *vb*, (person) presentar *vb*
inventory *n* inventario *nm* **inventory control** control de inventario *nm*, control público de existencias *nm*
invest *vb* (money) invertir *vb*
investment *n* inversión *nf*, inversiones *nfpl*, investidura *nf* **investment adviser** asesor, -ora de inversiones *nm,f* **investment portfolio** cartera de valores *nf* **investment programme, investment program** (US) plan de inversiones *nm* **investment strategy** estrategia de inversion *nf*
investor *n* inversionista *nmf*, inversor, -ora *nm,f*
invisible *adj* invisible *adj* **invisible exports** exportaciones invisibles *nfpl* **invisible imports** importaciones invisibles *nfpl*
invitation *n* invitación *nf*
invite *vb* invitar *vb*, llamar a *vb*, convidar *vb*
invoice *n* factura *nf* **duplicate invoice** copia de la factura *nf* **to issue an invoice** emitir una factura *vb* **to settle an invoice** pagar una factura *vb*, liquidar una factura *vb*
invoicing *n* facturación *nf*
irrecoverable *adj* (loss) irrecuperable *adj*
irrevocable *adj* irrevocable *adj* **irrevocable letter of credit** carta de crédito irrevocable *nf*
issue 1. *n* **bank of issue** banco emisor *nm* **share issue, stock issue** (US) emisión de nuevas acciones *nf* **2.** *vb* (cheques, shares, notes) emitir *vb*, extender *vb*, (policy) publicar *vb*, (tickets) expedir *vb* **to issue sb with sth** proporcionar algo a alguien *vb*
issuing *adj* **issuing bank** banco emisor *nm*
item *n* artículo *nm*, punto *nm*
itemize *vb* detallar *vb*, desglosar *vb*
itemized *adj* **itemized account** cuenta desglosada *nf*
itinerary *n* itinerario *nm*
jackpot *n* gordo *nm*
jingle *n* tonadilla *nf* **advertising jingle** jingle publicitario *nm*, tonadilla de un anuncio *nf*
job *n* **job analysis** evaluación de puestos de trabajo *nf* **job creation** creación de empleo *nf* **job description** descripción del puesto de trabajo *nf* **job offer** oferta de trabajo *nf* **job rotation** trabajo por turnos *nm* **job satisfaction** satisfacción laboral *nf*, satisfacción por el trabajo *nf*

job shop oficina de empleo *nf*, agencia de colocaciones *nf*, bolsa de empleo *nf*
jobber *n* trabajador, -ora eventual *nm,f*, intermediario, -ria *nm,f*, agente de bolsa *nmf*
Jobcentre (GB) *n* oficina de empleo *nf*, bolsa de empleo *nf*, agencia de colocaciones *nf*
jobless *adj* desempleado *adj*, sin trabajo *prep*, en paro *prep*, cesante (LAm) *adj* **the jobless** los desempleados *nmpl*, los desocupados *nmpl*, los cesantes (LAm) *nmpl*
joint *adj* conjunto *adj* **joint account** cuenta en participación *nf* **joint obligation** obligación conjunta *nf* **joint ownership** copropiedad *nf* **joint responsibility** responsabilidad conjunta/colectiva *nf*, responsabilidad en común *nf* **joint-stock company** sociedad anónima *nf* **joint venture** empresa conjunta *nf*, negocio en participación *nm*, agrupación temporal de empresas *nf*
jointly *adv* en común *prep*
journal *n* revista *nf*, boletín *nm*
journalism *n* periodismo *nm*
judicial *adj* judicial *adj*
junior *adj* auxiliar *adj*, menor *adj*
junk *n* **junk bond** obligación desvalorizada *nf*
jurisdiction *n* jurisdicción *nf*, competencia *nf*
juror *n* miembro de un jurado *nm*
jury *n* jurado *nm*
K *abbr* (1000) K *abbr*, mil libras esterlinas *nf*, kilobyte *nm*
keen *adj* (competition) afilado *adj*, fuerte *adj*, (price) competitivo *adj*, adecuado *adj*, chévere (LAm) *adj*
keep *vb* (goods) guardarse *vb*, guardar *vb* **to keep an appointment** acudir a una cita *vb* **to keep the books** llevar la contabilidad *vb* **to keep the business running** asegurar la marcha de la empresa *nf*
keep back *vb* (money) quedarse con dinero *vb*, guardarse dinero *vb*
keep down *vb* (prices) mantener bajos los precios *vb*
keep up *vb* (with events) no perder el hilo de los sucesos *vb*, estar al día *vb*
key *adj* **key currency** moneda clave *nf* **key industry** industria clave *nf* **key person** persona clave *nf* **key question** cuestión principal *nf*, pregunta clave *nf*
key in *vb* teclear *vb*, pasar a máquina *vb*

keyboard *n* teclado *nm*
keynote *adj* **keynote speech** discurso en el que se intenta establecer la tónica de... *nm*
keyword *n* (computer) palabra clave *nf*
kg *abbr* Kg *nm*, kilo *nm*, kilogramo *nm*
kill *vb* **to kill a project** acabar con un proyecto *vb*, poner fin prematuro a un proyecto *vb*
kilowatt *n* kilovatio *nm*
kind 1. *adj* amable *adj* **would you be so kind as to...** ¿tendría la amabilidad de...? **2.** *n* clase *nf*, tipo *nm*
king-size(d) *adj* extragrande *adj*, descomunal *adj*
kiosk *n* (phone) cabina (de teléfonos) *nf*
kit *n* (equipment) equipo *nm*
kite *n* **kite mark (GB)** marca de calidad *nf*
km, kilometer (US) *abbr* Km. *abbr*, kilómetro *nm*
knock *vb* (disparage) criticar *vb*, hablar mal de *vb*
knock down *vb* (price) rebajar *vb*, recortar *vb*, reducir *vb*, rematar (LAm) *vb*
knock off* *vb* (finish work) salir del trabajo *vb*
knock-for-knock *adj* **knock-for-knock agreement** acuerdo de pago respectivo *nm*
knock-on *adj* **knock-on effect** repercusiones *nfpl*, efecto secundario *nm*, reacción en cadena *nf*
knockdown *adj* **knockdown price** precio mínimo *nm*, precio de ganga *nm*, precio rematado (LAm) *nm*
know-how *n* conocimientos y experiencia *nmpl & nf*, pericia *nf*, "know-how" *nm*
knowledge *n* conocimiento *nm*, conocimientos *nmpl*, saber *nm* **knowledge base** base de conocimientos *nf* **it is common knowledge** se sabe muy bien *vb*, es bien sabido *vb* **to have a thorough knowledge of sth** conocer algo a fondo *vb* **to have a working knowledge of sth** defenderse bastante bien en algo *vb* dominar los principios básicos de algo *vb* **to my knowledge** que yo sepa *rel pron*
knowledgeable *adj* informado *adj*, culto *adj*
known *adj* sabido *adj* **known facts** hechos ciertos *nmpl*
krona *n* (Swedish) corona sueca *nf*
krone *n* (Danish, Norwegian) corona danesa *nf*, corona noruega *nf*
kudos *n* prestigio *nm*
kW *abbr* kW *abbr*, kilovatio *nm*

kWh *abbr* kwh *abbr*, kilovatio-hora *nm*
label 1. *n* etiqueta *nf* **2.** *vb* etiquetar *vb*, calificar *vb*
labour, labor (US) *n* trabajo *nm*, labor *nf*, mano de obra *nf*, esfuerzos *nmpl* **labour costs** costes de la mano de obra *nmpl*, costos de la mano de obra (LAm) *nfpl* **labour dispute** conflicto laboral *nm* **labour-intensive** con un alto coeficiente de mano de obra *prep*, que requiere mucha mano de obra *rel pron* **labour law** derecho laboral *nm* **labour market** mercado de trabajo *nm* **labour relations** relaciones laborales *nfpl*
labourer *n* trabajador, -ora *nm,f*, obrero, -era *nm,f*, peón (LAm) *nmf*
lack *n* falta *nf*, carencia *nf*, escasez *nf* **lack of investment** falta de inversión *nf*
land *n* **land purchase** compra de tierras *nf* **land reform** reforma agraria *nf* **land register** registro catastral *nm* **land tax** impuesto territorial *nm*, contribución territorial rústica *nf* **land tribunal** tribunal agrario *nm*
landlord *n* arrendador, -ora *nm,f*, propietario, -ria *nm,f*, hacendado, -ada (LAm) *nm,f*
landowner *n* terrateniente *nmf*, latifundista *nmf*
language *n* lenguaje *nm*, lengua *nf*, idioma *nm* **language specialist** especialista en idiomas *nmf*
large *adj* grande *adj* **large-scale** a gran escala *prep*
launch 1. *n* **product launch** lanzamiento de un producto *nm* **2.** *vb* (product) lanzar *vb*, introducir *vb*
law *n* derecho *nm*, ley *nf*, leyes *nfpl* **business law** derecho mercantil *nm* **civil law** derecho civil *nm* **criminal law** derecho penal *nm* **international law** derecho internacional *nm* **law of diminishing returns** ley de rendimientos decrecientes *nf* **public law** derecho público *nm*
lawsuit *n* juicio *nm*, pleito *nm*, proceso *nm*
lay off *vb* (workers) despedir temporalmente *vb*
LBO (leveraged buy-out) *abbr* LBO (compra apalancada de empresas *nf*, adquisición apalancada de empresas *nf*
leader *n* **market leader** empresa líder del mercado *nf*, artículo de mayor venta *nm*
leadership *n* liderazgo *nm*, dirección *nf*
leading *adj* importante *adj*, principal *adj*

leading product producto líder *nm*, producto principal *nm*
lease *vb* arrendar *vb*, ceder en arriendo *vb*
leasehold *n* arrendamiento *nm*
leaseholder *n* arrendatario, - ria *nm,f*
leave 1. *n* permiso *nm*, vacaciones *nfpl*, licencia (LAm) *nf* **leave of absence** excedencia *nf*, permiso *nm*, licencia (LAm) *nf* **sick leave** permiso por enfermedad *nm*, baja por enfermedad *nf*, licencia por enfermedad (LAm) *nf* **to take leave** tomarse permiso *vb*, estar de licencia (LAm) *vb* **to take leave of sb** despedirse de alguien *vb* **2.** *vb* irse *vb*, marcharse *vb* (resign from), dimitir *vb* dejar atrás *vb*
ledger *n* libro mayor *nm* **bought ledger** libro mayor de compras *nm* **ledger entry** asiento contable *nm*
left *adj* **left luggage** consigna *nf* **left-luggage locker** casilla de la consigna automática *nf*, locker de la consigna (LAm) *nm* **left-luggage office** consigna *nf*, consigna de equipajes (LAm) *nf*
legacy *n* legado *nm*
legal *adj* legal *adj* **legal tender** moneda de curso legal *nm* **to take legal action** entablar un pleito *vb*, proceder en contra de *vb*
legislate *vb* legislar *vb*
legislation *n* legislación *nf* **to introduce legislation** introducir legislación *vb*
lend *vb* prestar *vb*, dejar *vb*
lender *n* prestamista *nmf*, entidad crediticia *nf*
lessee *n* arrendatario, -ria *nm,f*, inquilino, -ina *nm,f*
lessor *n* arrendador, -dora *nm,f*
let *vb* (property) alquilar *vb*
letter *n* **letter of application** carta de solicitud *nf* **letter of credit** carta de crédito *nf* **letter of introduction** carta de recomendación *nf*
letterhead *n* membrete *nm*, papel con membrete *nm*
level *n* nivel *nm*, grado *nm* **level of employment** nivel de empleo *nm* **level of inflation** nivel de inflación *nm* **level of prices** nivel de precios *nm*
levy *vb* (tax) imponer *vb*, recaudar *vb*, gravar *vb*
liability *n* responsabilidad *nf*, propensión *nf* **current liabilities** pasivo circulante *nm* **fixed liability** pasivo a largo plazo *nm* **limited liability** responsabilidad limitada *nf*

liable *adj* responsable *adj*, propenso *adj*, sujeto *adj* **liable for damages** responsable de daños y perjuicios *adj* **liable for tax** sujeto a impuestos *adj*
libel *n* difamación *nf*, libelo *nm*
licence *n* licencia *nf*, permiso *nm*, autorización *nf* **licence fee** cuota de licencia *nf*, tasa de licencia *nf*
license *vb* conceder un permiso *vb*, autorizar *vb*
licensee *n* titular de una licencia *nmf*, concesionario, -ria *nm,f*
licensor *n* persona que concede un permiso o una licencia *nf*
life *n* **life assurance/insurance** seguro de vida *nm* **life member** miembro vitalicio *nm*
LIFO (last in first out) *abbr* primeras entradas, primeras salidas *nfpl & nfpl*, método contable para valorar las existencias *nm*
limit *n* límite *nm*, acotación *nf* **credit limit** límite de crédito *nm*
limited *adj* limitado *adj* **limited capital** capital limitado *nm* **limited company** compañía limitada *nf* **limited liability** responsabilidad limitada *nf* **limited partnership** asociación limitada *nf*
line *n* **above the line** incluido *adj* **assembly line** cadena de montaje *nf*, línea de montaje *nf* **below the line** no incluido *adj* **line management** orden jerárquico *nm*, dirección lineal *nf* **line manager** jefe, -efa de línea *nm,f* **line of business** ramo profesional *nm* **product line** gama de productos *nf*
liquid *adj* líquido *adj* **liquid assets** activo disponible *nm* **liquid capital** capital líquido *nm*
liquidate *vb* liquidar *vb*, cancelar *vb*, saldar *vb*
liquidation *n* liquidación *nf* **liquidation value** valor de liquidación *nm*
liquidity *n* liquidez *nf*
list 1. *n* lista *nf*, relación *nf* **list price** precio de catálogo *nm* **2.** *vb* hacer una lista *vb*
listed *adj* **listed share, listed stock** (US) acción cotizada *nf*
litigant *n* litigante *nmf*
litigate *vb* litigar *vb*
litigation *n* litigio *nm*
load 1. *n* carga *nf*, peso *nm*, montón *nm* **2.** *vb* cargar *vb*
loan *n* préstamo *nm*, crédito *nm* **loan agreement** contrato de préstamo *nm*

bank loan préstamo bancario *nm* **bridging loan, bridge loan** (US) crédito puente *nm* **personal loan** crédito personal *nm*, préstamo personal *nm* **to grant a loan** conceder un préstamo *vb* **to request a loan** pedir crédito *vb*
local *adj* local *adj*, municipal *adj* **local taxes** impuestos locales *nm*
location *n* posición *nf*, situación *nf*, ubicación (LAm) *nf*
lockout *n* (of strikers) cierre patronal *nm*, "lockout" *nm*, paro patronal (LAm) *nm*
logistics *n* logística *nf*
Lombard Rate *n* tasa Lombard *nf*
long *adj* **long capital** capital a largo plazo *nm* **long credit** crédito a largo plazo *nm* **long deposit** depósito a largo plazo *nm* **long-distance** interurbano *adj*, de largo recorrido *prep* **long-range** de largo alcance *prep*, a distancia *prep*, a largo plazo *prep* **long-term** a largo plazo *prep*, prolongado *adj* **long-term planning** planificación a largo plazo *nf*
lose *vb* (custom) perder *vb*
loss *n* pérdida *nf* **financial loss** pérdida financiera *nf* **gross loss** pérdida bruta *nf* **loss leader** artículo de gancho *nm* **net(t) loss** pérdida neta *nf* **loss of earnings** pérdida de ingresos *nf* **loss of job** pérdida de empleo *nf* **to minimise losses** reducir al mínimo las pérdidas *vb*
lost-property *adj* **lost-property office** oficina de objetos perdidos *nf*
lot *n* (at auction) lote *nm*
low *adj* (price) barato *adj*, económico *adj*
lower *vb* (price, interest rate) bajar *vb*
lucrative *adj* lucrativo *adj*
luggage *n* **excess luggage** exceso de equipaje *nm* **luggage insurance** seguro de equipaje *nm*
lump *n* **lump sum settlement** ajuste por suma fija *nm*
luxury *n* lujo *nm* **luxury goods** artículos de lujo *nmpl* **luxury tax** impuesto de lujo *nm*
machine 1. *n* máquina *nf*, aparato *nm* 2. *vb* trabajar a máquina *vb*, coser a máquina *vb*
machinery *n* maquinaria *nf*, mecanismo *nm*, aparato *nm* **machinery of government** aparato estatal *nm*
macroeconomics *n* macroeconomía *nf*
made *adj* fabricado *adj*, hecho *adj* **made in France** fabricado en Francia *adj*
magazine *n* (journal) revista *nf*

magnate *n* magnate *nmf*, potentado, -ada *nm,f*
magnetic *adj* **magnetic tape** (DP) cinta magnética *nf*
mail order *n* venta por correo *nf*, pedido efectuado por correo *nm*
mailing *n* **mailing list** banco de direcciones *nm*, lista de destinatarios *nf*
main *adj* principal *adj*, mayor *adj*, fundamental *adj* **main office** sede social *nf* **main supplier** proveedor, -ora principal *nm,f*, suministrador, -ora clave *nm,f*
mainframe *n* (DP) unidad principal *nf*, macrocomputadora *nf*, ordenador central *nm*, computadora central (LAm) *nf*
maintenance *n* mantenimiento *nm*, manutención *nf* **maintenance costs** costes de mantenimiento *nmpl*, costos de mantenimiento (LAm) *nmpl*
major *adj* mayor *adj*, principal *adj*, más importante *adj*
majority *n* mayoría *nf* **majority holding** participación mayoritaria *nf* **in the majority** mayoritariamente *adv*
make *vb* **to make a fortune** hacer una fortuna *vb*, hacerse rico *vb* **to make a living** ganarse la vida *vb* **to make money** hacer dinero *vb* **to make use** aprovechar *vb*
malingerer *n* enfermo, -rma fingido, -ida *nm,f*, simulador,- ora *nm,f*
mall *n* **shopping mall** centro comercial *nm*
malpractice *n* negligencia *nf*, mala práctica *nf*
man-made *adj* artificial *adj*, sintético *adj*
manage *vb* dirigir *vb*, administrar *vb*, manejar *vb*, gestionar (LAm) *vb*
management *n* dirección general *nf*, administración de empresas *nf*, gerencia *nf*, gestión (LAm) *nf* **business management** dirección comercial *nf*, gestión de empresas *nf* **management buy-out** adquisición de una empresa por sus propios directivos *nf* **management by objectives** dirección por objetivos *nf* **management consultant** asesor, -ora de empresas *nm,f*, consultor, -ora de empresas *nm,f* **financial management** dirección financiera *nf* **middle management** mandos intermedios *nmpl*, cuadros medios *nmpl* **personnel management** dirección de personal *nf*, gestión de personal *nf* **top management** altos cargos *nmpl*, alta dirección *nf*

management training formación de directivos *nf*

manager *n* director, -ora *nm,f*, gerente *nmf*, jefe, -efa *nm,f*

manpower *n* recursos humanos *nmpl*, personal *nm*, mano de obra *nf*

manual *adj* **manual worker** obrero, -era *nm,f*, trabajador, -ora manual *nm,f*

manufacture 1. *n* producción *nf*, fabricación *nf* **2.** *vb* manufacturar *vb*, fabricar *vb*

manufacturer *n* fabricante *nmf*

margin *n* margen *nm* **profit margin** margen de beneficio *nm*

marginal *adj* marginal *adj* **marginal cost** coste marginal *nm*, costo marginal (LAm) *nm* **marginal revenue** ingresos marginales *nmpl*

marine 1. *adj* marítimo *adj*, marino *adj* **marine engineering** ingeniería marina *nf* **marine insurance** seguro marítimo *nm* **2.** *n* **merchant marine** marina mercante *nf*

mark *n* marco *nm* **Deutsche Mark** marco alemán *nm*

mark down *vb* (price) rebajar *vb*, reducir *vb*

mark up *vb* aumentar *vb*, recargar *vb*

markdown *n* rebaja *nf*, reducción *nf*

market 1. *adj* **market analysis** análisis de mercado *nm* **down-market** (product) de mercado abajo *prep*, de mercado popular *prep* **market economy** economía de mercado *nf* **market forces** tendencias del mercado *nfpl*, fuerzas del mercado *nfpl* **market leader** empresa líder del sector *nf*, artículo líder *nm* **market opportunity** oportunidad comercial *nf* **market price** precio de mercado *nm* **market research** análisis de mercados *nm*, estudio de mercado *nm*, investigación de mercado *nf* **market research questionnaire** cuestionario para realizar investigaciones de mercado *nm* **market segmentation** división del mercado *nf* **market share** parte del mercado *nf*, cuota de mercado *nf*, participación en el mercado *nf* **up-market** (product) de mercado selecto *prep*, de mercado de élite *prep* **market value** valor de mercado *nm* **2.** *n* mercado *nm* **bear market** mercado bajista *nm* **black market** mercado negro *nm* **bond market** mercado de bonos *nm* **bull market** mercado con tendencia a subir *nm*, mercado alcista *nm* **buyer's market** mercado de oferta *nm* **capital market** mercado de capitales *nm* **Common Market** Mercado

Común *nm* **domestic market** mercado nacional *nm*, mercado interior *nm* **falling market** mercado con tendencia a la baja *nm* **firm market** mercado firme *nm* **foreign market** mercado exterior *nm*, mercado extranjero *nm* **futures market** mercado de futuros *nm* **labour market** mercado de trabajo *nm* **money market** mercado monetario *nm*, mercado financiero *nm* **property/real estate (US) market** mercado inmobiliario *nm* **retail market** mercado al por menor *nm* **seller's market** mercado favorable al vendedor *nm* **stock market** mercado de valores *nm*, bolsa de valores *nf* **the bottom has fallen out of the market** el mercado se ha desfondado *vb*, los precios han caído en picada (LAm) *vb* **to play the market** especular *vb* **3.** *vb* vender *vb*, comercializar *vb*

marketable *adj* comercializable *adj*, comercial *adj*, mercadeable (LAm) *adj*

marketing *n* márketing *nm*, mercadeo (LAm) *nm* **marketing consultant** asesor, -ora comercial *nm,f* **marketing department** departamento de márketing *nm*, departamento de comercialización *nm* **marketing director** director, -ora de márketing *nm,f*

markup *n* aumento *nm*, recargo *nm*, margen de beneficio *nm*

mart *n* mercado *nm*, lonja *nf*

mass *adj* **mass marketing** márketing de masas *nm*, mercadeo de masas (LAm) *nm* **mass media** medios de comunicación de masas *nmpl* **mass production** fabricación en serie *nf* **mass unemployment** desempleo masivo *nm*, paro generalizado *nm*, cesantía general (LAm) *nf*

material 1. *adj* **material needs** necesidades materiales *nfpl* **2.** *n* material *n* **building materials** materiales de construcción *nmpl* **raw materials** materias primas *nfpl*

maternity *n* **maternity leave** licencia por maternidad *nf*

matrix *n* matriz *nf*

mature *vb* (business, economy) madurar *vb*, vencer *vb*

maximise *vb* potenciar al máximo *vb*

maximum *adj* **maximum price** precio máximo *nm*

MBA (Master of Business Administration) *abbr* MBA (Máster en Administración de Empresas) *abbr*

mean 1. *adj* (average) medio *adj* **2.** *n*
(average) promedio *nm*, medio *nm*
means *npl* medios *nmpl*, recursos *nmpl*
financial means ingresos *nmpl*, recursos
financieros *nmpl* **to live beyond one's
means** llevar un tren de vida que los
ingresos no permiten *vb* **we do not have
the means to...** no disponemos de los
medios para... *vb*
measure 1. *n* medida *nf* **financial
measure** medida financiera *nf* **safety
measure** medida de seguridad *nf* **2.** *vb*
medir *vb*, calcular *vb*
mechanical *adj* mecánico *adj* **mechanical
engineering** ingeniería mecánica *nf*
media *n* **mass media** medios de
comunicación *nmpl*
median *adj* medio *adj*, intermedio *adj*
mediate *vb* mediar *vb*, lograr *vb*
mediation *n* mediación *nf*
mediator *n* mediador, -ora *nm,f*
medical *adj* médico *adj* **medical insurance** seguro médico *nm*
medium 1. *adj* mediano *adj*, medio *adj*
medium-sized firm empresa mediana *nf*,
empresa de tamaño mediano *nf* **medium
term** medio plazo *nm*, mediano plazo *nm*
2. *n* **advertising medium** medio
publicitario *nm*, medio de publicidad *nm*
meet *vb* conocer *vb*, encontrarse con *vb*
meeting *n* reunión *nf*, encuentro *nm*,
mitin *nm* **board meeting** reunión del
consejo de administración *nf* **business
meeting** reunión de negocios *nf* **to hold
a meeting** celebrar una reunión *vb*
megabyte *n* megabyte *nm*, megaocteto
nm
member *n* miembro *nmf*, socio, -cia *nm,f*
Member of Parliament (MP) (GB) diputado, -ada *nm,f* **Member of the European
Parliament (MEP)** eurodiputado, -ada
nm,f
memo *n* memorándum *nm*, nota *nf*
memorandum *n* memorándum *nm*, nota
nf, circular *nf*
memory *n* (DP) memoria *nf*, recuerdo *nm*
memory capacity capacidad de memoria
nf
mercantile *adj* mercantil *adj*
merchandise 1. *n* géneros *nmpl*,
mercancías *nfpl* **2.** *vb* comercializar *vb*
merchandizer *n* promotor, -ora de ventas
nm,f
merchandizing *n* comercialización *nf*,
mercadeo (LAm) *nm*
merchant *n* negociante *nmf*, comerciante

nmf **merchant bank** banco de negocios
nm, banco mercantil *nm* **merchant navy**,
merchant marine (US) marina mercante
nf **merchant ship** buque mercante *nm*
merge *vb* fusionarse *vb*, unirse *vb*,
fundirse *vb*
merger *n* fusión *nf*, unión *nf*
merit *n* mérito *nm* **merit payment** gratificación por méritos *nf*
message *n* mensaje *nm*, nota *nf*, dicho
(LAm) *nm*, mandado (LAm) *nm*
messenger *n* mensajero, -era *nm,f*,
recadista *nmf*
metal *n* metal *nm*
meter *n* contador *nm*, medidor (LAm) *nm*
method *n* **method of payment** modo de
pago *nm*, forma de pago *nf* **production
method** método de producción *nm*
metre, meter (US) *n* metro *nm* **cubic
metre** metro cúbico *nm* **square metre**
metro cuadrado *nm*
metric *adj* métrico *adj*
metrication *n* conversión al sistema
métrico *nf*
metropolis *n* metrópoli(s) *nf*
microchip *n* (micro)chip *nm*, pastilla de
silicio *nf*
microcomputer *n* microordenador *nm*,
microcomputador (LAm) *nm*, microcom-
putadora (LAm) *nf*
microeconomics *n* microeconomía *nf*
microfiche *n* microficha *nf*
microprocessor *n* microprocesador *nm*
middle *adj* **middle management** cuadros
medios *nmpl*, mandos intermedios *nmpl*
middle manager mando intermedio *nm*
middleman *n* intermediario, -ria *nm,f*
migrant *adj* **migrant worker** trabajador,
-ora extranjero, -era *nm,f*, trabajador, -ora
itinerante *nm,f*
mile *n* milla *nf* **nautical mile** milla marina
nf
mileage *n* kilometraje *nm*, provecho *nm*
million *n* millón *nm*
millionaire *n* millonario, -ria *nm,f*
mine *n* mina *nf* **coal mine** mina de carbón
nf
mineral *n* mineral *nm*
minimal *adj* mínimo *adj*
minimum *adj* mínimo *nm* **index-linked
minimum wage** salario mínimo indexado
nm **minimum lending rate** tipo de interés mínimo establecido por el banco
central *nm*, tasa de interés mínima
establecida por el banco central (LAm) *nf*

mining *n* minería *nf* **mining industry** industria minera *nf*
minister *n* ministro, -tra *nm,f*, secretario, -ria *nm,f*, pastor, -ora *nm,f*
ministry *n* ministerio *nm*, gestión ministerial *nf*, secretaría (LAm) *nf* **Ministry of Transport** Ministerio de Transporte *nm*, Secretaría de Transporte (LAm) *nf*
minor *adj* menor *adj*, secundario *adj*, pequeño *adj*
minority *n* minoría *nf* **minority holding** participación minoritaria *nf* **in the minority** en minoría *prep*
mint 1. *n* casa de la moneda *nf* **2.** *vb* acuñar *vb* **he/she mints money** hace una fortuna *vb*, hace un dineral *vb*
minutes *npl* **the minutes of the meeting** el acta de la reunión *nm*
misappropriation *n* malversación *nf*
miscalculation *n* error de cálculo *nm*
misconduct *n* (bad management) mala conducta *nf*
mishandling *n* maltrato *nm*
mismanagement *n* mala dirección *nf*
mistake *n* error *nm*, equivocación *nf* **to make a mistake** cometer un error *vb*, equivocarse *vb*
mix *n* **marketing mix** combinación de medios de márketing *nf* **product mix** combinación de productos *nf*
mixed *adj* **mixed economy** economía mixta *nf*
mode *n* (method) modo *nm*, medio *nm*
model *n* (person) modelo *nmf*
modem *n* módem *nm*
moderate 1. *adj* moderado *adj* **2.** *vb* moderar *vb*, aliviar *vb*
moderation *n* moderación *nf*
modern *adj* moderno *adj*
modernization *n* modernización *nf*
modernize *vb* modernizar *vb*
module *n* módulo *nm*
monetarism *n* monetarismo *nm*
monetary *adj* monetario *adj* **European Monetary System (EMS)** Sistema Monetario Europeo (SME) *nm* **International Monetary Fund (IMF)** Fondo Monetario Internacional (FMI) *nm* **monetary policy** política monetaria *nf*
money *n* **dear money** dinero caro *nm* **money market** mercado monetario *nm* **money order** giro postal *nm* **public money** dinero público *nm*, fondos públicos *nmpl* **money supply** oferta monetaria *nf* **to raise money** recaudar

fondos *vb* **money trader** cambista *nmf*, operador, -ora de cambios *nm,f*
moneymaking *adj* (profitable) rentable *adj*
monopoly *n* monopolio *nm* **Monopolies and Mergers Commission** Comisión de Monopolios y Fusiones *nf*
monthly *adj* mensual *adj*
moonlight* *vb* estar pluriempleado *vb*, practicar el pluriempleo *vb*
moor *vb* amarrar *vb*
mooring *adj* **mooring rights** derechos de amarre *nmpl*
mortgage *n* hipoteca *nf*, préstamo hipotecario *nm* **mortgage deed** contrato hipotecario *nm* **mortgage loan** préstamo hipotecario *nm*
mortgagee *n* acreedor, -ora hipotecario, -ria *nm,f*
mortgagor *n* deudor, -ora hipotecario, -ria *nm,f*
motor *n* **motor industry** industria del automóvil *nf*, industria automovilística *nf*
multilateral *adj* multilateral *adj*
multinational *adj* multinacional *adj* **multinational corporation** empresa multinacional *nf*
multiple *adj* **multiple store** sucursal de una cadena de grandes almacenes *nf*
multiply *vb* multiplicar *vb*
multipurpose *adj* multiuso *adj*, polivalente *adj*
municipal *adj* **municipal bonds** bonos municipales *nmpl*
mutual *adj* mutuo *adj* **mutual fund (US)** fondos mutuos *nmpl*
mutually *adv* mutuamente *adv*
N/A (not applicable) *abbr* no corresponde *vb*
name 1. *n* nombre *nm*, apellido *nm* **brand name** marca comercial *nf* **by name** de nombre *prep* **full name** nombre y apellidos *nm & nmpl* **in the name of** en el nombre de *prep* **registered trade name** marca registrada *nf* **2.** *vb* nombrar *vb*
named *adj* **named person** persona mencionada *nf*
narrow *adj* **narrow margin** margen reducido *nm* **narrow market** mercado reducido *nm*
nation *n* nación *nf* **the United Nations** las Naciones Unidas *nf*
national *adj* **national debt** deuda nacional *nf* **national income** renta nacional *nf* **national insurance (NI) (GB)** seguridad social *nf* **national interest** interés nacional *nm* **National Bureau of**

Economic Research (US) Departamento Nacional de Investigación Económica *nm* **nationality** *n* nacionalidad *nf* **nationalization** *n* nacionalización *nf* **nationalize** *vb* nacionalizar *vb* **nationalized** *adj* **nationalized industry** industria nacionalizada *nf* **nationwide** *adj* a escala nacional *prep*, de ámbito nacional *prep* **natural** *adj* **natural rate of increase** tasa natural de incremento *nf* **natural resources** recursos naturales *nmpl* **necessary** *adj* necesario *adj*, preciso *adj* **necessary qualifications** títulos adecuados *nmpl*, cualificaciones necesarias *nfpl* **necessity** *n* necesidad *nf* **need** *n* **needs assessment** análisis de necesidades *nm* **needs of industry** requisitos de la industria *nmpl* **to be in need** estar necesitado de *vb* **negative** *adj* **negative cash flow** flujo de caja negativo *nm*, "cash-flow" negativo *nm* **negative feedback** reacción negativa *nf* **negative (US)** *vb* rechazar *vb*, no aprobar *vb* **neglect** *n* abandono *nm*, negligencia *nf*, incumplimiento *nm* **neglect clause** cláusula de incumplimiento *nf* **negligence** *n* negligencia *nf* **negligence clause** cláusula de negligencia *nf* **contributory negligence** culpa concurrente *nf* **gross negligence** imprudencia temeraria *nf* **negligent** *adj* negligente *adj*, despreocupado *adj* **negotiable** *adj* negociable *adj*, superable *adj* **negotiable bill** factura negociable *nf* **negotiable cheque** cheque negociable *nm* **negotiate** *vb* negociar *vb* **negotiated** *adj* **negotiated price** precio negociado *nm* **negotiating** *adj* **negotiating session** sesión de negociaciones *nf* **negotiating skills** capacidad de negociación *nf* **negotiation** *n* negociación *nf* **by negotiation** mediante negociaciones *prep* **to begin negotiations** entablar negociaciones *vb* **under negotiation** en negociación *prep* **wage negotiations** negociaciones salariales *nfpl* **negotiator** *n* negociador, -ora *nm,f* **net(t)** **1.** *adj* neto *adj*, global *adj* **net(t) amount** importe neto *nm*, suma global *nf*

net(t) assets activo neto *nm* **net(t) cost** coste neto *nm*, costo neto (LAm) *nm* **net(t) earnings** ingresos netos *nmpl* **net(t) interest** interés neto *nm* **net(t) investment** inversión neta *nf* **net(t) loss** pérdida neta *nf* **net(t) price** precio neto *nm* **net(t) proceeds** recaudación neta *nf* **net(t) profit** beneficio neto *nm* **net(t) result** resultado neto *nm* **net(t) sales** ventas netas *nfpl* **net(t) saving** ahorro neto *nm* **terms strictly net(t)** términos estrictamente netos *nmpl* **net(t) wage** sueldo neto *nm*, salario neto *nm* **net(t) weight** peso neto *nm* **2.** *vb* obtener *vb*, producir *vb*, embolsar *vb* **network** **1.** *n* red *nm* **banking network** red bancaria *nf* **computer network** red de ordenadores *nf*, red de computadoras (LAm) *nf* **distribution network** red de distribución *nf* **2.** *vb* interconectar *vb*, transmitir en cadena *vb* **neutral** *adj* neutral *adj* **new** *adj* **new account** cuenta nueva *nf* **new business** nuevos negocios *nmpl*, empresa de creación reciente *nf* **new product** producto nuevo *nm* **new technology** nueva tecnología *nf* **newly** *adv* **newly-appointed** recién contratado *adj* **newly-industrialised** de reciente industrialización *prep* **news** *n* noticias *nfpl* **news agency** agencia de prensa *nf* **bad news** malas noticias *nfpl* **news bulletin** diario hablado *nm* **news coverage** reportaje de las noticias *nm* **financial news** noticias financieras *nfpl* **good news** buenas noticias *nfpl* **newsdealer (US)** *n* vendedor, -ora de periódicos y revistas *nm,f* **newsletter** *n* boletín informativo *nm* **newspaper** *n* periódico *nm*, diario *nm* **newspaper advertisement** anuncio (publicitario) *nm*, aviso (LAm) *nm* **daily newspaper** diario *nm*, periódico *nm* **newspaper report** reportaje de prensa *nm* **nil** *n* cero *nm* **nil profit** beneficio nulo *nm* **no** *det* **no agents wanted** no se admiten agentes **no-claims bonus** prima por ausencia de siniestralidad *nf* **no commercial value** sin valor comercial **nominal** *adj* nominal *adj* **nominal amount** suma simbólica *nf* **nominal assets** capital nominal *nm*, activo nominal *nm* **nominal damages** resarcimiento no compensatorio *nm* **nominal inflation** inflación nominal *nf* **nominal price** valor

nominal *nm*, precio simbólico *nm* **nominal value** valor nominal *nm*
nominate *vb* proponer *vb*, nombrar *vb*, postular (LAm) *vb* **nominate sb to a board/committee** nombrar a alguien a un consejo, una comisión *vb*, postular a alguien a un consejo, una comisión (LAm) *vb*
nomination *n* nombramiento *nm*, candidatura *nf*, postulación (LAm) *nf*
nominee *n* candidato, -ata *nm,f*, postulado, -ada (LAm) *nm,f* **nominee shareholder** accionista apoderado, -ada *nm,f*
non-acceptance *n* no aceptación *nf*
non-attendance *n* no asistencia *nf*
non-completion *n* no formalización *nf*, no terminación *nf*
non-contributory *adj* sin aportaciones por parte del empleado *prep*
non-convertible *adj* inconvertible *adj*
non-delivery *n* falta de entrega *nf*
non-discriminatory *adj* no discriminatorio *adj*
non-essential *adj* dispensable *adj*
non-interest-bearing *adj* que no devenga interés *rel pron*
non-intervention *n* no intervención *nf*
non-negotiable *adj* no negociable *adj*
non-payment *n* impago *nm*
non-profitmaking *adj* no rentable *adj*, sin fines de lucro *prep*
non-returnable *adj* no retornable *adj*, de usar y tirar *prep*
non-stop *adj* sin escalas *prep*, sin parar *prep*, directo *adj*
non-transferable *adj* intransferible *adj*
norm *n* norma *nf*
normal *adj* **normal trading hours** horario normal de venta al público *nm*
not *adv* no *adv* **not applicable** no pertinente *adj*, no corresponde *vb* **not available** no disponible *adj* **not dated** sin fecha *prep*
notary *n* notario, -ria *nm,f*
note 1. *n* nota *nf* **advice note** aviso de envío *nm*, aviso de expedición *nm* **cover note** póliza provisional *nf*, nota de cobertura *nf*, póliza provisoria (LAm) *nf* **credit note** nota de crédito *nf* **debit note** nota de débito *nf* **delivery note** nota de entrega *nf* **dispatch note** nota de envío *nf*, nota de expedición *nf* **open note (US)** pagaré del Tesoro *nm* **to compare notes** cambiar impresiones *vb* **to make a note of sth** apuntar algo *vb*, tomar nota de algo *vb* **2.** anotar *vb*

noteworthy *adj* notable *adj*, digno de notarse *adj*
notice *n* antelación *nf*, aviso *nm* **advance notice** aviso previo *nm*, preaviso *nm*, aviso por adelantado *nm* **at short notice** a última hora *prep* **final notice** última notificación *nf* **notice period** período de aviso *nm* **term of notice** plazo de preaviso *nm* **to come to the notice of sb** llegar al conocimiento de alguien *vb* **to give notice of sth** avisar de algo *vb*, notificar de algo *vb* **to take notice** prestar atención *vb*, hacer caso *vb* **until further notice** hasta nuevo aviso *prep*
notification *n* notificación *nf*
notify *vb* notificar *vb*, informar *vb*, avisar *vb*
null *adj* **null and void** nulo y sin valor *adj* + *prep*
number *n* **account number** número de cuenta *nm* **opposite number** homólogo, -oga *nm,f* **order number** número de pedido *nm* **serial number** número de serie *nm* **telephone number** número de teléfono *nm* **wrong number** (phone) número equivocado *nm*
numeracy *n* nociones elementales de cálculo aritmético *nfpl*
numerate *adj* capaz de realizar cálculos aritméticos elementales *adj*
numeric *adj* **alpha-numeric** numérico-alfabético *adj* **numeric character** carácter numérico *nm*
numerical *adj* numérico *adj* **numerical analysis** análisis numérico *nm*
NYSE (New York Stock Exchange) *abbr* Bolsa de Nueva York *nf*
object *vb* oponerse *vb*
objection *n* objeción *nf* **to make/raise an objection** poner una objeción *vb*, expresar una objeción *vb*
objective *n* objetivo *nm* **to reach an objective** lograr un objetivo *vb*
obligation *n* obligación *nf*, compromiso *nm*, deber *nm* **to meet one's obligations** hacer frente a sus obligaciones *vb*, cumplir sus compromisos *vb*
obligatory *adj* obligatorio *adj*
oblige *vb* **to be obliged to do sth** estar obligado a hacer algo *vb*
observation *n* comentario *nm* **under observation** bajo vigilancia *prep*, en observación *prep*
observe *vb* observar *vb* **observe the rules** respetar las reglas *vb*, acatar las normas *vb*

obsolescence n caducidad nf, obsolescencia nf **built-in obsolescence** obsolescencia planificada nf
obsolete adj anticuado adj, caído en desuso adj
obtain vb obtener vb, conseguir vb **to obtain credit** conseguir crédito vb
occupant n ocupante nmf, inquilino, -ina nm,f, titular nmf
occupation n ocupación nf, profesión nf, tenencia nf
occupational adj laboral adj, ocupacional adj **occupational disease** enfermedad profesional nf **occupational hazard** riesgo de la profesión nm
occupier n ocupante nmf
occupy vb (premises) ocupar vb, llevar vb
off-the-job adj **off-the-job training** capacitación fuera del puesto de trabajo nf
offence, offense (US) n infracción nf, delito nm, ataque nm
offer n **firm offer** oferta en firme nf **offer in writing** oferta por escrito nf **offer subject to confirmation** oferta sujeta a confirmación nf **offer valid until...** oferta válida hasta... nf
offeree n receptor, -ora de la oferta nm,f
offeror n oferente nmf
office n oficina nf, despacho nm, cargo nm **office equipment** equipo de oficina nm, mobiliario de oficina nm **office hours** horas de oficina nfpl, horario de oficina nm **office management** dirección de oficina nf **office staff** personal administrativo nm **to hold office** ocupar un cargo vb **to resign from office** dimitir el cargo vb
official n funcionario, -ria nm,f, cargo nm **official strike** huelga oficial nf, huelga autorizada por el sindicato nf, paro oficial (LAm) nm
offshore adj **offshore company** empresa extraterritorial nf, compañía en un paraíso fiscal nf
oil n **oil industry** industria petrolífera nf, industria petrolera (LAm) nf **oil state** país productor de petróleo nm
oilfield n yacimiento petrolífero nm
oligopoly n oligopolio nm
ombudsman n defensor, -ora del pueblo nm, f
on-line adj en conexión directa con el ordenador central prep
on-the-job en el puesto de trabajo prep **on-the-job training** capacitación en el puesto de trabajo nf

onus n **the onus is on us to...** nos incumbe... vb, nos corresponde... vb
open 1. adj **open cheque** cheque abierto nm **open credit** crédito abierto nm **open market** mercado libre nm **open shop** empresa donde los trabajadores no tienen obligación de afiliarse al sindicato nf 2. vb **to open an account** abrir una cuenta vb
open up vb (market) abrir vb, flexibilizar vb
opening adj **opening price** cotización de apertura nf **opening times** horario comercial nm, horario de atención al público nm
operate vb operar vb, explotar vb **to operate a business** llevar un negocio vb
operating adj **operating expenditure** gastos de explotación nmpl, costes de explotación nm, costos de operación (LAm) nmpl **operating expenses** gastos de explotación nmpl, costes de explotación nm, gastos de operación nm, costos de operación (LAm) nmpl **operating income** ingresos de explotación nmpl, ingresos de operación (LAm) nmpl **operating profit** beneficios de explotación nmpl, beneficios de operación (LAm) nmpl **operating statement** cuenta de pérdidas y ganancias nf
operation n (of business) explotación nf, dirección nf, gestión nf, (of machine) funcionamiento nm, manejo nm, uso nm
operator n operador, -ora nm,f, operario, -ria nm,f, telefonista nmf
opportunity n oportunidad nf, posibilidad nf **market opportunities** oportunidades de mercado nfpl **to seize an opportunity** aprovecharse de la ocasión vb
option n opción nf, posibilidad nf, elección nf **share option, stock option** (US) opción de compra de acciones a cierto precio para el futuro nf, opción de venta de acciones a cierto precio para el futuro nf **options market** mercado de opciones de compra y venta de acciones nm **option to buy** opción de compra nf **option to cancel** opción de anular nf
optional adj optativo adj
order n orden nf, pedido nm, mandamiento nm **order book** libro de pedidos nm **order form** formulario de pedido nm **order number** número de pedido nm **pay to the order of...** pagar a la orden de... vb **to cancel an order** anular un pedido vb, dar orden de no

pagar *vb* **to place an order** hacer un pedido *vb*, encargar *vb*
ordinary *adj* **ordinary general meeting** junta general ordinaria *nf* **ordinary share, ordinary stock** (US) acción ordinaria *nf*
organization *n* organización *nf*, método *nm*, sistema *nm*
organize *vb* organizar *vb*, ordenar *vb*, sindicar *vb*, sindicalizar (LAm) *vb*
organized *adj* **organized labour** (trade unions) obreros sindicados *nmpl*
origin *n* (of a product) fuente *nf* **country of origin** país de origen *nm* **statement of origin** relación de procedencia *nf*
original *adj* **original cost** coste original *nm*, costo original (LAm) *nm*
outbid *vb* sobrepujar *vb*, ofrecer más *vb*
outcome *n* resultado *nm*, consecuencias *nfpl*
outgoings *npl* gastos *nmpl*, desembolsos *nmpl*, salidas *nfpl*
outlay *n* **capital outlay** gastos de capital *nmpl*
outlet *n* **market outlet** salida de mercado *nf* **sales outlet** punto de venta *nm*
outlook *n* **business outlook** perspectivas comerciales *nfpl*
output *n* producción *nf*, rendimiento *nm* **to increase output** potenciar la producción *vb*, aumentar la producción *vb*
outstanding *adj* **outstanding amount** importe a pagar *nm* **outstanding debt** deuda pendiente *nf* **outstanding stock** existencias pendientes *nfpl*
overcharge *vb* cobrar de más *vb* recargar *vb*
overdraft *n* sobregiro *nm* **to request an overdraft** pedir un sobregiro *vb*
overdraw *vb* girar en descubierto *vb*, sobregirarse *vb*, rebasar *vb*
overdrawn *adj* **overdrawn account** cuenta rebasada *nf*
overdue *adj* vencido *adj*, atrasado *adj*
overhead *adj* **overhead costs** gastos generales *nmpl*, gastos indirectos *nmpl*
overheads *npl* gastos generales *nmpl*
overheating *n* (of economy) recalentamiento *nm*
overload *vb* sobrecargar *vb*
overlook *vb* pasar por alto *vb*, dejar pasar *vb*
overman *vb* tener mano de obra excesiva *vb*
overmanned *adj* con demasiado personal *prep*

overmanning *n* (excess staff) exceso de personal *nm*
overnight *adj* **overnight delivery** distribución de noche *nf*
overpay *vb* pagar de más *vb*
overpayment *n* pago en exceso *nm*
overpopulation *n* superpoblación *nf*, sobrepoblación (LAm) *nf*
overproduce *vb* producir en exceso *vb*
overproduction *n* sobreproducción *nf*
overseas *adj* extranjero *adj*, exterior *adj* **overseas market** mercado exterior *nm* **overseas territory** territorio de ultramar *nm* **overseas trade** comercio exterior *nm*, comercio de ultramar *nm*
oversell *vb* vender en exceso *vb*, exagerar los méritos de *vb*
oversight *n* descuido *nm*, supervisión *nf* **due to an oversight** debido a un error *adv*
oversold *adj* sobrevendido *adj*, vendido en exceso *adj*
oversubscribed *adj* sobrevendido *adj*, con demanda que supera a la oferta *prep*
oversupply *vb* proveer en exceso *vb*
overtime *n* horas extra(s) *nfpl*, sobretiempo (LAm) *nm*
overvalue *vb* sobrevalorar *vb*, sobrestimar *vb*
overworked *adj* con trabajo excesivo *prep*, explotado *adj*
owe *vb* deber *vb*
own *vb* poseer *vb*, tener *vb*, ser dueño de *vb*
owner *n* dueño, -eña *nm,f*, propietario, -ria *nm,f*, amo, -a *nm,f*
owner-occupier *n* propietario, -ria ocupante de una vivienda *nm,f*
ownership *n* propiedad *nf*
pack *vb* envasar *vb*, embalar *vb*
package *n* paquete *nm*, embalaje *nm*, envase *nm* **package deal** acuerdo global *nm*, oferta combinada *nf* **package tour** vacaciones organizadas *nfpl*
packaging *n* embalaje *nm*, envase *nm*, presentación *nf*
packet *n* paquete *nm*, dineral *nm*
paid *adj* pagado *adj*, remunerado *adj*, asalariado *adj* **paid holiday** vacaciones pagadas *nfpl*
paid-up *adj* **paid-up capital** capital desembolsado *nm*
pallet *n* paleta *nf*, bandeja *nf*, gama *nf*
palletized *adj* **palletized freight** carga paletizada *nf*, mercaderías empaletizadas (LAm) *nfpl*
paper *n* papel *nm*, documento *nm*

commercial paper papel comercial *nm*, efectos negociables *nm* **paper loss** pérdida sobre el papel *nf* **paper profit** beneficio ficticio *nm*, beneficio no realizado *nm*

paperwork *n* papeleo *nm*, trámites burocráticos *nmpl*

par *n* par *nf* **above par** por encima de la par *prep* **below par** por debajo de la par *prep*

parent *n* **parent company** oficina central *nf*, empresa matriz *nf*

parity *n* paridad *nf*, igualdad *nf*, tipo de cambio *nm*, tasa de cambio (LAm) *nf*

part *n* (of a machine) pieza *nf* **part payment** pago parcial *nm* **part shipment** envío parcial *nm*, cargamento parcial *nm* **spare part** (for machine) pieza de recambio *nf*, refacción (LAm) *nf*

part-time 1. *adj* a tiempo parcial *prep*, a jornada reducida *prep* **2.** *adv* a tiempo parcial *prep*

participation *n* **worker participation** participación obrera *nf*, participación de los trabajadores en la gestión de la empresa *nf*

partner *n* socio, -cia *nm,f*, asociado, -ada *nm,f* **sleeping partner** socio, -cia comanditario, -ria *nm,f*, socio, -cia en comandita *nm,f*

partnership *n* sociedad colectiva *nf*, asociación *nf* **trading partnership** asociación comercial *nf*

passenger *n* pasajero, -era *nm,f*, viajero, -era *nm,f*

patent *n* patente *nf*

patented *adj* patentado *adj*

patronage *n* clientela *nf*, patrocinio *nm*, influencia *nf*

pattern *n* **spending patterns** pautas de gasto *nfpl*, pautas de consumo *nfpl*

pay 1. *n* (salary, wages) paga *nf*, salario *nm*, sueldo *nm* **equal pay** igualdad salarial *nf* **pay rise** aumento de sueldo *nm*, incremento salarial *nm* **severance pay** indemnización por despido *nf* **unemployment pay** subsidio de paro *nm*, subsidio de desempleo (LAm) *nm* **2.** *vb* pagar *vb*, abonar *vb* **to pay an invoice** pagar una factura *vb* **to pay by credit card** pagar con tarjeta de crédito *vb* **to pay for a service** pagar por un servicio *vb* **to pay in advance** pagar por adelantado *vb* **to pay in cash** pagar al contado *vb*, pagar en efectivo *vb*

payable *adj* pagadero *adj* **accounts payable** cuentas a pagar *nfpl*

payee *n* portador, -ora *nm,f*, beneficiario, -ria *nm,f*

payer *n* pagador, -ora *nm,f* **prompt payer** pagador, -ora puntual *nm,f* **slow payer** pagador, -ora moroso, -osa *nm,f*

payload *n* (of vehicle) carga útil *nf*

payment *n* pago *nm*, plazo *nm*, recompensa *nf*, cuota (LAm) *nf* **down payment** entrada *nf*, depósito *nm*, pago inicial *nm*, pie (LAm) *nm*

payola (US) *n* soborno *nm*, coima (LAm) *nf*, mordida (LAm) *nf*

payroll *n* nómina *nf*, plantilla *nf*, planilla (LAm) *nf* **to be on the payroll** estar en plantilla *vb*, estar en planilla (LAm) *vb*

peak *n* punto máximo *nm*, pico *nm* **peak demand** demanda máxima *nf* **peak period** horas punta *nfpl*, período de mayor afluencia *nm*

pecuniary *adj* **for pecuniary gain** con afán de lucro *prep*

peddle *vb* vender en la calle *vb*

peg *vb* (prices) sujetar *vb*, congelar *vb* **the HK dollar is pegged to the US dollar** el dólar de Hong Kong está vinculado al dólar norteamericano *nm*

penetration *n* **market penetration** penetración en el mercado *nf*

pension *n* pensión *nf* **pension fund** fondo de pensiones *nm* **retirement pension** pensión *nf*, jubilación *nf*, pensión de jubilación *nf* **pension scheme** plan de pensiones *nm*

per *prep* **per annum** al año, por año *prep* **per capita** per cápita *prep,* por persona *prep* **per cent** por ciento *prep*

percentage *n* porcentaje *nm* **percentage of profit** tanto por ciento de los beneficios *nm*

performance *n* (behaviour) actuación *nf* **performance appraisal** evaluación del rendimiento *nf* **performance-related bonus** plus según rendimiento *nm*

period *n* **cooling-off period** período de reflexión *nm* **period of grace** período de gracia *nm*

peripheral *adj* periférico *adj*

perishable *adj* **perishable goods** artículos perecederos *nmpl*, mercaderías perecederas (LAm) *nfpl*

perk *n* gratificación *nf*

permanent *adj* **permanent employment** empleo fijo *nm*

permit *n* permiso *nm*, licencia *nf*, carné *nm* **building permit** licencia de obras *nf*

perquisite *n* ((formal)) beneficio extra *nm*, incentivo *nm*

person *n* persona *nf* **third person** tercero *nm*, tercera persona *nf*

personal *adj* personal *adj*

personnel *n* **personnel department** departamento de personal *nm* **personnel management** dirección del personal *nf*

peseta *n* peseta *nf*

petrodollar *n* petrodólar *nm*

petroleum *n* **petroleum industry** industria petrolera *nf*

pharmaceutical *adj* **pharmaceutical industry** industria farmacéutica *nf*

phoney* *adj* falso *adj*, fingido *adj* **phoney* company** empresa ficticia *nf*

photocopier *n* fotocopiadora *nf*

photocopy 1. *n* fotocopia *nf* 2. *vb* fotocopiar *vb*

pick up *vb* (improve) mejorar *vb*, recuperarse *vb*

picket *n* (strike) piquete *nm*

piecework *n* trabajo a destajo *nm*

pig iron *n* hierro en lingotes *nm*

pilferage *n* pequeño hurto *nm*

pilot *n* **pilot plant** planta piloto *nf*, fábrica piloto *nf* **pilot scheme** programa piloto *nm*

pipeline *n* conducto *nm*, ducto (LAm) *nm*

piracy *n* (at sea) piratería *nf* **software piracy** piratería de software *nf*, piratería de programa informático *nf*

place 1. *n* lugar *nm*, sitio *nm* 2. *vb* poner *vb*, colocar *vb* **to place an order** hacer un pedido *vb*

plan 1. *n* **economic plan** plan económico *nm*, programa económico *nm* **plan of campaign** plan de campaña *nm* **to make plans** hacer planes *vb* 2. *vb* planificar *vb*, planear *vb*, proyectar *vb*, concertar *vb*

planned *adj* **planned economy** economía planificada *nf* **planned obsolescence** obsolescencia planificada *nf*

planning *n* planificación *nf* **regional planning** planificación regional *nf*

plant *n* (machinery) maquinaria *nf* **plant hire** alquiler de maquinaria *nm* **plant manager** director, -ora de fábrica *nm,f*, director, -ora de planta *nm,f*

plastics *npl* **plastics industry** industria del plástico *nf*

pledge *n* promesa *nf*, garantía *nf*, prenda *nf*

plenary *adj* (assembly, session) plenario *adj*

plough back, plow back (US) *vb* (profits) reinvertir *vb*

point *n* **point of sale** punto de venta *nm*

policy *n* **insurance policy** póliza de seguros *nf* **pricing policy** política de precios *nf*

political *adj* político *adj*

politics *n* política *nf*

port *n* puerto *nm*

portable *adj* portátil *adj*

portfolio *n* **investment portfolio** cartera de inversiones *nf*

post 1. *n* (job) puesto *nm* 2. *vb* mandar por correo *vb*, remitir por correo *vb*

post office *n* oficina de correos *nf*, correo (LAm) *nm*

postal *adj* **postal services** servicios postales *nmpl*

postdate *vb* tener lugar después de *vb*, poner fecha adelantada *vb*, diferir (LAm) *vb*

poste restante *n* lista de correos *nf*, poste restante (LAm) *nm*

poster *n* (advertising) cartel *nm*, póster *nm*

postpone *vb* aplazar *vb*, posponer *vb*, postergar (LAm) *vb*

potential *n* potencial *nm*, posibilidades *nfpl* **sales potential** posibilidades de ventas *nfpl*

pound *n* (weight) libra *nf* **pound sterling** libra esterlina *nf*

power *n* poder *nm*, potencia *nf*, fuerza *nf* **power of attorney** poder notarial *nm*

preference *n* **community preference** preferencia comunitaria *nf*

preferential *adj* preferencial *adj*

premises *npl* local *nm* **office premises** local de una oficina *nm*

premium *n* prima *nf*, recargo *nm* **at a premium** por encima de la par *prep*

prepayment *n* pago anticipado *nm*, pago por adelantado *nm*

president *n* (of company) presidente, -nta *nm,f*

press *n* **press baron** magnate de la prensa *nmf* **press conference** rueda de prensa *nf*

price *n* precio *nm*, cotización *nf* **market price** precio de mercado *nm* **stock exchange prices** cotizaciones de la bolsa *nfpl* **threshold price** precio umbral *nm*, precio mínimo al que pueden venderse en la UE *nm*

pricing *adj* **pricing policy** política de precios *nf*

primary *adj* primario *adj* **primary industry** industria de base *nf*
prime *adj* **prime lending rate** tipo preferencial de interés bancario *nm*, tasa preferencial de interés bancario (LAm) *nf*
priority *n* prioridad *nf*, preferencia *nf*, antelación *nf*
private *adj* **private sector** sector privado *nm*
privatization *n* privatización *nf*
privatize *vb* privatizar *vb*
pro 1. *n* **pros and cons** pros y contras *nmpl* & *nmpl* **2.** *prep* **pro rata** a prorrata *prep*, a prorrateo *prep*, proporcionalmente *adv*
probate *n* legalización *nf*, trámite para obtener la legitimación de un testamento *nm*
proceeds *npl* beneficios *nmpl*, ganancias *nfpl*
process 1. *n* proceso *nm*, procedimiento *nm*, curso *nm* **2.** *vb* elaborar *vb*, tramitar *vb*
produce 1. *n* productos *nmpl* **2.** *vb* producir *vb*, fabricar *vb*, presentar *vb*
producer *n* fabricante *nmf*
product *n* producto *nm* **primary product** producto primario *nm*
production *n* producción *nf*, fabricación *nf*, presentación *nf* **production line** cadena de montaje *nf*, cadena de producción *nf*
productive *adj* productivo *adj*
productivity *n* productividad *nf* **productivity gains** aumentos de productividad *nmpl*
profession *n* profesión *nf* **the professions** las profesiones liberales *nfpl*
profit *n* beneficio(s) *nm(pl)*, ganancia(s) *nf(pl)*, provecho *nm*, utilidades (LAm) *nfpl* **profit and loss** ganancias y pérdidas *nfpl* & *nfpl* **profit margin** margen de beneficio *nm* **net(t) profit** beneficio neto *nm* **operating profit** beneficio(s) de explotación *nm(pl)*, beneficio(s) de operación (LAm) *nm(pl)* **profit-sharing scheme** programa de participación en los beneficios *nm* **to make a profit** obtener beneficios *vb*
profitability *n* rentabilidad *nf*
profiteer *vb* especular *vb*, realizar ganancias excesivas *vb*
program *n* (DP) programa *nm*
programmer *n* (DP) programador, -ora *nm,f*
programming *n* (DP) programación *nf*

progress 1. *n* progreso *nm*, adelanto *nm*, marcha *nf* **2.** *vb* (research, project) avanzar *vb*, desarrollar *vb*
project *n* proyecto *nm*
promissory *adj* **promissory note** pagaré *nm*, letra al propio cargo *nf*
promote *vb* (person) ascender *vb*, promover *vb* (product) promocionar *vb*, fomentar *vb*, potenciar *vb*
promotion *n* (of product) promoción *nf* (of person) ascenso *nm*, promoción *nf*, fomento *nm*
promotional *adj* publicitario *adj* **promotional budget** presupuesto publicitario *nm*, presupuesto promocional *nm*
prompt *adj* rápido *adj*, pronto *adj*, puntual *adj*
property *n* propiedad *nf*, propiedades *nfpl*, bienes inmuebles *nmpl* **property company** sociedad inmobiliaria *nf* **property developer** promotor, -ora inmobiliario, -ria *nm,f* **private property** propiedad privada *nf*
proprietary *adj* patentado *adj*, de marca registrada *prep* **proprietary brand** marca registrada *nf*
proprietor *n* propietario, -ria *nm,f*, dueño, -eña *nm,f*
prospect *n* perspectiva *nf*, posibilidad *nf*, panorama *nm* **future prospects** perspectivas futuras *nfpl*
prospectus *n* folleto informativo *nm*, folleto publicitario *nm*
prosperous *adj* próspero *adj*
protectionism *n* proteccionismo *nm*
protectionist *adj* proteccionista *adj*
provide *vb* (supply) proveer *vb*, suministrar *vb*, proporcionar *vb*, disponer *vb*
provision *n* (stipulation) provisión *nf*, disposición *nf*
proxy *n* (power) poderes *nmpl*, apoderado, -ada *nm,f*
public *adj* público *adj* **public company** sociedad cotizada en bolsa *nf* **public funds** fondos públicos *nmpl* **public relations** relaciones públicas *nfpl* **public sector** sector público *nm* **public service** servicio público *nm*
publicity *n* publicidad *nf*
publishing *n* campo editorial *nm*, mundo editorial *nm* **desk-top publishing** autoedición *nf*
purchase 1. *adj* **purchase price** precio de compra *nm* **2.** *n* compra *nf*, adquisición *nf* **3.** *vb* comprar *vb*, adquirir *vb*

purchasing *adj* **purchasing power** poder adquisitivo *nm*
pyramid *n* **pyramid scheme** plan piramidal *nm* **pyramid selling** venta piramidal *nf*
qualification *n* cualificación *nf*, competencia *nf*, título *nm*, calificación (LAm) *nf* **academic qualification** título académico *nm* **educational qualification** título docente *nm* **professional qualification** cualificación profesional *nf*
qualified *adj* cualificado *adj*, capacitado *adj*, calificado (LAm) *adj*, capacitado (LAm) *adj* **qualified acceptance** aceptación con reservas *nf* **qualified personnel** personal cualificado *nm*, personal calificado (LAm) *nm*
qualitative *adj* cualitativo *adj*
quality *n* calidad *nf*, categoría *nf* **quality control** control de calidad *nm* **quality report** informe de calidad *nm*, informe sobre la calidad *nm* **quality standard** nivel de calidad *nm*, norma de calidad *nf*
quantitative *adj* cuantitativo *adj*
quantity *n* cantidad *nf* **quantity discount** descuento por grandes cantidades *nm* **quantity theory of money** teoría cuantitativa del dinero *nf*
quarter *n* (of year) trimestre *nm*
quarterly *adj* trimestral *adj* **quarterly interest** interés trimestral *nm* **quarterly trade accounts** contabilidad comercial trimestral *nf*
quasi-contract *n* cuasicontrato *nm*
quasi-income *n* cuasingresos *nmpl*
quay *n* muelle *nm*
quayage *n* derechos de muelle *nmpl*, espacio disponible en un muelle *nm*
questionnaire *n* cuestionario *nm*, encuesta *nf* **questionnaire design** diseño de cuestionarios *nm*
queue *n* cola *nf*
quick *adj* **quick assets** activo disponible *nm*
quiet *adj* **quiet market** mercado poco móvil *nm*
quit *vb* (resign) abandonar *vb*, dejar de *vb*
quittance *n* descargo *nm*, compensación *nf*
quorate *adj* (meeting) con quórum *prep*
quorum *n* quórum *nm* **quorum of creditors** quórum de acreedores *nm*
quota *n* cupo *nm*, cuota *nf* **quota agreement** acuerdo de cuotas *nm* **quota buying** compra de cupos *nf* **import quota** cupo de importación *nm* **sales quota**

cupo de ventas *nm* **quota sampling** muestreo de cuotas *nm* **quota system** sistema de cuotas *nm*
quotation *n* (price) cotización *nf*, presupuesto *nm*
quoted *adj* **quoted company** sociedad cuyas acciones se cotizan en Bolsa *nf* **quoted investment** inversión cotizada *nf* **quoted share, quoted stocks** (US) acciones que se cotizan en Bolsa *nfpl*
racket *n* chanchullo *nm*, estafa *nf*, timo *nm*
racketeer *n* estafador, -ora *nm,f*, mafioso, -osa *nm,f*
racketeering *n* crimen organizado *nm*, negocio ilícito *nm*
rag *n* **the rag trade** (informal) el comercio textil *nm*, la industria del vestido *nf*
rail *n* **by rail** en tren *prep*
railway, railroad (US) *n* ferrocarril *nm*
raise *vb* (price, interest rate) subir *vb*, aumentar *vb*, incrementar *vb*, (capital, loan) subir *vb*, elevar *vb*
RAM (random access memory) *abbr* (DP) RAM *nf*, memoria RAM *nf*
random *adj* **at random** al azar *prep* **random selection** selección aleatoria *nf*
range *n* (of products) gama *nf*, alcance *nm*, línea *nf*
rate *n* **base rate** tipo base *nm*, tasa base (LAm) *nf* **rate of exchange** tipo de cambio *nm*, tipo/tasa de paridad *nm/f*, tasa de cambio (LAm) *nf* **rate of expansion** ritmo de expansión *nm*, coeficiente de expansión *nm*, tasa de expansión (LAm) *nf* **rate of growth** tasa de crecimiento *nf* **rate of inflation** tasa de inflación *nf* **rate of interest** tipo de interés *nm*, tasa de interés (LAm) *nf* **rate of investment** ritmo de inversiones *nm*, tasa de inversión (LAm) *nf* **rate of return** tasa de rendimiento *nf*, tasa de rentabilidad *nf*
rates (tax) tarifas *nfpl*, contribuciones municipales *nfpl*, tasas (LAm) *nfpl*
ratification *n* ratificación *nf*
ratify *vb* ratificar *vb*
ratio *n* ratio *nm*, relación *nf*
rationale *n* lógica *nf*
rationalization *n* racionalización *nf*, reconversión *nf* **rationalization measures** medidas de reconversión *nfpl*
rationalize *vb* racionalizar *vb*, sistematizar *vb*
raw *adj* (unprocessed) crudo *adj*, sin analizar *prep*
re *prep* con referencia a *prep*, con relación a *prep*, Asunto *nm*

re-elect *vb* reelegir *vb*
re-election *n* reelección *nf*
ready *adj* listo *adj*, dispuesto *adj* **ready for despatch** listo para entrega *adj*
real *adj* **real estate** propiedad inmobiliaria *nf*, bienes raíces *nmpl* **real price** precio real *nm* **real time** tiempo real *nm* **real value** valor real *nm* **real wages** ingreso real *nm*, salario real *nm*
realization *n* **realization of assets** liquidación de activo *nf*
realize *vb* (profit) realizar *vb*
reallocate *vb* (funds) redistribuir *vb*, readjudicar *vb*
reallocation *n* (of funds) redistribución *nf*, reasignación *nf*
realtor (US) *n* agente inmobiliario *nmf*, agente de la propiedad inmobiliaria *nmf*, corredor, -ora de propiedades (LAm) *nm,f*
reappoint *vb* volver a nombrar *vb*, volver a contratar *vb*
reappointment *n* recontratación *nf*
reasonable *adj* (price) razonable *adj*, bien de precio *adv*
rebate *n* desgravación *nf*, reembolso *nm*, descuento *nm* **to grant a rebate** conceder una desgravación *vb*
receipt *n* **to acknowledge receipt** acusar recibo *vb* **to issue a receipt** expedir un recibo *vb*, extender un recibo *vb*
receive *vb* recibir *vb*, cobrar *vb*
receiver, administrator (US) *n* (bankruptcy) síndico, -ica *nm,f*
recession *n* recesión *nf*
recipient *n* receptor, -ora *nm,f*, destinatario, -ria *nm,f*, beneficiario, -ria *nm,f*
reciprocal *adj* recíproco *adj*, mutuo *adj*
reclaimable *adj* (materials) reciclable *adj*, reutilizable *adj*
recommend *vb* recomendar *vb*, aconsejar *vb*
recommendation *n* recomendación *nf*
recompense *n* indemnización *nf*, recompensa *nf*
record **1.** *n* archivo *nm*, acta *nm*, antecedentes *nmpl*, historial (LAm) *nm* **according to our records** según nuestros registros *prep* **2.** *vb* anotar *vb*
recover *vb* **to recover money from sb** recuperar dinero a alguien *vb*
recovery *n* (of debt) cobro *nm* (economic) reactivación *nf*, repunte *nm*
recruit *vb* reclutar *vb*, contratar *vb*
recruitment *n* contratación *nf* **recruitment campaign** campaña de reclutamiento *nf*

recyclable *adj* reciclable *adj*
recycle *vb* reciclar *vb*
red *adj* **red tape** burocracia *nf*, trámites burocráticos *nmpl*, papeleo *nm* **to be in the red** estar en números rojos *vb*, entrar en déficit *vb*
redeem *vb* amortizar *vb*, liquidar *vb*, redimir *vb*
redeemable *adj* **redeemable bond** bono amortizable *nm*
redemption *n* amortización *nf*, pago *nm*, rescate *nm* **redemption fund** fondo para amortizaciones *nm*
redirect *vb* (mail) reexpedir *vb*
reduce *vb* (prices) reducir *vb*, rebajar *vb* (taxes) recortar *vb*
reduced *adj* rebajado *adj* **at a greatly reduced price** a un precio muy rebajado *prep*
reduction *n* reducción *nf*, rebaja *nf*, recorte *nm*
redundancy *n* despido *nm*, cese *nm*, baja *nf*
redundant *adj* desempleado *adj*, excesivo *adj*, superfluo *adj*, parado (LAm) *adj* **to make sb redundant** despedir a alguien por reducción de plantilla *vb*
refer *vb* referir *vb*, hacer referencia *vb* **we refer to our letter of...** hacemos referencia a nuestra carta de *vb*, con relación a nuestra carta de *prep* **we refer you to our head office** le remitimos a nuestra oficina central *vb*, le referimos a nuestra sede *vb*
referee *n* evaluador, -ora *nm,f*, persona que da referencias sobre otra *nf*, árbitro *nm* **to act as referee** estar dispuesto a dar referencias sobre *vb*
reference *n* referencia *nf*, informe *nm* **credit reference** referencia de crédito *nf* **reference number** número de referencia *nm* **to take up a reference** pedir una referencia *vb* **with reference to** con referencia a *prep*
referendum *n* referéndum *nm*
reflation *n* reflación *nf*, reactivación *nf*
reflationary *adj* reflacionario *adj*
reform *n* reforma *nf* **currency reform** reforma monetaria *nf*
refund **1.** *n* reembolso *nm*, reintegro *nm* **2.** *vb* reembolsar *vb*, devolver *vb*, reintegrar *vb*
refundable *adj* reembolsable *adj*
refurbish *vb* renovar *vb*, hacer reformas en *vb*
refurbishment *n* renovación *nf*, restauración *nf*

refusal *n* negativa *nf*, rechazo *nm*, plante (LAm) *nm*
refuse *vb* rehusar *vb*, negarse a *vb*, denegar *vb* **to refuse a claim** negarse a pagar una reclamación *vb* **to refuse goods** rechazar mercancías *vb* **to refuse payment** negarse a pagar *vb*, rehusar pagar (LAm) *vb*
regard *n* **with regard to...** en cuanto a *prep*, con relación a *prep*
regarding *prep* respecto a *prep*, por lo que se refiere a *prep*
regional *adj* **regional office** oficina regional *nf*, dirección general *nf*
register *n* registro *nm*, lista *nf*, archivo *nm*
registered *adj* **registered bond** obligación registrada *nf*, título nominativo *nm* **registered capital** capital certificado *nm*, capital nominal *nm* **registered company** compañía registrada *nf*, sociedad legalmente constituida *nf* **registered letter** carta certificada *nf*, carta registrada (LAm) *nf*, carta recomendada (LAm) *nf* **registered mail** correo certificado *nm*, correo recomendado (LAm) *nm* **registered office** domicilio social *nm*, sede *nf* **registered share** acción nominativa *nf* **registered trademark** marca registrada *nf*
regret *vb* **we regret to inform you that...** lamentamos informarle que *vb*
regular *adj* **regular customer** cliente, -nta habitual *nm,f*
regulation *n* regulación *nf*, reglamento *nm* **according to the regulations** según las normas *prep*, de acuerdo con las disposiciones *prep*
reimburse *vb* reembolsar *vb*
reimbursement *n* reembolso *nm*
reimport *vb* reimportar *vb*
reimportation *n* reimportación *nf*
reinsurance *n* reaseguro *nm*
reinsure *vb* reasegurar *vb*
reject *vb* (goods) rechazar *vb*, negarse a aceptar *vb*
relations *npl* **business relations** relaciones comerciales *nfpl* **industrial relations** relaciones industriales *nfpl*
relationship *n* **working relationship** relación de trabajo *nf*
relax *vb* (restrictions) relajar *vb*, flexibilizar *vb*
relevant *adj* pertinente *adj*, apropiado *adj*
reliability *n* fiabilidad *nf*, formalidad *nf*
reliable *adj* fidedigno *adj*, responsable *adj*, formal *adj*, fiable (LAm) *adj*, confiable (LAm) *adj*

relocate *vb* trasladar *vb*, trasladarse *vb*
relocation *n* traslado *nm*
remaining *adj* (sum) restante *adj*
reminder *n* recordatorio *nm*, advertencia *nf*
remittance *n* remesa *nf*, envío *nm*, giro *nm* **remittance advice** aviso de expedición *nm*
remunerate *vb* remunerar *vb*, pagar *vb*
remuneration *n* remuneración *nf*
renew *vb* (policy, contract) renovar *vb*, reanudar *vb*
renewable *adj* renovable *adj*
rent **1.** *n* alquiler *nm*, arrendamiento *nm*, renta (LAm) *nf*, arriendo (LAm) *nm* **2.** *vb* (house, office) alquilar *vb*, arrendar *vb*, rentar (LAm) *vb*
rental *n* alquiler *nm*, arrendamiento *nm*, renta (LAm) *nf*, arriendo (LAm) *nm*
repair **1.** *n* **costs of repair** costes de reparación *nmpl*, costos de reparación (LAm) *nmpl* **2.** *vb* reparar *vb*, arreglar *vb*
reparation *n* indemnización *nf*
repatriation *n* repatriación *nf*
repay *vb* reembolsar *vb*, devolver *vb*, pagar *vb*
repayment *n* (of loan) reembolso *nm*
repeat *adj* **repeat order** pedido suplementario *nm*
replace *vb* reemplazar *vb*, reponer *vb*
replacement *n* (person) sustituto, -uta *nm,f*, suplente *nmf*
reply *n* **in reply to your letter of...** en contestación a su carta de *prep*
report *n* informe *nm*, noticia *nf*, reportaje *nm*, reporte (LAm) *nm* **annual report** memoria anual *nf* **to draw up a report** redactar un informe *vb*, elaborar un informe *vb*, hacer un reporte (LAm) *vb* **to submit/present a report** presentar un informe *vb*, reportear (LAm) *vb*
repossess *vb* confiscar *vb*, recobrar *vb*
repossession *n* recuperación *nf*, confiscación *nf*
representative *n* representante *nmf*, agente *nmf*, viajante *nmf* **area representative** representante regional *nmf* **sales representative** agente comercial *nmf*
repudiate *vb* (contract) cancelar *vb*, rechazar *vb*
reputation *n* fama *nf* **to enjoy a good reputation** tener buena reputación *vb*
request *n* solicitud *nf*, petición *nf*, pedido (LAm) *nm* **request for payment** solicitud de pago *nf*, pedido de pago (LAm) *nm*
requirement *n* necesidad *nf*, requisito *nm*,

estipulación *nf* **in accordance with your requirements** según sus requisitos *prep,* de acuerdo con sus estipulaciones *prep* **it is a requirement of the contract that...** exige el contrato que *vb*

resale *n* reventa *nf*

rescind *vb* anular *vb,* cancelar *vb*

research *n* investigación *nf,* estudio *nm* **research and development (R&D)** investigación y desarrollo (I y D) *nf & nm* **market research** investigación de mercado *nf,* estudio de mercado *nm*

reservation *n* reserva *nf,* reservación (LAm) *nf* **to make a reservation** hacer una reserva *vb,* hacer una reservación (LAm) *vb*

reserve 1. *adj* **reserve currency** divisa de reserva *nf* **reserve stock** existencias de reserva *nfpl* **2.** *n* **currency reserve** reserva de divisas *nf* **to hold sth in reserve** tener algo en reserva *vb* **3.** *vb* reservar *vb*

residual *adj* residual *adj,* sobrante *adj*

resign *vb* dimitir *vb,* presentar la dimisión *vb,* renunciar *vb*

resignation *n* dimisión *nf,* renuncia *nf* **to hand in one's resignation** presentar la carta de renuncia *vb*

resolution *n* (decision) resolución *nf,* propósito *nm* **to make a resolution** tomar la determinación *vb,* decidirse *vb*

resolve *vb* (sort out) resolver *vb,* aclarar *vb* **to resolve to do sth** resolver hacer algo *vb,* optar por hacer algo *vb*

resort to *vb* (have recourse) recurrir a *vb,* no tener más remedio que *vb*

resources *npl* recursos *nmpl,* medios *nmpl*

respect *n* respeto *nm* **in respect of...** respecto a *prep*

response *n* **in response to...** en respuesta a *prep*

responsibility *n* **to take responsibility for sth** asumir responsabilidad *vb,* responsabilizarse de algo *vb*

responsible *adj* responsable *adj,* formal *adj,* serio *adj*

restrict *vb* restringir *vb,* limitar *vb*

restriction *n* restricción *nf,* límite *nm* **to impose restrictions on** imponer restricciones a *vb*

restrictive *adj* restrictivo *adj* **restrictive practices** prácticas restrictivas *nfpl*

restructure *vb* remodelar *vb,* reconvertir *vb,* replantear *vb*

retail *adj* **retail outlet** comercio al por menor *nm,* tienda al por menor *nf* **retail price** precio de venta al público *nm* **retail sales tax** impuesto sobre las ventas al detalle *nm* **retail trade** comercio al por menor *nm,* comercio minorista *nm*

retain *vb* retener *vb,* conservar *vb,* contratar *vb*

retention *n* retención *nf,* mantenimiento *nm* **retention of title** retención de título *nf*

retire *vb* jubilarse *vb,* retirarse *vb*

retirement *n* jubilación *nf,* retiro *nm* **to take early retirement** tomar la jubilación anticipada *vb*

retrain *vb* hacer un curso de reconversión *vb,* hacer un curso de recapacitación (LAm) *vb*

retraining *n* reciclaje profesional *nm,* reconversión *nf* **retraining programme, retraining program** (US) programa de reciclaje *nm,* curso de reciclaje *nm,* plan de recapacitación (LAm) *nm*

return 1. *n* vuelta *nf,* rendimiento *nm,* retorno (LAm) *nm* **in return** a cambio *prep* **return on capital** rendimiento del capital *nm,* rendimiento de la inversión *nm* **return on equity** rendimiento del capital social *nm,* rendimiento del patrimonio neto *nm* **return on investment** rendimiento de la inversión *nm* **return on sales** rendimiento de las ventas *nm* **returns** cifras *nfpl,* datos *nmpl,* resultados *nmpl* **2.** *vb* volver *vb,* regresar *vb,* retornar *vb*

returnable *adj* (deposit) reembolsable *adj*

revaluation *n* (of currency) revalorización *nf,* revaluación (LAm) *nf*

revalue *vb* (currency) revalorizar *vb,* revaluar (LAm) *vb*

revenue *n* ingresos *nmpl,* rentas públicas *nfpl*

reverse *vb* invertir *vb,* cambiar radicalmente *vb*

revert *vb* revertir *vb*

revert to *vb* volver a *vb,* revertir a *vb*

revise *vb* revisar *vb,* repasar *vb*

revocable *adj* **revocable letter of credit** carta de crédito revocable *nf*

revoke *vb* (offer) revocar *vb* (licence) revocar *vb*

right *n* derecho *nm,* derecha *nf* **right of recourse** derecho a recurrir *nm* **right of way** derecho de paso *nm,* preferencia *nf* **the right to do sth** el derecho a hacer algo *nm* **the right to sth** el derecho a algo *nm,* el derecho de algo *nm*

rights *npl* **rights issue** emisión de derechos *nf* **sole rights** derechos exclusivos *nmpl*
rise, raise (US) **1.** *n* (in earnings) subida *nf*, aumento *nm*, suba (LAm) *nf* (in inflation) subida *nf*, aumento *nm*, incremento *nm* (in unemployment) subida *nf*, aumento *nm*, crecimiento *nm* **2.** *vb* subir *vb*, levantarse *vb*, aumentar *vb*
risk *n* riesgo *nm*, peligro *nm* **all-risks insurance** seguro a todo riesgo *nm* **risk analysis** análisis de riesgos *nm* **risk assessment** valoración de riesgos *nf* **at the buyer's risk** por cuenta y riesgo del comprador *prep* **risk capital** capital de especulación *nm* **risk management** gestión de riesgos *nf* **the policy covers the following risks...** la póliza cubre los riesgos siguientes *nf*
road *n* **by road** por carretera *prep*, por tierra *prep* **road haulage** transporte por carretera *nm* **road haulage company** empresa de transportes por carretera *nf*, compañía de transportes *nf* **road traffic** circulación en la carretera *nf*, tráfico por carretera *nm*, tránsito en la carretera (LAm) *nm* **road transport** transporte por carretera *nm*
ROM (read only memory) *abbr* ROM *abbr,nf*, memoria de lectura *nf*
Rome *n* **the Treaty of Rome** El Tratado de Roma *nm*
room *n* **room for manoeuvre** espacio para maniobrar *nm*
royal *adj* real *adj* **the Royal Mint** (GB) casa real de la moneda *nf*
RSVP (répondez s'il vous plaît) *abbr* s.r.c. (se ruega contestación) *abbr* R.S.V.P. (LAm) *abbr*
run *vb* correr *vb* (manage) dirigir *vb*, poner *vb*, poner un servicio *vb*
run down *vb* (stocks) ir recortando *vb*
run low *vb* (stocks) ir agotándose *vb*, reducir al mínimo *vb*
running *adj* **running costs** gastos de explotación *nmpl*, costes corrientes *nmpl*, costos de operación (LAm) *nmpl*
rush *adj* **rush hour** hora punta *nf*, hora pico (LAm) *nf* **rush job** trabajo hecho de prisa *nm* **rush order** pedido urgente *nm*
sack, fire* (US) *vb* despedir *vb*, echar del trabajo *vb*, botar del trabajo (LAm) *vb*
safe *adj* seguro *adj*, fiable *adj*, sin riesgo *prep*
safety *n* **safety officer** responsable de la seguridad *nmf*

salary *n* sueldo *nm*, remuneración *nf*, salario *nm* **salary scale** escala salarial *nf*
sale *n* venta *nf* **closing-down sale, closing-out sale** (US) liquidación por cierre *nf* **sales** *npl* ventas *nfpl* **sales campaign** campaña de ventas *nf* **sales conference** reunión de ventas *nf* **sales department** departamento de ventas *nm* **export sales** ventas al exterior *nfpl* **sales figures** cifras de ventas *nfpl*, volumen de ventas *nm* **sales forecast** previsión de ventas *nf* **home sales** ventas nacionales *nfpl*, ventas en el mercado interior *nfpl* **sales ledger** libro mayor de ventas *nm* **sales management** gestión de ventas *nf*, dirección comercial *nf*
salesperson *n* dependiente, -nta *nm,f*, vendedor, -ora *nm,f*, representante *nmf*, corredor, -ora (LAm) *nm,f*
salvage *vb* salvar *vb*, rescatar *vb*
sample 1. *n* muestra *nf*, ejemplo *nm* **2.** *vb* probar *vb*, tomar muestras *vb*
sampling *n* muestreo *nm*
sanction *n* sanción *nf* **trade sanctions** sanciones económicas *nfpl*
saving *n* ahorro *nm*, economía *nf* **savings bank** caja de ahorros *nf*
scab* *n* rompehuelgas *nmf*, esquirol *nm*, carnero,- era (LAm) *nm,f*
scale *n* escala *nf*, balanza *nf*, tarifa *nf*, banda *nf*
scarcity *n* escasez *nf*, carestía *nf*
schedule 1. *n* programa *nm*, horario *nm*, lista *nf* **2.** *vb* programar *vb*, proyectar *vb*
scheme *n* **pension scheme** plan de pensiones *nm* **recovery scheme** plan de reactivación *nm*, programa de recuperación *nm*
scrap *n* (metal) chatarra *nf*
scrip *n* acción gratuita *nf*, título provisional *nm*
SDRs (special drawing rights) *abbr* DEG (derechos especiales de giro) *abbr*
sea *n* mar *nm* & *nf* **by sea** en barco, por vía marítima *prep* **sea freight** flete marítimo *nm*, carga marítima *nf*
seal 1. *n* sello *nm*, cierre *nm*, aprobación *nf* **2.** *vb* sellar *vb*, cerrar *vb*
sealed *adj* cerrado *adj*, sellado *adj* **sealed bid** oferta en pliego cerrado *nf*
season *n* temporada *nf*, estación *nf*, época *nf* **high season** temporada alta *nf* **low season** temporada baja *nf*
seasonal *adj* estacional *adj*
SEC (Securities and Exchange Commission) (GB) *abbr* Comisión de Valores y

Cambios (La) *nf,* Comisión de Bolsa y Valores *nf*

secondary *adj* **secondary industry** sector secundario *nm* **secondary market** mercado subsidiario *nm*

secondment *n* traslado temporal *nm*

secretary *n* secretario, -ria *nm,f* **executive secretary** secretario, -ria ejecutivo, -iva *nm,f*

sector *n* sector *nm* **primary sector** sector primario *nm* **secondary sector** sector secundario *nm* **tertiary sector** sector terciario *nm*

secure *adj* seguro *adj*

secured *adj* **secured loan** préstamo garantizado *nm*

securities *npl* valores *nmpl,* titulos *nmpl,* acciones *nfpl* **gilt-edged securities** títulos del Estado *nmpl,* valores del Estado *nmpl* **listed securities** valores bursátiles *nmpl,* acciones cotizables en bolsa *nfpl* **unlisted securities** valores no admitidos a cotización *nmpl*

security *n* seguridad *nf,* valor *nm* **Social Security (GB)** Seguridad Social *nf*

self-assessment *n* autoevaluación *nf*

self-employed *adj* autónomo *adj,* que trabaja por cuenta propia *rel pron*

self-financing *adj* autofinanciado *adj*

self-management *n* autogestión *nf*

self-sufficient *adj* autosuficiente *adj*

sell 1. *n* **hard sell** venta agresiva *nf* **soft sell** venta blanda/suave *nf* **2.** *vb* vender *vb* **to sell sth at auction** subastar algo *vb,* rematar (LAm) *vb* **to sell sth in bulk** vender algo a granel *vb* **to sell sth on credit** vender algo a crédito *vb* **to sell sth retail** vender algo al por menor *vb* **this article sells well** este artículo se vende bien *vb* **to sell sth wholesale** vender algo al por mayor *vb*

sell off *vb* liquidar *vb,* vender barato *vb*

sell up *vb* liquidar *vb,* vender un negocio con todas sus existencias *vb*

seller *n* vendedor, -ora *nm,f*

semi-skilled *adj* semicualificado *adj*

send *vb* enviar *vb,* mandar *vb,* remitir *vb*

send back *vb* devolver *vb*

sendee *n* destinatario, -ria *nm,f*

sender *n* remitente *nmf*

senior *adj* mayor *adj,* superior *adj,* principal *adj* **senior management** alta dirección *nf*

seniority *n* antigüedad *nf*

service *n* **after-sales service** servicio postventa *nm* **civil service** administra-

ción pública *nf* **service included** servicio incluido *nm* **service industry** industria de servicios *nf,* sector servicios *nm* **National Health Service (GB)** Seguridad Social *nf*

set up *vb* (company) montar *vb,* fundar *vb,* poner *vb*

settle *vb* (dispute) resolver *vb* (account) pagar *vb,* saldar *vb,* solventar *vb*

severance *n* **severance pay** indemnización por despido *nf*

shady* *adj* (dealings) sospechoso *adj,* turbio *adj*

share 1. *n* participación *nf,* cuota *nf,* acción *nf* **share in the profits** una parte de las ganancias *nf* **market share** participación en el mercado *nf,* cuota de mercado *nf* **ordinary share** acción ordinaria *nf* **2.** *vb* compartir *vb* **to share the responsibilities** compartir las responsabilidades *vb*

shareholder *n* accionista *nmf,* tenedor, -ora de acciones *nm,f*

shark* *n* usurero, -era *nm,f,* explotador, -ora *nm,f*

sharp *adj* **sharp practice** triquiñuelas *nf*

shift *n* cambio *nm,* turno *nm,* desplazamiento *nm* **the three-shift system** el sistema de tres turnos *nm* **shift work** trabajo por turnos *nm*

shipbuilding *n* construcción naval *nf*

shipment *n* (consignment) carga *nf,* consignación *nf*

shipper *n* expedidor, -ora *nm,f,* remitente *nmf*

shipping *n* **shipping agent** consignatario, -ria *nm,f,* agencia de transportes *nf* **shipping broker** agente expedidor *nm,* corredor marítimo *nm* **shipping line** compañía naviera *nf*

shipyard *n* astillero *nm*

shirker* *n* vago, -aga *nm,f,* flojo, -oja *nm,f,* fiacún, -una (LAm) *nm,f,* flojonazo,-aza (LAm) *nm,f*

shoddy* *adj* de baja calidad

shop *n* **shop assistant** dependiente, -nta *nm,f,* vendedor, -ora *nm,f,* empleado, -ada de tienda (LAm) **closed shop** plantilla sindicada *nf* **shop steward** representante sindical *nmf,* enlace sindical *nmf,* delegado, -ada sindical *nm,f* **to shut up shop** (informal) cerrar *vb,* cerrar la tienda *vb,* dar por terminado un asunto *vb* **to talk shop** (informal) hablar del trabajo *vb*

shopping *n* **shopping centre** centro comercial *nm*
short *adj* breve *adj*, corto *adj* **short delivery** entrega insuficiente *nf* **to be on short time** trabajar a jornada reducida *vb*
shortage *n* falta *nf*, escasez *nf*
show *n* (exhibition) exposición *nf*, exhibición *nf*, feria *nf*
showroom *n* salón de exposición *nm*, sala de exposiciones *nf*
shredder *n* trituradora *nf*
shrink *vb* recortar *vb*, contraerse *vb*
shrinkage *n* **stock shrinkage** pérdidas de estoc *nfpl*, fugas de existencias *nfpl*
shutdown *n* cese *nm*, paralización *nf*
shuttle *n* servicio de enlace *nm*, puente aéreo *nm*
SIB (Securities and Investment Board) (GB) *abbr* Comisión de Bolsa y Valores *nf*
sick *adj* **sick leave** baja por enfermedad *nf*, licencia por enfermedad (LAm) *nf*
sickness *n* **sickness benefit** subsidio de enfermedad *nm*
sight *n* **sight draft** letra a la vista *nf*, efecto a la vista *nm*
sign *vb* firmar *vb*, fichar *vb*
signatory *n* firmante *nmf*, signatario, -ria *nm,f*
signature *n* firma *nf*
silent *adj* **silent partner** socio, -cia comanditario, -ria *nm,f*
sinking *n* hundimiento *nm*, amortización *nf* **sinking fund** fondo de amortización *nf*
sit-in *n* (strike) encierro en señal de protesta *nm*
size *n* tamaño *nm*, talla *nf*, talle (LAm) *nm*
skill *n* habilidad *nf*, técnica *nf*
skilled *n* (worker) cualificado *adj*, especializado *adj*, capacitado (LAm) *adj*
slackness *n* (laxity) falta de actividad *nf*, falta de movimiento *nf*
sliding *adj* **sliding scale** escala móvil *nf*
slogan *n* consigna *nf*, eslogan *nm*
slow down *vb* desacelerar *vb*, frenarse *vb*
slowdown *n* desaceleración *nf*, reducción *nf*, huelga de celo *nf*
slump 1. *n* depresión *nf*, caída repentina *nf* 2. *vb* caer en picado *vb*, sufrir un bajón *vb*
slush *adj* **slush fund** fondo para sobornos *nm*, fondo de reptiles *nm*
small *adj* pequeño *adj* **small ads** anuncios clasificados *nmpl*, avisos clasificados (LAm) *nmpl* **small scale** pequeña escala *nf*

smuggle *vb* contrabandear *vb*
society *n* sociedad *nf* **building society** sociedad hipotecaria *nf*, sociedad de crédito hipotecario *nf*, sociedad de ahorro y préstamo para la vivienda *nf* **consumer society** sociedad de consumo *nf*
socio-economic *adj* **socio-economic categories** grupos socioeconómicos *nmpl*
software *n* software *nm*, programa informático *nm* **software package** paquete de software *nm*
sole *adj* exclusivo *adj*, único *adj* **sole agent** representante en exclusiva *nmf*
solicitor, lawyer (US) *n* abogado, -ada *nm,f*
solvency *n* solvencia *nf*
solvent *adj* solvente *adj*
source *n* fuente *nf*, origen *nm*, raíz *nf*
sourcing *n* aprovisionamiento *nm*, procedencia *nf*
specialist *n* especialista *nmf*
speciality *n* especialidad *nf*
specialize *vb* especializar *vb*
specification *n* especificación *nf*, requisito *nm*
specify *vb* precisar *vb*, indicar *vb*
speculate *vb* especular *vb*
speculator *n* especulador, -ora *nm,f*
spend *vb* gastar *vb*, pasar *vb*, emplear *vb*
spending *n* gastos *nmpl*
spendthrift *adj* despilfarrador *adj*
sphere *n* ámbito *nm*, campo *nm*, esfera *nf* **sphere of activity** ámbito de actividad profesional *nm*
spin-off *n* efecto indirecto *nm*
split 1. *adj* **split division** fraccionamiento *nm* 2. *vb* escindirse *vb*, desintegrar *vb*, dividir *vb*, partir *vb*, romper *vb*
spoilage *n* desechos *nmpl*, desperdicios *nmpl*
spoils *npl* botín *nm*
spokesperson *n* portavoz *nmf*, vocero, -era (LAm) *nm,f*
sponsor *n* patrocinador, -ora *nm,f*, espónsor *nmf*
sponsorship *n* patrocinio *nm*, mecenazgo *nm*
spot *adj* **spot cash** pago al contado *nm*, dinero en mano *nm* **spot market** mercado de entrega spot *nm* **spot price** precio de entrega inmediata *nm*, tarifa de entrega inmediata *nf* **spot rate** precio de entrega inmediata *nm*, tarifa de entrega inmediata *nf*
spread *vb* (payments) distribuir *vb*
spreadsheet *n* hoja de cálculo *nf*
squander *vb* despilfarrar *vb*, derrochar *vb*

squeeze 1. *n* **credit squeeze** restricciones de crédito *nfpl* **2.** *vb* (spending) restringir *vb*, recortar *vb*

stable *adj* (economy) estable *adj*

staff *n* personal *nm*, plantilla *nf*, empleados *nmpl*

staffing *n* dotación de personal *nf*

stage *n* etapa *nf* **in stages** por etapas *prep*

staged *adj* **staged payments** pagos por etapas *nmpl*

stagger *vb* (holidays) escalonar *vb*

stagnation *n* estancamiento *nm*

stake *n* participación *nf*, inversión *nf*, paquete accional autónomo *nm*

stakeholder *n* inversor, -ora *nm,f*, apostador, -ora *nm,f*

stalemate *n* punto muerto *nm*

standard 1. *adj* normal *adj* **standard agreement** contrato-tipo *nm* **2.** *n* **gold standard** patrón-oro *nm* **standard of living** nivel de vida *nm*

standardization *n* estandarización *nf*, normalización *nf*

standardize *vb* normalizar *vb*, tipificar *vb*

standing 1. *adj* **standing charges** cuotas fijas *nfpl* **standing order** orden permanente de pago *nf*, pedido fijo *nm* **2.** *n* standing *nm*

staple *adj* **staple commodities** productos básicos *nmpl*, artículos de primera necesidad *nmpl*

start-up *n* inicio *nm* **start-up capital** capital de puesta en marcha *nm*

state *n* **state-owned enterprise** empresa estatal *nf*, empresa de propiedad pública *nf*

statement *n* afirmación *nf*, declaración *nf*, instrucción *nf* **bank statement** estado de cuentas *nm*

statistics *n* estadísticas *nfpl*, cifras *nfpl*

status *n* **financial status** situación económica *nf* **status quo** statu quo *nm*

statute *n* estatuto *nm*, ley *nf*

steel *n* **steel industry** industria del acero *nf*

sterling *n* esterlina *nf*, libra esterlina *nf* **sterling area** zona de la libra esterlina *nf* **sterling balance** reserva de libras esterlinas *nf* **pound sterling** libra esterlina *nf*

stock, inventory (US) *n* (goods) existencias *nfpl*, estoc *nm*, stock *nm* **stock control** control de existencias *nm* **stock exchange** bolsa *nf* **in stock** en almacén *prep*, en estoc *prep* **stock market** mercado de valores *nm*, bolsa de

valores *nf* **out of stock** con las existencias agotadas **stocks and shares** acciones *nfpl*, valores inmobiliarios *nmpl*

stockbroker *n* corredor, -ora de Bolsa *nm,f*, agente de Bolsa *nmf*, corredor (LAm) *nm*

stockholder *n* accionista *nmf*, tenedor, -ora de acciones *nm,f*

stocktaking *n* inventario de existencias *nm*, balance *nm*

stoppage *n* (strike) paro *nm*, cese *nm*

storage *n* almacenaje *nm*, almacenamiento *nm* **storage capacity** capacidad de almacenaje *nf* **cold storage plant** planta de almacenaje frigorífico *nf*

store 1. *n* (shop) almacén *nf*, tienda *nf* **chain store** tienda que forma parte de una cadena *nf* **department store** grandes almacenes *nmpl* **2.** *vb* guardar *vb*

stowage *n* gastos de estiba *nmpl*, bodega *nf*

strategic *adj* estratégico *adj*

strategy *n* estrategia *nf*

stress *n* **executive stress** estrés profesional *nm*

strike 1. *adj* **strike action** acción laboral *nf*, huelga *nf*, paro (LAm) *nm* **strike ballot** votación para decidir si se hace huelga *nf*, votación para decidir si se va al paro (LAm) *nf* **2.** *n* huelga *nf*, paro (LAm) *nm* **wildcat strike** huelga salvaje *nf*, paro incontrolado (LAm) *nm*, paro imprevisto (LAm) *nm* **3.** *vb* declararse en huelga *vb*, hacer huelga *vb*, ir al paro (LAm) *vb*, declararse en paro (LAm) *vb*

strikebreaker *n* rompehuelgas *nmf*, carnero,-era (LAm) *nm,f*

striker *n* huelguista *nmf*, trabajador,-ora en paro (LAm) *nm,f*

subcontract *vb* subcontratar *vb*

subcontractor *n* subcontratista *nmf*

subordinate *n* subalterno, -rna *nm,f*

subscribe *vb* contribuir *vb*, suscribir *vb*

subsidiary *n* empresa filial *nf*, sucursal *nf* (LAm)

subsidize *vb* subvencionar *vb*, subsidiar (LAm)

subsidy *n* subvención *nf* **state subsidy** subvención estatal *nf*, subsidio del gobierno *nm*, subsidio del estado (LAm) *nm*

suburb *n* afueras *nfpl*, colonias (LAm) *nfpl* **outer suburbs** barrios residenciales de las afueras *nmpl*

supermarket *n* supermercado *nm*, autoservicio *nm*

supertanker *n* superpetrolero *nm*

supertax n impuesto elevadísimo nm
supervisor n supervisor, -ora nm,f, revisor, -ora nm,f, director, -ora nm,f
supervisory adj **supervisory board** comité de supervisión nm
supplementary adj suplementario adj
supplier n suministrador, -ora nm,f, proveedor, -ora nm,f, abastecedor, -ora nm,f
supply 1. n oferta nf, suministro nm, reserva nf **supply and demand** oferta y demanda nf & nf **2.** vb proveer vb, abastecer vb
surplus n excedente nm, exceso nm, superávit nm **budget surplus** superávit presupuestario nm **trade surplus** superávit comercial nm
surtax n recargo del impuesto sobre la renta nm
survey n encuesta nf, sondeo nm **market research survey** estudio de mercado nm, investigación de mercado nf
swap 1. n canje nm, cambio nm, intercambio nm **2.** vb canjear vb, intercambiar vb
sweetener* n (bribe) soborno nm, coima (LAm) nf, mordida (LAm) nf
swindle* n estafa nf
swindler* n estafador, -ora nm,f, timador, -ora nm,f
switchboard n centralita de teléfonos nf, conmutador (LAm) nm **switchboard operator** telefonista nmf
syndicate n agrupación nf, sindicato nm, consorcio nm
synergy n sinergia nf
synthesis n síntesis nf
synthetic adj sintético adj
system n sistema nm **expert system** sistema experto nm **systems analyst** analista de sistemas nm
table vb (motion, paper) presentar vb
tabulate vb (data) tabular vb, presentar en forma de tabla vb
tabulated adj **tabulated data** datos tabulados nmpl
tacit adj tácito adj **by tacit agreement** por acuerdo tácito prep
tactic n táctica nf **delaying tactics** táctica de demora nf **selling tactics** táctica de ventas nf
tailor vb (adapt) adaptar vb
take vb **to take legal action** entablar un pleito vb **to take notes** tomar apuntes vb, tomar notas vb, sacar apuntes (LAm) vb **to take part in** participar en vb **to take the chair** presidir vb **to take the lead** tomar la

delantera vb, tomar el mando vb **to take one's time** tomarse tiempo vb, tardar vb
take over vb (company) adquirir vb
takeover n adquisición nf, absorción nf
takeup n solicitud nf, interés nm
takings npl ingresos nmpl, recaudación nf, entrada nf
talk 1. n **sales talk** argumentos de venta nmpl, reunión de ventas nf, conversación sobre ventas nf **2.** vb hablar vb **to talk business** hablar de negocios vb, hablar en serio vb
tally 1. n cuenta nf, registro nm **2.** vb coincidir vb, cuadrar vb
tally up vb hacer la cuenta vb, cuadrar vb
tally with vb concordar con vb, coincidir con vb
tangible adj **tangible asset** activo tangible nm, activo material nm
tap vb **to tap a market** aprovechar un mercado vb **to tap resources** explotar recursos vb
target n objetivo nm, meta nf **target date** fecha objetivo nf **target market** mercado previsto nm **production target** objetivo de producción nm **sales target** objetivo de ventas nm **to set a target** fijar una meta vb
targeted adj **targeted campaign** campaña dirigida nf
tariff n arancel nm, tarifa nf, precio nm **tariff barrier** barrera arancelaria nf **tariff negotiations** negociaciones arancelarias nfpl **tariff quota** cupo arancelario nm **tariff reform** reforma arancelaria nf **to raise tariffs** incrementar aranceles vb, subir tarifas vb
task n tarea nf, faena nf **task management** gestión de tareas nf
tax n impuesto nm, tributo nm **after tax** después de deducir impuestos prep, neto adj **tax allowance** desgravación fiscal nf, deducción impositiva nf **before tax** antes de deducir impuestos prep, bruto adj **capital gains tax** impuesto sobre las plusvalías nm **tax claim** reclamación de impuestos nf **tax-deductible** desgravable adj **direct tax** impuesto directo nm **tax-free** libre de impuestos adj, exento de impuestos adj **income tax** impuesto sobre la renta personal nm **indirect tax** impuesto indirecto nm **tax liability** deuda fiscal nf **tax rate** tipo impositivo nm **to levy taxes** cobrar impuestos vb **value-added tax, sales tax** (US) impuesto sobre

el valor añadido/agregado (IVA) *nm* **tax year** año fiscal *nm*, ejercicio fiscal *nm*
taxable *adj* **taxable income** ingresos gravables *nmpl*
taxation *n* imposición *nf*, cargas fiscales *nfpl* **corporate taxation** imposición de sociedades *nf*
taxpayer *n* contribuyente *nmf*
team *n* **research team** equipo de investigación *nm*
technical *adj* **technical director** director, -ora técnico, -ica *nm,f*
technician *n* técnico, -ica *nm,f*
technique *n* **sales technique** técnica de ventas *nf*
technology *n* tecnología *nf* **information technology** informática *nf*, tecnología de datos *nf* **technology transfer** transferencia de tecnología *nf*
telebanking *n* telebanca *nf*
telecommunications *npl* telecomunicaciones *nfpl*
telecopier *n* telecopiadora *nf*, teletipo *nm*
telefax *n* telefax *nm*
telephone *n* teléfono *nm* **telephone box, telephone booth** (US) cabina de teléfonos *nf* **telephone call** llamada telefónica *nf*, llamado (LAm) *nm* **telephone directory** guía telefónica *nf*, directorio telefónico (LAm) *nm* **telephone number** número de teléfono *nm*
teleprocessing *n* teleproceso *nm*
telesales *npl* televentas *nfpl*
televise *vb* televisar *vb*, transmitir *vb*
teleworking *n* trabajo por teléfono *nm*
telex **1.** *n* télex *nm* **2.** *vb* (message) poner un télex *vb*
teller *n* cajero, -era de banco *nm,f*
temporary *adj* temporal *adj*, provisional *adj*, temporario (LAm) *adj*, provisorio (LAm) *adj* **temporary employment** empleo eventual *nm*, trabajo temporario (LAm) *nm*
tenant *n* inquilino, -ina *nm,f*, arrendatario, -ria *nm,f*
tend *vb* **to tend toward** tender a *vb*, tener tendencia a *vb*
tendency *n* tendencia *nf*, propensión *nf* **market tendencies** tendencias del mercado *nfpl*
tender *n* oferta *nf*, concurso *nm*, licitación *nf* **tender offer** oferta pública de adquisición (OPA) *nf* **tender price** precio de oferta *nm* **sale by tender** venta por concurso *nf* **to lodge a tender** presentar

una oferta *vb*, licitar (LAm) *vb* **to put sth out for tender** sacar algo a licitación *vb*
tenderer *n* postor, -ora *nm,f*, licitador,-ora (LAm) *nm,f*
tendering *n* licitación *nf*, oferta *nf*
tentative *adj* **tentative offer** oferta provisional *nf*, oferta provisoria (LAm) *nf* **tentative plan** plan provisional *nm*, plan provisorio (LAm) *nm*
tenure *n* tenencia *nf*, ocupación *nf*, posesión *nf*
term *n* **at term** a término *prep* **long term** largo plazo *nm* **medium term** medio plazo *nm* **term of office** mandato *nm* **terms and conditions** términos y condiciones *nmpl* & *nfpl* **short term** corto plazo *nm* **terms of reference** atribuciones y responsabilidades *nfpl* & *nfpl*, competencia *nf*, ámbito *nm* **terms of trade** relación real de intercambio *nf*
terminal **1.** *adj* terminal *adj*, final *adj* **terminal bonus** bonificación recibida al concluir un seguro *nf* **terminal market** mercado terminal *nm* **2.** *n* **air terminal** terminal aérea *nf* **computer terminal** terminal de ordenador *nm*
termination *n* caducidad *nf*, cese *nm* **termination date** fecha de caducidad *nf* **termination of employment** baja *nf*, cese *nm*, despido *nm*
tertiary *adj* **tertiary industry** sector terciario *nm*, sector de los servicios *nm*
test *n* prueba *nf*, ensayo *nm* **test case** caso que sienta jurisprudencia *nm* **test data** datos de prueba *nmpl* **to put sth to the test** someter algo a prueba *vb*, poner algo a prueba *vb* **to stand the test** pasar la prueba *vb*
test-market *vb* someter a prueba de mercado *vb*
testimonial *n* recomendación *nf*, tributo *nm*, homenaje *nm*
textile *n* **textile industry** industria textil *nf*
theory *n* **in theory** en teoría *prep*, teóricamente *adv*
third *adj* **third party** tercero *nm*, tercera parte *nf* **third-party insurance** seguro contra terceros *nm*, seguro de responsabilidad civil *nm* **the Third World** el Tercer Mundo *nm*
thirty *adj* **Thirty-Share Index** (GB) índice de cotización de acciones *nm*
thrash out *vb* (agreement, policy) tratar de resolver *vb*, llegar a un acuerdo *vb*
three *adj* **three-way split** división triple *nf*
threshold *n* umbral *nm* **tax threshold**

nivel en el que la tasa de impuestos cambia *nm*
thrive *vb* prosperar *vb*, crecer *vb*
through *prep* **to get through to sb** (phone) comunicarse con alguien *vb*, entenderse con alguien *vb* **to put sb through (to sb)** (phone) conectar *vb*
tick over *vb* ir tirando *vb*
ticket *n* billete *nm*, ticket *nm*, entrada *nf*, pasaje (LAm) *nm*, boleto (LAm) *nm*, tiquete (LAm) *nm* **ticket agency** agencia de venta de localidades *nf* **ticket office** taquilla *nf*, despacho de billetes *nm*, boletería (LAm) *nf*, taquilla (LAm) *nf* **price ticket** etiqueta del precio *nf* **return ticket, round-trip ticket** (US) billete de ida y vuelta *nm*, pasaje de vuelta *nm* **season ticket** billete de abono *nm*, boleto de abono (LAm) *nm* **single/one-way ticket** (rail/flight) billete de ida *nm*, pasaje sencillo *nm*, boleto sencillo (LAm) *nm*
tide over *vb* ayudar a salir de un apuro *vb*
tie up *vb* (capital) inmovilizar *vb*
tied *adj* **tied loan** préstamo inmovilizado *nm*
tier *n* **two-tier system** sistema de dos niveles *nm*
tight *adj* **to be on a tight budget** tener un presupuesto muy limitado *vb*
time *n* tiempo *nm*, vez *nf* **time and a half** paga y media *nf* **double time** paga doble *nf* **time frame** plazo de tiempo *nm* **lead time** plazo de entrega *nm*, período de gestación *nm* **time limit** plazo *nm*, término *nm*, fecha tope *nf* **time management** gestión del tiempo *nf*
time-consuming *adj* que lleva mucho tiempo *rel pron*
time-saving *adj* que ahorra tiempo *rel pron*
timescale *n* programa *nm*, calendario *nm*, escala de tiempo *nf*
timeshare *n* multipropiedad *nf*, copropiedad *nf*
timetable *n* horario *nm*, programa *nm*, agenda *nf*
timing *n* ritmo *nm*, cronometraje *nm*
tip *n* (suggestion) consejo práctico *nm*, aviso *nm* **market tip** información confidencial acerca del mercado *nf*
title *n* (to goods) título *nm* **title deed** escritura de propiedad *nf*
token *n* **token payment** pago simbólico *nm* **token strike** huelga de advertencia *nf*
toll *n* peaje *nm*, tasa *nf*, efecto *nm*, cuota (LAm) *nf*

ton *n* tonelada *nf* **metric ton** tonelada métrica *nf*
tone *n* tono *nm* **dialling tone, dial tone** (US) (phone) tono de marcar *nm*, tono de discado (LAm) *nm*
tonnage *n* tonelaje *nm*, peso *nm* **bill of tonnage** declaración de tonelaje *nf* **gross tonnage** tonelaje bruto *nm* **net(t) tonnage** tonelaje neto *nm*
top *adj* **top management** alta dirección *nf* **top prices** precios de punta *nmpl* **top priority** prioridad absoluta *nf*
top-level *adj* de primera categoría *prep*, de alto standing *prep*
top-of-the-range *adj* mejor de la gama *adj*
total 1. *adj* total *adj*, absoluto *adj*, rotundo *adj* **total sales** ventas totales *nfpl* **2.** *n* total *nm*, totalidad *nf* **the grand total** total global *nm*, suma global *nf*
tough *adj* **tough competition** competencia fuerte *nf*, competencia intensa *nf*
tour *n* **tour of duty** período de servicio *nm*
tourism *n* turismo *nm*
tourist *n* turista *nmf* **the tourist trade** la industria del turismo *nf*, turismo *nm*, el mercado turístico *nm*
town *n* **town centre** centro ciudad *nm* **town council** ayuntamiento *nm*, municipio *nm* **town hall** ayuntamiento *nm*, municipio *nm*, presidencia municipal (LAm) *nf*, intendencia (LAm) *nf* **town planning** urbanismo *nm*
TQM (Total Quality Management) *abbr* gestión total de calidad *nf*
track *n* pista *nf* **track record** antecedentes *nmpl*, registro de antecedentes *nm*, historial (LAm) *nm* **to be on the right track** ir por buen camino *vb*
trade 1. *adj* **trade agreement** acuerdo comercial *nm* **trade balance** balanza comercial *nf* **trade barrier** barrera comercial *nf*, barrera arancelaria *nf* **trade cycle** ciclo económico *nm* **trade directory** guía comercial *nf*, guía de fabricantes y comerciantes *nf* **trade fair** feria de muestras *nf* **trade figures** estadísticas de la balanza comercial *nfpl* **trade name** nombre comercial *nm*, razón social *nf* **trade price** precio al detallista *nm* **trade restrictions** restricciones comerciales *nfpl* **trade secret** secreto comercial *nm* **trade talks** conversaciones comerciales *nfpl*, negociaciones comerciales *nfpl* **Trade Descriptions Act** ley que regula la descripción comercial de productos *nf* **Trades Union Congress** Confederación de

118   Business Glossary: English–Spanish

Sindicatos *nf* **trade union** sindicato *nm*, gremio (LAm) *nm* **2.** *n* comercio *nm* **balance of trade** balanza comercial *nf* **by trade** de profesión *prep*, de oficio *prep* **fair trade** comercio con reciprocidad arancelaria *nm* **foreign trade** comercio exterior *nm*, comercio de ultramar *nm* **retail trade** comercio al por menor *nm* **to be in the trade** (informal) dedicarse al negocio de *vb* **3.** *vb* comerciar *vb*, negociar *vb* **to trade as** (name) comerciar como *vb* **to trade with sb** comerciar con alguien *vb*

trademark *n* marca *nf* **registered trademark** marca registrada *nf*

trader *n* comerciante *nmf*, vendedor, -ora *nm,f*, operador, -ora *nm,f*, feriante (LAm) *nmf*, puestero, -era (LAm) *nm,f*

trading *adj* **trading area** zona de comercio *nf* **trading capital** capital de explotación *nm*, capital circulante *nm* **trading company** sociedad comercial *nf* **trading estate** zona industrial *nf*, polígono industrial *nm* **trading loss** pérdida de ejercicio *nf* **trading margin** margen comercial *nm* **trading nation** país comerciante *nm* **trading partner** empresa que comercia con otra *nf*, país que comercia con otro *nm*, socio, -cia *nm,f* **trading standards** normas comerciales *nfpl* **Trading Standards Office (US)** departamento de control de prácticas comerciales *nm* **trading year** ejercicio comercial *nm*

traffic *n* tráfico *nm*, tránsito *nm* **air traffic** tráfico aéreo *nm* **rail traffic** tráfico por ferrocarril *nm* **road traffic** tráfico por carretera *nm* **sea traffic** tráfico marítimo *nm*

train **1.** *n* **goods train, freight train** (US) tren de mercancías *nm* **passenger train** tren de pasajeros *nm* **2.** *vb* (staff) formar *vb*, capacitar *vb*

trainee *n* aprendiz *nmf*, persona en aprendizaje *nf* **trainee manager** aspirante a un puesto directivo *nmf*

training *n* formación *nf*, capacitación *nf*, aprendizaje *nm* **advanced training** capacitación avanzada *nf* **training centre** centro de formación *nm* **training course** cursillo de actualización *nm*

transaction *n* transacción *nf*, operación *nf*, negociación *nf* **cash transaction** operación al contado *nf* **transaction management** gestión de transacciones *nf*

transcribe *vb* transcribir *vb*

transfer **1.** *adj* **transfer desk** (transport) mostrador de transbordos *nm* **transfer duty** impuesto de transferencia *nm* **transfer lounge** (transport) sala de tránsito *nf* **transfer payments** pagos de transferencia *nmpl* **transfer price** precio de transferencia *nm* **transfer tax** impuesto sobre transferencias *nm* **2.** *n* **bank transfer** transferencia bancaria *nf* **capital transfer** transferencia de capital *nf* **credit transfer** transferencia de fondos *nf* **3.** *vb* (call) pasar a *vb*, poner con *vb* (ownership, technology) transferir *vb*, traspasar *vb* (transport) trasladar *vb*, hacer transbordo *vb*

transferable *adj* transferible *adj*

transit *n* **transit goods** mercancías en tránsito *nfpl* **in transit** en tránsito *prep* **lost in transit** perdido en tránsito *adj* **transit lounge** (transport) sala de tránsito *nf*, sala para pasajeros en tránsito *nf* **transit passenger** (transport) pasajero en tránsito *nm*

transmit *vb* transmitir *vb*, emitir *vb*, comunicar *vb*

transnational *adj* transnacional *adj*

transport *n* **transport agent** agente de transportes *nmf* **air transport** transporte aéreo *nm* **transport company** compañía de transportes *nf*, empresa de transportes *nf* **public transport** transporte público *nm* **rail transport** transporte por ferrocarril *nm* **road transport** transporte por carretera *nm*

transportation *n* transporte *nm*

transship *vb* transbordar *vb*

travel **1.** *adj* **travel agency** agencia de viajes *nf* **travel insurance** seguro de viaje *nm* **2.** *n* **air travel** viajes en avión *nmpl*, viajar por avión *vb* **business travel** viajes de negocios *nmpl* **3.** *vb* viajar *vb*, desplazarse *vb*

traveller, traveler (US) *n* viajero, -era *nm,f*, pasajero, -era *nm,f*, viajante comercial *nmf* **traveller's cheque, traveler's check** (US) cheque de viajero *nm*, cheque de viaje *nm*

travelling, traveling (US) *n* **travelling expenses, travel expenses** (US) gastos de viaje *nmpl*

treasurer *n* **treasurer check (US)** cheque de tesorero *nm* **company treasurer** director, -ora de finanzas de la empresa *nm,f*

treasury *n* tesoro *nm* **Treasury bill** pagaré del Tesoro *nm* **the Treasury** el Tesoro público *nm*, la Hacienda Pública *nf* **the Treasury Department (US)** Departamento del Tesoro *nm*, el Ministerio de Hacienda *nm*

treaty *n* tratado *nm*, acuerdo *nm*, convenio *nm* **commercial treaty** tratado comercial *nm*, acuerdo comercial *nm* **to make a treaty** suscribir un tratado *vb*, llegar a un acuerdo *vb*

trend *n* tendencia *nf*, coyuntura *nf*, moda *nf* **trend analysis** análisis de tendencias *nm* **current trend** moda actual *nf* **economic trend** tendencia económica *nf* **market trend** tendencia del mercado *nf* **price trend** tendencia de precios *nf* **to buck a trend** ir contracorriente *vb* **to set a trend** iniciar una moda *vb*

trial *n* **trial and error** ensayo y error *nm* & *nm* **trial offer** muestra de oferta *nf* **trial period** período de prueba *nm* **to carry out trials** poner a prueba *vb*, realizar ensayos *vb*

tribunal *n* tribunal *nm*, comisión *nf* **industrial tribunal** tribunal Magistratura del Trabajo *nf*

trim *vb* (investment) recortar *vb* (workforce) reducir la plantilla *vb*

trimming *n* **cost trimming** reducción de costes *nf*

trip *n* viaje *nf*, recorrido *nm* **business trip** viaje de negocios *nm* **round trip** viaje de ida y vuelta *nm*, viaje redondo (LAm) *nf*

triplicate *n* **in triplicate** por triplicado *prep*

trust *n* **trust agreement** acuerdo fiduciario *nm* **trust company** compañía fiduciaria *nf* **trust estate** herencia fiduciaria *nf* **trust fund** fondo de fideicomiso *nm*, fondo de custodia *nm* **investment trust** sociedad de inversión *nf* **to hold sth in trust** estar encomendado de algo *vb* **to set up a trust** establecer un fideicomiso *vb* **to supply sth on trust** suministrar algo bajo palabra *vb*, abastecer algo a crédito *vb* **unit trust** sociedad inversora por obligaciones *nf*, fondos mutuos *nmpl*, fondo de inversión mobiliaria *nm*

trustee *n* fideicomisario, -ria *nm,f* **trustee department** (bank) oficina de administración fiduciaria *nf*

trusteeship *n* fideicomiso *nm*, cargo de administrador *nm*

try out *vb* probar *vb*, poner a prueba *vb*

turn *vb* (market) cambiar *vb*, fluctuar *vb*

turn down *vb* (offer) rechazar *vb*

turn on *vb* (machine) poner en marcha *vb*, conectar *vb*, prender (LAm) *vb*

turn out *vb* (end) salir *vb*, resultar *vb*, acabar *vb*

turn over *vb* facturar *vb*, dar la vuelta a *vb*, voltear (LAm) *vb*, dar vuelta (LAm) *vb*

turn round, turn around (US) *vb* (company) sanear *vb*

turnabout *n* giro *nm*, cambio *nm*

turning *adj* **turning point** vuelta de la marea *nf*, momento decisivo *nm*

turnover *n* volumen de ventas *nm*, cifra de facturación *nf* **capital turnover** volumen de capital facturado *nm* **turnover rate** ritmo de facturación *nm*, índice de rotación de existencias *nm* **turnover ratio** ratio de facturación *nm*, ratio de renovación *nm* **turnover tax** impuesto sobre el volumen de ventas y negocios *nm*

twenty-four *adj* **twenty-four-hour service** servicio de veinticuatro horas *nm*

two *adj* **two-speed** de velocidad doble *prep* **two-tier** de dos niveles *prep* **two-way** de doble sentido *prep*, bilateral *adj* de doble mano (LAm) *prep*, de doble vía (LAm) *prep*

tycoon *n* magnate *nmf*

type 1. *n* **bold type** negrita *nf* **italic type** cursiva *nf* **large type** letra grande *nf* **small type** caracteres pequeños *nmpl* **2.** *vb* escribir a máquina *vb*, pasar a máquina *vb*, tipear (LAm) *vb*

typewriter *n* máquina de escribir *nf*

typing *adj* **typing error** error tipográfico *nm*

typist *n* mecanógrafo, -afa *nm,f*

ultimo *adj* del pasado mes *prep*

unanimous *adj* unánime *adj*

uncleared *adj* (customs) sin despachar *prep*, (cheque) sin pagar *prep*

unconditional *adj* incondicional *adj*

unconfirmed *adj* sin confirmar *prep*

undeclared *adj* (goods) sin declarar *prep*

undercapitalized *adj* infracapitalizado *adj*

undercharge *vb* cobrarle de menos a *vb*

undercut *vb* vender más barato *vb*

underdeveloped *adj* **underdeveloped country** país subdesarrollado *nm*

underemployed *adj* subempleado *adj*, infrautilizado *adj*

underinsured *adj* infrasegurado *adj*

underpay *vb* pagar de menos *vb*

underpayment *n* pago insuficiente *nm*

undersell *vb* vender más barato *vb*

understanding *n* comprensión *nf*, entendimiento *nm*, acuerdo *nm*

undersubscribed adj no cubierto por entero adj

undertake vb emprender vb, comprometerse vb, encargarse vb

undertaking n empresa nf, compromiso nm

undervalue vb infravalorar vb

underwrite vb (risk) asegurar vb

underwriter n suscriptor, -ora nm,f, asegurador, -ora nm,f

undischarged adj (bankrupt) no rehabilitado adj

unearned adj **unearned income** rendimientos del capital nmpl, renta no salarial nf

unemployed adj desempleado adj, parado adj, sin trabajo prep, cesante (LAm) adj

unemployment n desempleo nm, paro nm, cesantía (LAm) nf **unemployment benefit** subsidio de paro nm **unemployment insurance** seguro de desempleo nm **level of unemployment** nivel de desempleo nm **rate of unemployment** tasa de paro nf

unexpected adj inesperado adj

unfair adj **unfair dismissal** despido improcedente nm, despido injustificado nm, despido injusto nm

unforeseen adj **unforeseen circumstances** circunstancias imprevistas nfpl

unification n unificación nf

unilateral adj (contract) unilateral adj

uninsurable adj no asegurable adj

union n sindicato nm, unión nf, asociación de estudiantes nf, gremio (LAm) nm **union membership** afiliación sindical nf **union representative** representante sindical nmf, delegado, -ada sindical nm,f **trade union, labor union** (US) sindicato laboral nm

unit n unidad nf, módulo nm, conjunto nm **unit cost** coste unitario nm, costo por unidad (LAm) nm, costo unitario (LAm) nm **unit of production** unidad de producción nf **unit price** precio por unidad nm **unit trust** fondos mutuos nmpl, fondo de inversión mobiliaria nm

united adj unido adj **United Nations** Naciones Unidas (la ONU) nfpl

unlimited adj **unlimited company** empresa ilimitada nf **unlimited credit** crédito ilimitado nm **unlimited liability** responsabilidad ilimitada nf

unload vb descargar vb, deshacerse de vb

unmarketable adj invendible adj

unofficial adj **unofficial strike** huelga no autorizada nf, huelga ilegal nf

unpack vb deshacer vb, desembalar vb, sacar vb, desempacar (LAm) vb

unpaid adj **unpaid balance** saldo deudor nm, saldo negativo nm, importe a pagar todavía nm **unpaid bill** factura sin saldar nf **unpaid cheque** cheque impagado nm

unprofessional adj contrario a la ética profesional adj

unprofitable adj no rentable adj, no lucrativo adj, infructuoso adj

unsaleable adj invendible adj, no comerciable adj

unsatisfactory adj insatisfactorio adj, deficiente adj

unsecured adj **unsecured bond** bono no garantizado nm **unsecured credit** crédito sin garantía nm

unskilled adj **unskilled worker** trabajador, -ora no cualificado, -ada nm,f, obrero, -era no especializado, -ada nm,f, obrero,-era no calificado,-ada (LAm) nm,f, peón (LAm) nmf

unsold adj invendido adj, sin vender prep

unsolicited adj **unsolicited offer** oferta no solicitada nf

up-to-date adj actual adj, al día prep, moderno (LAm) adj **to bring sth up-to-date** actualizar algo vb, poner algo al día vb, modernizar algo vb

update vb (records) actualizar vb

upgrade vb mejorar vb, ascender vb

upswing n reactivación nf, repunte nm

upturn n mejora nf, reactivación nf, giro positivo nm

upward adj & adv alcista adj, hacia arriba prep & adv

urban adj **urban renewal** remodelación urbana nf **urban sprawl** expansión urbana descontrolada nf

urgency n urgencia nf **a matter of urgency** asunto urgente nm

urgent adj urgente adj, apremiante adj

urgently adv urgentemente adv

usage n **intensive usage** uso intensivo nm

use n **to make use of sth** usar algo vb, hacer uso de algo vb

user-friendly adj fácil de utilizar adj, amigable adj

usury n usura nf

utility n utilidad nf **marginal utility** utilidad marginal nf **public utility** empresa de utilidad pública nf

utilization n utilización nf, empleo nm

utilize vb utilizar vb, usar vb, emplear vb

vacancy n vacante nf, habitación libre nf
vacant adj vacante adj, libre adj, desocupado adj
valid adj vigente adj, legítimo adj
validate vb convalidar vb
validity n validez nf, legitimidad nf
valuable adj valioso adj, precioso adj
valuation n valoración nf, tasación nf, evaluación nf, avalúo (LAm) nm
value n valor nm **face value** valor nominal nm **market value** valor de mercado nm **to gain value** aumentar de valor vb, revalorizarse vb **to get value for one's money** conseguir buen precio vb **to lose value** depreciarse vb, perder valor vb
variable adj **variable costs** costes variables nmpl, costos variables (LAm) nmpl **variable rate** tasa variable nf, tipo variable nm
variance n varianza nf, discrepancia nf, variación nf **budget variance** variación presupuestaria nf
VAT (value added tax) abbr IVA (impuesto al valor agregado, impuesto sobre el valor añadido) abbr,nm
vendee n comprador, -ora nm,f
vending machine n máquina expendedora automática nf
vendor n vendedor, -ora nm,f **vendor capital** capital de vendedor, -ora nm,f **joint vendor** vendedor, -ora nm,f, asociado, ada nm,f
verbatim adv palabra por palabra nf, al pie de la letra prep
vertical n **vertical integration** integración vertical nf
vested adj personal adj, adquirido adj **vested interests** interés personal nm **vested rights** derechos adquiridos nmpl
veto 1. n veto nm 2. vb vetar vb
viability n viabilidad nf
video n vídeo nm **video facilities** equipo de vídeo nm
viewer n telespectador, -ora nm,f
VIP (very important person) abbr VIP abbr,nmf
visa n visado nm, visa (LAm) nf
visible adj **visible exports** exportaciones visibles nfpl
visit 1. n visita nf 2. vb visitar vb, hacer una visita vb
visitor n visita nmf, invitado, -ada nm,f
visual adj visual adj **visual display unit (VDU)** unidad de despliegue visual nf, pantalla de visualización nf **visual telephone** teléfono visual nm

vocational adj profesional adj
volatile adj (prices) inestable adj, fluctuante adj
volume n volumen nm, cantidad nf, capacidad nf **volume discount** descuento por volumen nm **trading volume** volumen comercial nm, volumen de negocios nm
voluntary adj voluntario nm **to go into voluntary liquidation** entrar en liquidación voluntaria vb **voluntary wage restraint** moderación voluntaria en las reivindicaciones salariales nf
vote 1. n voto nm, votación nf **vote of no confidence** voto de censura nm **vote of thanks** voto de gracias nm 2. vb votar vb, aprobar vb
voting adj **voting right** derecho de voto nm
voucher n vale nm, bono nm, comprobante nm
wage 1. adj **wage demand** reivindicación salarial nf **wage earner** asalariado, -ada nm,f **wage increase** aumento de sueldo nm, incremento salarial nm, mejora salarial nf **wage negotiations** negociaciones salariales nfpl **wage packet, salary package** (US) sueldo neto nm **wage policy** política salarial nf **wage restraint** moderación salarial nf **wage rise** aumento de sueldo nm, incremento salarial nm **wage(s) agreement** acuerdo salarial nm **wage(s) bill** coste total de los salarios nm **wage scale** escala salarial nf **wage(s) claim** reivindicación salarial nf, demanda salarial nf **wage(s) freeze** congelación salarial nf **wage(s) settlement** convenio salarial nm, acuerdo salarial nm 2. n salario nm, sueldo nm, paga nf **average wage** salario medio nm **minimum wage** salario mínimo nm **net(t) wage** sueldo neto nm, salario neto nm **real wage** salario real nm **starting wage** salario de entrada nm 3. vb librar vb, hacer vb **to wage a campaign** hacer una campaña vb
waiting n **waiting list** lista de espera nf
waive vb renunciar vb, repudiar vb
waiver n renuncia nf, exención nf **waiver clause** cláusula de renuncia nf
wall n **tariff wall** barrera arancelaria nf **to go to the wall** quebrar vb, ser declarado en quiebra vb **Wall Street (US)** Wall Street n, centro financiero de Nueva York nm
war n **price war** guerra de precios nf **trade war** guerra comercial nf

warehouse n almacén nm, depósito nm, bodega (LAm) nf **bonded warehouse** depósito aduanero nm, bodega aduanera (LAm) nf

warehousing n almacenaje nm, depósito nm

wares npl mercancías nfpl, mercaderías (LAm) nfpl

warn vb avisar vb, advertir vb, aconsejar vb **to warn sb against doing sth** prevenir a alguien contra algo vb

warning n aviso nm, advertencia nf **due warning** debido aviso nm **warning sign** señal de alerta nf **without warning** sin previo aviso prep

warrant 1. n orden nf, autorización nf, derecho de suscripción de nuevas acciones nm **warrant for payment** mandato de pago nm **2.** vb justificar vb, garantizar vb, asegurar vb

warranty n garantía nf **under warranty** bajo garantía prep

wastage n pérdida nf, desgaste nm, desperdicio nm **wastage rate** tasa de abandono nf, ritmo de reducción de la plantilla nm

waste 1. adj **waste products** material sobrante nm, productos de desecho nmpl, desechos nmpl **2.** n desperdicio nm, pérdida nf **industrial waste** residuos industriales nmpl, desechos industriales nmpl **waste of time** pérdida de tiempo nf **to go to waste** echarse a perder vb **3.** vb malgastar vb, despilfarrar vb

wasting adj **wasting asset** activo amortizable nm

watch vb **to watch developments** seguir de cerca los sucesos vb

watchdog n (fig.) perro guardián nm, guardián, -ana nm,f **watchdog committee** comisión de control nf

water down vb diluir vb, suavizar vb

watered adj **watered capital** acciones emitidas sin aumento de capital nfpl **watered stock** valores emitidos sin aumento de capital nmpl

watertight adj (fig.) infalible adj, hermético adj

wave n (of mergers, takeovers) oleada nf

wavelength n **to be on the same wavelength** sintonizar con vb

weaken vb (market) debilitarse vb, caer vb, aflojar vb

wealth riqueza nf, patrimonio nm, abundancia nf, fortuna nf **national**

wealth patrimonio nacional nm **wealth tax** impuesto sobre el patrimonio nm

week n **twice a week** dos veces a la semana nfpl **working week** semana laboral nf

weekly adj **weekly wages** salario semanal nm

weigh vb pesar vb **to weigh the pros and cons** pesar ventajas y desventajas vb, sopesar vb

weight n **dead weight** peso muerto nm **excess weight** exceso de peso nm **gross weight** peso bruto nm **net(t) weight** peso neto nm **weights and measures** pesos y medidas nmpl & nfpl

weighted adj **weighted average** promedio ponderado nm **weighted index** índice ponderado nm

weighting n suplemento salarial nm, bonificación nf

weighty adj importante adj, serio adj

welfare 1. adj **welfare benefits** subsidios sociales nmpl **welfare state** estado asistencial nm, estado benefactor nm **2.** n bienestar nm, asistencia social nf

well-advised adj sensato adj

well-informed adj muy al corriente prep, muy interiorizado (LAm) adj

well-known adj conocido adj, bien sabido adj

well-made adj de buena fabricación prep, fuerte adj

well-paid adj bien remunerado adj

well-tried adj probado adj

WEU (Western European Union) abbr UEO (Unión de la Europa Occidental) (La) abbr,nf

white adj **white-collar worker** administrativo, -iva nm,f, empleado, -ada de oficina nm,f, oficinista nmf

wholesale n **at/by wholesale** al por mayor prep **wholesale price** precio al por mayor nm **wholesale trade** comercio al por mayor nm

wholesaler n mayorista nmf, comerciante al por mayor nmf

wholly adv totalmente adv, completamente adv **wholly-owned subsidiary** filial de entera propiedad nf

wide-ranging adj amplio adj, diverso adj, de gran alcance prep

will n voluntad nf, testamento nm

win vb ganar vb, conseguir vb, lograr vb **win customers** hacerse con clientes vb **to win support** ganarse apoyo vb

wind up vb terminar vb, concluir vb, liquidar vb

windfall n suerte imprevista nf **windfall profit** beneficio inesperado nm

winding-up n conclusión nf, liquidación nf **winding-up arrangements** disposiciones de liquidación nfpl **winding-up order** liquidación judicial nf

window n **window of opportunity** marco de oportunidad nm

withdraw vb retirar vb, sacar vb, cancelar vb **to withdraw an offer** retirar una oferta vb

withdrawal n retirada nf, abandono nm, retiro (LAm) nm **withdrawal of funds** reintegro de fondos nm, retiro de fondos (LAm) nm

withhold vb retener vb, negar vb **to withhold a document** retener un documento vb, no dar a conocer un documento vb

withstand vb resistir vb, soportar vb

witness 1. n testigo nm, testimonio nm **2.** vb atestiguar vb, ser testigo de vb, presenciar vb **to witness a signature** atestiguar una firma vb

word n palabra nf **word processing** procesamiento de textos nm **word processor** procesador de palabras nm **to give one's word** dar su palabra vb, comprometerse vb **to keep one's word** cumplir su palabra vb

wording n texto nm, redacción nf

work 1. adj **work experience** experiencia laboral nf, prácticas nfpl **work permit** permiso de trabajo nm **work schedule** plan de trabajo nm **work study** estudio del trabajo nm **2.** n **casual work** trabajo eventual nm **day off work** día libre nm **day's work** jornada nf **factory work** trabajo manual nm **office work** trabajo de oficina nm **works** obras nfpl, fábrica nf, mecanismo nm **works committee** comité de la empresa nm, comité de empresa nm **works council** consejo de obreros nm **works manager** jefe, -efa de taller nm,f, director, -ora de fábrica nm,f **public works programme (GB)** programa de obras públicas nm **to be in work** tener trabajo vb **to be out of work** estar desempleado vb, estar en paro vb, estar en cesantía (LAm) vb **to look for work** buscar trabajo vb **3.** vb trabajar vb **to work to rule** hacer huelga de celo vb, hacer huelga de trabajo lento vb, trabajar

a reglamento (LAm) vb **to work unsocial hours** trabajar fuera de horas normales vb

workable adj factible adj, viable adj

workaholic n trabajoadicto, -cta nm,f

workday (US) n día laborable nm

worker n **casual worker** trabajador, -ora eventual nm,f **clerical worker** oficinista nmf, administrativo, -iva nm,f, empleado, -ada de oficina nm,f **worker-director** director, -ora obrero, -era nm,f **manual worker** obrero, -era manual nm,f, trabajador, -ora manual nm,f, peón (LAm) nmf **worker participation** participación obrera nf **skilled worker** obrero, -era especializado, -ada nm,f, obrero, -era calificado, -ada nm,f **unskilled worker** obrero, -era no cualificado, -ada nm,f, peón nmf, obrero, -era no calificado, -ada (LAm) nm,f

workforce n personal nm, plantilla nf, fuerza laboral nf

working adj **working agreement** acuerdo laboral nm **working area** área de trabajo nf, campo de trabajo nm **working capital** capital circulante nm **working conditions** condiciones de trabajo nfpl **working environment** ambiente laboral nm **working hours** horario de trabajo nm **working knowledge** conocimientos básicos nmpl **working language** idioma de trabajo nm **working life** vida activa nf, vida laboral nf **working majority** mayoría suficiente nf **working model** maqueta nf **working paper** documento de trabajo nm **working party** equipo de trabajo nm **working population** población activa nf **working week (GB)** semana laboral nf, semana de trabajo nf

workload n trabajo asignado nm, carga de trabajo nf

workmate n compañero, -era de trabajo nm,f

workplace n lugar de trabajo nm, trabajo nm

workshop n taller nm, estudio nm

workweek (US) n semana laboral nf, semana de trabajo nf

world n mundo nm **the commercial world** el mundo de los negocios nm, el mundo comercial nm **world consumption** consumo global nm **world exports** exportaciones mundiales nfpl **world fair** exposición universal nf **World Bank** Banco Mundial nm **World Court** Tribunal Internacional de Justicia nm

worldwide adj mundial adj, global adj

worth 1. *adj* que vale *rel pron* **to be worth** valer *vb*, merecer *vb* **2.** *n* valor *nm*

wpm (words per minute) *abbr* palabras por minuto *nfpl*

wreck *vb* destrozar *vb*, echar por tierra *vb*

writ *n* orden judicial *nf*, mandato judicial *nm*, mandamiento judicial *nm* **to issue a writ** dictar un mandato judicial *vb*

write down *vb* (depreciation) depreciar *vb*, amortizar *vb*

write off *vb* (debts) anular *vb*, dar por perdido *vb*, (vehicle) declarar siniestro total *vb*

write-off *n* anulación *nf*, depreciación *nf*, fracaso *nm*

wrongful *adj* **wrongful dismissal** despido injusto *nm*

xerox *vb* fotocopiar *vb*, xerografiar *vb*

Xerox (R) *n* (machine) fotocopiadora *nf*

year *n* año *nm* **year-end dividend** dividendo de fin de año *nm* **year-end inventory** inventario por cierre de ejercicio *nm* **financial year** ejercicio financiero *nm* **fiscal year** ejercicio fiscal *nm*, año fiscal *nm* **tax year** año fiscal *nm*, ejercicio fiscal *nm*

yearly *adj* anual *adj* **yearly income** renta anual *nf*

yellow *adj* **the Yellow pages (R) (GB)** las páginas amarillas *nfpl*

yen *n* (currency) yen *nm* **yen bond** bono de yen *nm*

yield 1. *adj* **yield curve** curva de rendimiento *nf* **2.** *n* **yield on shares** rendimiento sobre acciones *nm* **3.** *vb* rendir *vb*, devengar *vb*, ceder *vb*

young *adj* **young economy** economía nueva *nf*

zenith *n* cenit *nm*, apogeo *nm*

zero *n* cero *nm* **zero address** sin dirección *prep* **below zero** bajo cero *prep* **zero defect** sin defecto *prep* **zero growth** crecimiento cero *nm* **zero hour** hora cero *nf* **zero rate/rating** imposición del 0% *nf*, exento de impuestos *adj* **zero-rate taxation** sistema tributario a tasa cero *nm* **to be zero-rated for VAT** estar exento de IVA *vb*

zip code (US) *n* código postal *nm*

zone 1. *n* zona *nf*, polígono *nm* **currency zone** zona monetaria *nf* **enterprise zone** zona de libre empresa *nf*, zona de desarrollo *nf* **postal zone** distrito postal *nm* **time zone** huso horario *nm* **wage zone** zona salarial *nf* **2.** *vb* zonificar *vb*

zoning *n* zonificación *nf*, división por zonas *nf*